Road Biking™ Colorado

Road Biking™ Series

Road Biking™ Colorado

A Guide to the State's Best Bike Rides

Robert Hurst

FALCONGUIDES

GUILFORD, CONNECTICUT
HELENA, MONTANA

FALCONGUIDES®

An imprint of Rowman & Littlefield
Falcon, FalconGuides, and Outfit Your Mind are registered trademarks of Rowman & Littlefield.

Distributed by NATIONAL BOOK NETWORK

Copyright © 2015 by Rowman & Littlefield

Maps by Melissa Baker © Rowman & Littlefield
All photos by the author unless otherwise noted

British Library Cataloguing-in-Publication Information Available

Library of Congress Cataloging-in-Publication Data

Hurst, Robert (Robert J.)
  Road biking Colorado : a guide to the State's best bike rides / Robert Hurst.
    pages cm. — (Road Biking Series)
  "Distributed by NATIONAL BOOK NETWORK"—T.p. verso.
  Includes index.
  ISBN 978-1-4930-0988-6 (paperback)—ISBN 978-1-4930-1911-3 (e-book) 1. Cycling—Colorado—Guidebooks. 2. Colorado—Guidebooks. I. Title.
  GV1045.5.C6H87 2015
  796.609788—dc23
                              2015013495

∞™ The paper used in this publication meets the minimum requirements of American National Standard for Information Sciences—Permanence of Paper for Printed Library Materials, ANSI/NISO Z39.48-1992.

Contents

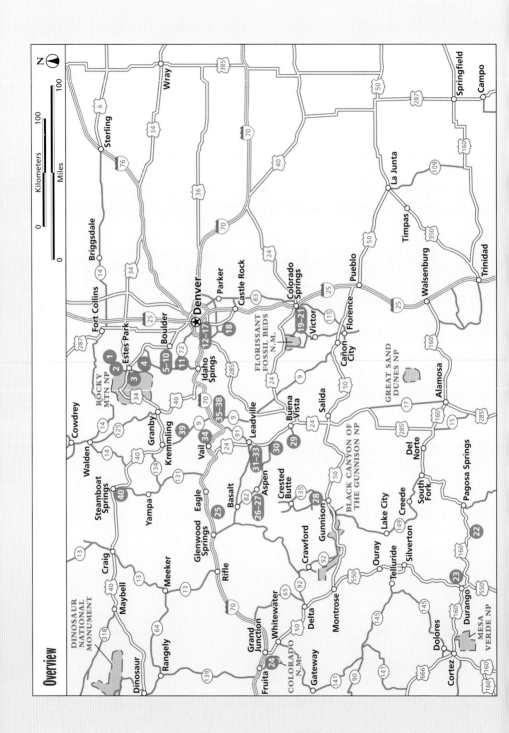

Overview

Acknowledgments

What a privilege it was to prepare this guide. Thank you for reading it. I hope I have done a job worthy of the material.

As usual I needed a lot of help finishing this book. My dad drove me out on several of the excursions, dropping me off to ride while he went to take pictures of wildflowers. We visited Steamboat, Grand Junction, Aspen, Leadville, Vail, and some other places I can't remember right now. Thanks, Dad. You made the work more pleasant, and your photos made the book a lot nicer too. And Christie, thank you. I know your patience was all used up while I went jaunting around the state doing the exact thing you wished you could be doing.

Thanks also to the folks at Falcon who agreed to let me write this and then edited it into respectability.

Introduction

The Rides

The rides featured in this book run the gamut from easy bike-path cruises to extreme mountain climbs. However, you'll probably notice my preference for hilly rides. There are a few longer rides, some shorter rides, and lots of medium-length rides between 20 and 40 miles long. Most are loops of some sort, but many are out-and-back or one-way routes, out of necessity or simply for convenience's sake.

There are rides from all over the state, but some areas received more attention. It makes sense to concentrate on the central mountains and Front Range, as that is where the people and road routes are also concentrated. I hit Boulder particularly hard, as it is arguably the world's best town for road biking. Some other areas don't get the treatment they deserve. I wish I had the time and resources to add more rides on the eastern plains and the southwest, which is a widely varied and super-rich road-biking sector in its own right. (The local riders down there, on the other hand, are probably glad that there isn't more coverage of their dearest routes.)

I was able to include many of my old favorites, and I found a few new favorites in the process of making this guide. The Mineral Belt Loop ringing Leadville (Ride 32), the Steamboat Gravel Grinder (Ride 40), the Colorado National Monument

The road to Bear Lake

(Ride 24), and Pikes Peak (Ride 21) were all new to me, and those are all absolutely amazing rides. I can't wait to get back and experience them again. But frankly it could be a while.

Bike Paths

Several of the rides use off-street paths for part of the route; others use off-street paths almost exclusively. It's important to realize that these paths, though we and everybody else know them as "bike paths," are actually multi-use paths (MUPs), and pedestrians own the right-of-way on them. Always pass pedestrians at a reasonable speed and give them a wide berth. And give them some kind of audible signal in advance of the pass.

Dirt Roads

Some of the rides in this book include sections of dirt road that are suitable for road bikes. There are one or two rougher roads that are best suited for cyclocross bikes (Chapman Cyclocross Loop [Ride 9] and North Cheyenne Canyon Loop [Ride 19], to be precise), but even these can be ridden without too much trouble on unmodified racing bikes.

If you're not yet a gravel grinder, I urge you to give dirt roads a chance. Embracing the dirt will not just expand your horizons, it will explode your horizons. It will open up a whole different world of possibilities. And the roads are generally not as rough as you might think. In some cases, you might even notice that the ride smooths

Yield to peds on the Bear Creek Trail and every so-called bike path.

out when you go from paved road (which is often a very crude chip-seal surface in the mountains) to unpaved.

There is no need to get a special "gravel bike" for riding dirt roads, although the bike industry may be trying, at this very moment, to convince you otherwise. Carbon frames and forks should be fine. When in doubt, baby your equipment and ride light. Big riders will run into many more issues with flat tires and equipment failure on rough dirt roads and will need to be much more mindful about bumps and surfaces, but that's true on pavement as well. Heavy riders will need wider tires and stouter wheels.

Dirt roads set you free.

The only components that I personally *wouldn't* use on gravel are carbon rims and super-delicate, exotic racing tires—things that I am unlikely to ever own anyway, incidentally. Lightweight aluminum rims, well-built wheels, and fast clinchers eat Colorado gravel for lunch, I can say without hesitation.

Riding dirt on a road bike is not without its special hazards. The quality of a dirt road's surface can vary quite a bit from week to week, even from hour to hour. Depending on the makeup of the soil in question, rain or snowmelt could turn a dirt road into an impassable slop, or at least make riding it extremely unpleasant. Sections of severe washboard can appear suddenly and surprisingly on what you thought was smooth dirt, damaging equipment or causing wrecks. Deep gravel could cause the front wheel to wash out. Huge, wheel-swallowing ruts can carve a dirt road to pieces.

These potentially dangerous surprises appear on dirt roads only slightly more often than analogous hazards appear on pavement, it seems. No riding surface is perfect for very long. No matter where you ride, keep your eyes open for surface hazards as well as for cars, trucks, pedestrians, and animals.

Riding Safe in Colorado

Most bicycling injuries occur when riders wipe out on potholes, slide out on sand, go over the bars after braking improperly, or some other circus of the absurd mishap that you hope nobody saw or recorded on their iPhone (according to statistics from the Consumer Products Safety Commission's National Electronic Injury Surveillance System). Most of the people who are reading this are probably beyond that floundering stage, but to those who aren't yet, I'll simply say, Watch where you're going. That will take care of most of it right there.

Awareness is what it's all about in traffic, too. Bring it. Don't assume others will. Hope for the best, but prepare for the worst.

Of course it's important to ride according to basic traffic rules—on the right-hand side of the road, with traffic, and obeying all traffic-control devices. But evidence shows clearly that following the law is not, by itself, a very effective measure to prevent collisions. In most reported car-bike collisions involving adult riders, the bicyclist was riding lawfully at the time of the wreck.

It's crucial to understand why these crashes occur in order to avoid them. These wrecks are caused by drivers who fail to notice bicyclists in their path. They're not malicious; it only seems that way at the time. They pull out of driveways and stop signs and parking spaces in front of bikes, turn left into them, turn right into them, and so on, thinking that they're driving into an empty gap. Some of these drivers are simply not paying proper attention. Some aren't even watching the road. Distracted driving. Other times, they're looking right at you but still don't see you somehow. It happens all the time.

Drivers are probably not even thinking about the possibility of cyclists (or pedestrians or motorcyclists or mule deer) on the road. When they look, they're looking for cars. Approaching a turn or crossing, their brains are working to quickly identify any large, fast-moving objects. Other objects will often get ignored. Sometimes their vision is just poor—humans in general have some pretty awful vision compared to other animals. We're just not very good at seeing things, especially bicyclists. And being a very nice, considerate person doesn't help any of this.

In the end, the nice person who doesn't notice you is far more dangerous than the jerk who does. (And the jerk who does should be avoided.)

A simple appreciation for the typical human's severe limitations in vision and awareness will go a long way toward keeping you in one piece. Instead of putting your safety into the hands of drivers who have such a poor track record of noticing bicyclists or, for that matter, huge semis, take back responsibility for your own well-being. Don't assume that any other road user notices your presence. If you can avoid it (you can't all the time), don't put yourself in a position where you are dependent on the awareness of other road users.

Pay special attention to oncoming cars that could turn left across your path, cars waiting to pull out on your right, and pedestrians waiting to cross the road. You can subtly adjust speed to avoid putting yourself in their possible path or adjust position to give more space, more of an escape hatch. Most often, simply being *ready* for the driver's encroachment is all that's needed to keep you safe. Be ready, not surprised. This is defensive driving for bicyclists, and it's critical.

That's the main thing. Beyond that, remember these suggestions:

- **Avoid the "door zone."** The "door zone" is the space within about 4 feet of any parked vehicle. Simply avoid it. If you can't, or don't want to, ride very slow so the inevitable crunch doesn't hurt as much.

- **Use lights and reflective gear.** It doesn't solve the basic problem, but we do what we can.
- **Take care on sidewalks.** Colorado municipalities tend to outlaw sidewalk bicycling by adults. This law is widely ignored. If you ignore the law, please give right-of-way as well as a stout comfort zone to any pedestrians and take great care when crossing driveways and alleys or entering the street. A high percentage of car-bike crashes occur when bikers on sidewalks ride into intersections without looking or stopping. Another sizable chunk could be prevented if wrong-way sidewalk riders would simply not ride in front of cars that are about to turn onto the street.

Colorado Bike Laws

The state of Colorado's bicycle laws are pretty typical. Which is to say, they're confusing as heck when you get into the details. Here are some highlights:

Follow basic traffic laws. Just like everywhere else, Colorado bicyclists "shall have all of the rights and duties applicable to the driver of any other vehicle ... except as to special regulations in this article and except as to those provisions which by their nature can have no application." Wait ... say that last part again? You know the drill: You're required to ride with traffic and obey traffic signals, and in return you won't be arrested and disappeared to a black site for interloping on (most) roadways. Different law-enforcement agencies around the state have different views on this fundamental law and very different approaches to enforcing the cyclist's requirements. Some police in Denver won't bat an eye at a bicyclist ignoring a red light; some local sheriffs will bust a rider for not putting a foot down at a deserted four-way stop.

Ride to the right (sometimes). The most fiddly and confusing aspect of bike law concerns the allowable lateral positioning of the bicyclist—a slow-moving vehicle unlike any other—on roadways with and without faster vehicles. Do you have to ride to the right? How far right? When are you allowed to "take the lane"? Lawmaking institutions have given a fair amount of attention to these questions over the decades. As in most other states, the Colorado legislature gave a lot of leeway to cyclists, listing a multitude of specific exceptions to the ride-to-the-right rule, as well as unspecific, deliberately ambiguous exemptions, in section 42-4-1412 (Operation of Bicycles and Other Human-Powered Vehicles) of the *Colorado Revised Statutes* (C.R.S.):

> *(5) (a) Any person operating a bicycle or an electrical assisted bicycle upon a roadway at less than the normal speed of traffic shall ride in the right-hand lane, subject to the following conditions:*
>> *(I) If the right-hand lane then available for traffic is wide enough to be safely shared with overtaking vehicles, a bicyclist shall ride far enough to the right as judged safe by the bicyclist to facilitate the movement of such overtaking vehicles unless other conditions make it unsafe to do so.*
>> *(II) A bicyclist may use a lane other than the right-hand lane when:*

(A) Preparing for a left turn at an intersection or into a private roadway or driveway;

(B) Overtaking a slower vehicle; or

(C) Taking reasonably necessary precautions to avoid hazards or road conditions.

(III) Upon approaching an intersection where right turns are permitted and there is a dedicated right-turn lane, a bicyclist may ride on the left-hand portion of the dedicated right-turn lane even if the bicyclist does not intend to turn right.

(b) A bicyclist shall not be expected or required to:

(I) Ride over or through hazards at the edge of a roadway, including but not limited to fixed or moving objects, parked or moving vehicles, bicycles, pedestrians, animals, surface hazards, or narrow lanes; or

(II) Ride without a reasonable safety margin on the right-hand side of the roadway.

(c) A person operating a bicycle or an electrical assisted bicycle upon a one-way roadway with two or more marked traffic lanes may ride as near to the left-hand curb or edge of such roadway as judged safe by the bicyclist, subject to the following conditions:

(I) If the left-hand lane then available for traffic is wide enough to be safely shared with overtaking vehicles, a bicyclist shall ride far enough to the left as judged safe by the bicyclist to facilitate the movement of such overtaking vehicles unless other conditions make it unsafe to do so.

(The law then specifies the same conditions and exceptions for left-side riding [legal on one-way streets] as it does for right-side riding.)

When you get right down to the proverbial nitty-gritty, there is plenty of ambiguity in this peculiar slow-moving vehicle law—in laws in general. Some riders take the ambiguous phrasing above, particularly the catchall (5)(II)(C) ("Taking reasonably necessary precautions to avoid hazards or road conditions"), to mean that they are ultimately allowed to ride wherever they want—that they could, for instance, take the lane on a busy road even if there is a shoulder or bike lane, just because they feel safer doing so.

In reality, the legality of the cyclist's actions is not determined by the cyclist alone. They will be held to a "standard of reasonableness" determined by society in general. So, if you get pulled over for taking the lane on a highway with a rideable shoulder, don't expect judges or juries to overturn the police officer's negative judgment about the reasonableness of your positioning.

If there are no faster vehicles approaching, you can ride in the middle of the lane no matter how wide it is, theoretically.

The three-foot passing rule. This is a relatively new and very welcome requirement for drivers: "(b) The driver of a motor vehicle overtaking a bicyclist proceeding in the same direction shall allow the bicyclist at least a three-foot separation between the right side of the driver's vehicle, including all mirrors or other projections, and the left side of the bicyclist at all times" (section 42-4-1003). There is also a similar statement for vehicles passing cyclists who are riding on the left side of one-way streets (section 42-4-1004) and another provision allowing motorists to cross double yellows in order to pass bicyclists (section 42-4-1005), provided they do so when no oncoming vehicles are approaching (section 42-4-1002). Don't get too excited, however. At high speed, a 3-foot pass will scare the Gu out of most riders.

The anti-terror law. See section 1008.5: "Crowding or threatening bicyclist. The driver of a motor vehicle shall not, in a careless and imprudent manner, drive the vehicle unnecessarily close to, toward, or near a bicyclist." Violators will be cheerfully bludgeoned with a frame pump. No, that's just a destructive fantasy. Violators will be charged with careless driving.

To report aggressive driving and harassment, notify the Colorado State Patrol by dialing ★CSP (★277). Without a license plate number, there won't be much, if any, response.

Single up. The laws governing two-abreast riding have been a source of confusion and frustration for recreational riders who like to have conversations with each other while pedaling down the road. It's hard to talk to a riding partner when rolling single file, no doubt about it. However, unless there is a shoulder or bike lane wide enough to contain two riders side by side, I recommend continuing the traditional practice of "singling up" when faster same-direction traffic approaches—especially other cyclists—for the sake of simple courtesy. This will also keep you on the right side of the law, which some exurban sheriffs have been particularly enthusiastic about enforcing on the roads between Boulder and Fort Collins:

> *(6) (a) Persons riding bicycles or electrical assisted bicycles upon a roadway shall not ride more than two abreast except on paths or parts of roadways set aside for the exclusive use of bicycles.*
> *(b) Persons riding bicycles or electrical assisted bicycles two abreast shall not impede the normal and reasonable movement of traffic and, on a laned roadway, shall ride within a single lane.*

So, no more than two abreast and ride single file when faster bike or motor traffic is present.

Signal your turns. Cyclists are supposed to signal their turns in Colorado, although hardly anybody does, and the law is rarely enforced. You can simply hold an arm out and point in the direction you intend to turn.

No helmet required. There is no statewide mandatory bike-helmet law, even for kids—as of 2015. We'll see what happens there. For now, wear one anyway.

Use lights. Headlights, rear reflectors or lights, and side reflectors are required between sundown and sunrise.

E-bikes. Electric bikes are not allowed on bike paths or sidewalks.

Bicyclists may be banned from some roads. State law (C.R.S. 42-4-109) dictates that local governments or the state department of transportation can restrict bicyclists from using a road if a "suitable bike path" is available near the road.

Roads through federal property, like Rim Rock Drive in Colorado National Monument, may have different rules for bicyclists.

Local laws rule (except when they don't). As in other states, Colorado law specifies that local governments are allowed to create and enforce their own special bike-specific laws. So, when you roll from the countryside into a town or city, the state laws are almost irrelevant. However, local laws must not contradict the overriding traffic laws set by the state, which in turn are based on national norms.

The most famous local law in the state, so far, belonged to the community of Blackhawk, which passed a law in 2010 forbidding bicyclists from riding through their town. The ban was vigorously challenged by the bike community, and ultimately it was overturned by the Colorado Supreme Court, on the grounds that no alternative route was available. I don't recommend riding through Blackhawk anyway.

Confusing though they may be, the bike laws need not become an issue in your life. By simply riding courteously and with a little sense, you'll avoid ever having to think about them.

Map Legend

Transportation

Interstate/Divided Highway	═══〔25〕═══
Featured US Highway	═══〔34〕═══
US Highway	──〔34〕──
Featured State Highway	═══〔72〕═══
State Highway	──〔72〕──
Featured Road	▪▪▪〔CR 24〕▪▪▪
County/Local Road	──〔CR 24〕──
Featured Bike Route	▪▪▪▪▪▪▪▪▪▪▪▪▪▪▪
Bike Route	▪▪▪▪▪▪▪▪▪▪▪▪▪▪▪
Featured Trail	‑ ‑ ‑ ‑ ‑ ‑ ‑ ‑
Trail/Dirt Road	‑ ‑ ‑ ‑ ‑ ‑ ‑ ‑
Railroad	┝━┿━┿━┿━┥

Symbols

Ride Start	🔟
Mileage Marker	17.1 ◆──
Direction Arrow	→
Capital	✪
Large City	◉
Small City/Town	○
Gate	⚑
Mountain	▲
Museum	🏛
Parking	🅿
Pass	)(
Point of Interest	■
Ski Area	⛷
Visitor Center	❷

Hydrology

Reservoir/Lake	⬭
River/Creek	～
Spring	⌀
Wetlands	‑ ‑ ‑

Land Use

National Forest	▭
State/Local Park	▮
Indian Reservation	▭
Archaeological Area	▭

1 Big Masonville Loop

Don't miss this Colorado classic, a beautiful and unique 42-mile loop with lots of climbing west of Fort Collins.

Start: Masonville, at the intersection of Buckhorn Road/Stove Prairie Road and CR 27
Length: 41.9 miles
Terrain: Rolling hills and forested canyons; also jagged, rocky hills around Horsetooth Reservoir

Traffic and hazards: Traffic is moderate all around the loop; some sharp turns and descents.
Things to see: Stove Prairie, Rist Canyon, Horsetooth Reservoir, Fort Collins from above

Getting there: From Denver, take I-25 north to US 34 and go west through Loveland. Take a right on CR 27 and go north until the road comes to a T intersection at Masonville. From Fort Collins, head west out of town toward Horsetooth Reservoir on Harmony Road, which becomes CR 38E. Continue past the reservoir on CR 38E to Masonville, at the intersection of CR 38E/Buckhorn Road and CR 27, and park on the side of CR 27. **GPS:** N 40 29'14.00" / W 105 12'38.81"

Ride Description

This awesome ride through the foothills west of Fort Collins could go by several different names. It could be called the Big Horsetooth Reservoir Loop, or the Stove Prairie Loop, or the Rist Canyon Loop just as easily as the Masonville Loop. You'll see a lot of territory on this classic.

The loop could go either direction and could be started niftily from the Fort, or any one of a number of parking areas along Horsetooth Reservoir. If you're starting from the Masonville crossroads and rolling clockwise, the first leg of the journey is a big climb, but a moderate, rolling one. There is a good deal of variety in the terrain northwest of Masonville. For the first several miles, the road bounces across dry golden, windswept hills. Then the canyon closes in and the road snakes through a pine forest.

Upon arrival at Stove Prairie, about 15 miles up the road, some riders will be alarmed to find out they aren't quite at the high point yet. The right turn toward Rist Canyon is followed by a straight, steep grunt. The rudest climb so far, no doubt. It doesn't last too long, and then you're looping down Rist Canyon Road (CR 52E) in classic fashion.

At the bottom, turn south on CR 23 to begin a distinctly different third phase of the loop. This road takes you past Horsetooth Reservoir, which is a huge bucket of water poised on top of a door over Fort Collins. The scenery here could be the finest of the ride, as the road climbs sharply to the water and dips and dives above the eastern shoreline in a series of leg-cracking 200-foot humps. These climbs can get really ugly for riders on the edge.

The road between Masonville and Stone Prairie

With the right lighting it's a spectacular tableau of flashing blue water and golden hills. The scene is mostly man-made, of course. Horsetooth was created in 1949 as part of the Colorado–Big Thompson project. Under the water lies the little town of Stout. The thriving industry here in the valley was rock harvesting.

Horsetooth Reservoir with its rollicking road is a natural destination for a shorter loop out of Fort Collins. And if you like a little hiking or mountain biking, the reservoir is surrounded by public lands and trails.

To end the loop, stay right as you reach the south tip of the reservoir. The road throws in a few more leg burners before suddenly arriving back at the Masonville crossroads. Nearly 42 miles in all, and hardly a dud among them. If you're looking for still more, tack on the Little Masonville Loop.

Miles and Directions

0.0 Start from Masonville (the intersection of CR 27 and Buckhorn Road/Stove Prairie Road).

14.4 Turn right onto Rist Canyon Road (CR 52E).

26.8 Turn right onto CR 23 (not CR 25, which takes you nowhere).

32.5 Pass an intersection with a road heading down to Fort Collins.

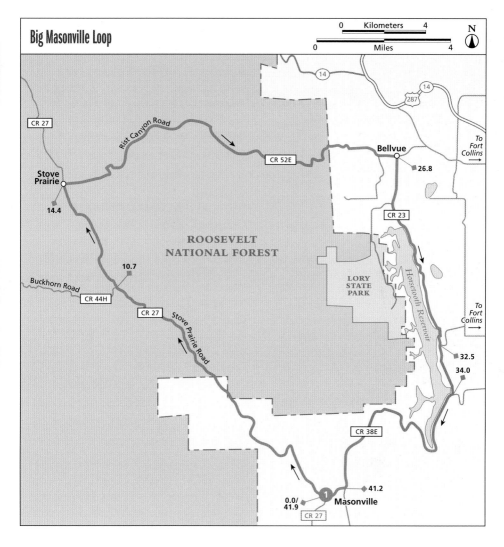

Big Masonville Loop

0 Kilometers 4
0 Miles 4

N

CR 27

Rist Canyon Road

CR 52E

Bellvue

26.8

To Fort Collins →

Stove Prairie

14.4

CR 23

ROOSEVELT NATIONAL FOREST

10.7

Buckhorn Road

CR 44H

CR 27

Stove Prairie Road

LORY STATE PARK

Horsetooth Reservoir

To Fort Collins →

32.5

34.0

CR 38E

41.2

0.0/41.9

Masonville

CR 27

34.0   Turn right and continue next to the water on CR 38E. (A left turn takes you down to Fort Collins.)

41.2   Pass the intersection with West Glade Road.

41.9   Arrive back at the Masonville crossroads.

Bike Shops

Brave New Wheel. 105 E. Myrtle, Fort Collins; (970) 416-0417; bravenewwheel.com.

Drake Cyclery. 2100 W. Drake Rd., Fort Collins; (970) 631-8326; drakecyclery.com.

Fort Collins Bicycle Co-op. 331 N. College Ave., Fort Collins; (970) 484-3804; fcbikecoop .org.

Lee's Cyclery. Two locations: 931 E. Harmony Dr., Fort Collins; (970) 226-6006; 202 W. Laurel St., Fort Collins; (970) 482-6006; leescyclery.com.

Ride 1 **Big Masonville Loop**   **3**

Peloton Cycles. 3027 E. Harmony Rd., Fort Collins; (970) 449-5595; peloton-cycles.com.
The Phoenix Cyclery. 152 E. Mulberry St., Fort Collins; (970) 493-4517; thephoenixcyclery .com.
ProVelo Bicycles. 4612 S. Mason St. #110, Fort Collins; (970) 204-9935; provelobikes .com.
REI. 4025 S. College Ave., Fort Collins; (970) 223-0123; REI.com.
Breakaway Cycles. 2237 W. Eisenhower Blvd., Loveland; (970) 663-1726; breakaway-cycles .com.
Rocky Mountain Cyclery. 504 N. Garfield Ave., Loveland; (970) 669-2361.

Food

Lupita's Mexican Restaurant. 1720 W. Mulberry St., Fort Collins; (970) 568-8363.
Maza Kabob. 2427 S. College Ave., Fort Collins; (970) 484-6292; mazakabob.com. For years I bought *bolani* from Sayed's cart in downtown Denver. Now he's got his own restaurant! Excellent.
Paninos. 310 W. Prospect Rd., Fort Collins; (970) 498-8292; paninos.com. Cheap Italian.
Restaurant 415. 415 S. Mason St., Fort Collins; (970) 407-0415; thefourfifteen.com.
Next Door Food & Drink. 222 E. 4th St. #100, Loveland; (970) 541-3020; nextdoorloveland .com.

Lodging

Fort Collins and Loveland both have the full complement of chain hotels.
Armstrong Hotel. 259 S. College Ave., Fort Collins; (970) 484-3883; thearmstronghotel .com. Refurbished old hotel.
Wilder-Nest Retreats Bed & Breakfast. 9144 N. Glade Rd., Loveland (closer to Masonville); (970) 481-2563; retreatsatwildernest.com.

2 Little Masonville Loop

Here's a compact sampler of fun cycling roads west of Loveland, near Masonville.

Start: Masonville, at the intersection of Buckhorn Road/Stove Prairie Road and CR 27
Length: 14.4 miles
Terrain: Rolling, with a few short, sharp climbs, along and around the hogbacks

Traffic and hazards: Traffic is moderate all around the loop. There is a short stint on US 34, with typical highway speeds.
Things to see: Big Thompson River, Green Ridge Glade Reservoir

Getting there: From Denver, take I-25 north to US 34 and go west, through Loveland. Take a right on CR 27 and go north until the road comes to a T intersection at Masonville. From Fort Collins, head west out of town toward Horsetooth Reservoir on Harmony Road, which becomes CR 38E. Continue past the reservoir on CR 38E to Masonville, at the intersection of CR 38E/Buckhorn Road and CR 27, and park on the side of CR 27. **GPS:** N 40 29'14.00" / W 105 12'38.81"

Ride Description

West and north of Loveland, west and south of Fort Collins, tucked into the area between the mountains and the hogbacks, is a crossroads called Masonville. Other than a vintage clothing store, some houses, and a green field filled with whimsical antiques, there isn't much going on here. But Masonville has a certain magic to it.

You can park here on the side of the road and begin the ride (be considerate and don't park in any spot that could remotely be considered a parking space for a local business or residence), as described below, but there are other places to start. For those driving up from the south, the elementary school at US 34 and CR 27 is a good staging area when school's not in session, during the summer, and on weekends. This shortish loop also makes a nice add-on to a longer ride. Try a remote start from Fort Collins, Loveland, Longmont, or Lyons. You could also combine this loop very nicely with a Carter Lake or Pole Hill Road outing. Those gorgeous, pain-inducing roads are lying in wait just on the other side of US 34.

Riders have been pedaling through Masonville for well over one hundred years, as the following passage from the June 19, 1912, *Fort Collins Weekly Courier* attests:

Late Sunday afternoon seven bicycle riders came hiking into town pushing their wheels through the mud. They had started for Estes Park but only one of them got through, the others explaining that they were delayed by an accident on the way up when C. M. Liggett had a nasty spill going down hill and broke the front rim of his wheel. Gephardt continued on his way and finally reached the park. The rest of the party got some distance beyond Montrose Inn before they turned back. On the return trip they were caught in the rain at Masonville and were forced to walk two miles of the distance between Masonville and this city. In spite of the reverses encountered, all reported a good time and a trip to Loveland is planned for next Sunday. . . .

How we wish it were so, Doctor Bob.

The Big Thompson ate this pavement structure.

With single-speed fixed-wheel bikes and dirt roads that became impassable after rainstorms, road riding was a bit more difficult back then.

Though the roads are now paved, those pavement structures can still get tossed around like saltine crackers after a heavy rain. In September 2013, a storm caused flash floods all up and down the Front Range. Just about every canyon from Colorado Springs to Fort Collins was ripped to shreds. The bridges and highways in those canyons were destroyed. Fixing them was a monumental task that was still far from finished as this book went to press. Over a year after the floods, many of the ruined roads and bridges were still awaiting the arrival of the first repair crews. A bridge on the west side of this loop was one of those. Blasted to smithereens by the raging Big Thompson River, it was still a pile of rubble in early 2015. The road should be fixed before too much longer, but if you're not sure, check with the Colorado Department of Transportation (CDOT) or the Larimer County road department before embarking on this ride.

The west half of this loop, along the river and Green Ridge Glade Reservoir, is certainly the more interesting and scenic half. CR 29 is a real delight. Those 4 miles on Glade Road are relatively straight and uneventful.

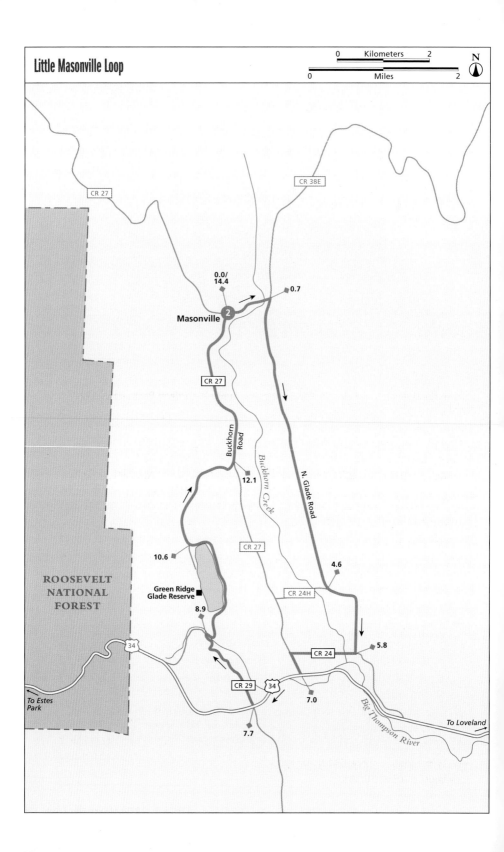

Kilometers

Miles

N

CR 27

CR 38E

0.0/
14.4

0.7

Masonville 2

CR 27

Buckhorn Road

Buckhorn Creek

N. Glade Road

12.1

CR 27

10.6

4.6

ROOSEVELT
NATIONAL
FOREST

Green Ridge
Glade Reserve

CR 24H

8.9

CR 24

5.8

34

CR 29

34

7.0

To Estes
Park

7.7

Big Thompson River

To Loveland

If this little loop turns your crank, think about coming back here and trying the Big Masonville Loop, which heads up to Stove Prairie and back to Fort Collins via Rist Canyon.

Miles and Directions

0.0   Start from the intersection of Buckhorn Road (CR 27) and CR 38E, aka Masonville, and ride east on CR 38E, toward Fort Collins.

0.7   Turn right onto North Glade Road.

4.6   Turn left onto Glade Road.

5.8   Turn right onto CR 24.

6.7   Turn left onto CR 27.

7.0   Turn right onto US 34.

7.7   Turn right onto CR 29.

8.9   The road turns sharply as it crosses the Big Thompson River.

10.6   Veer right, continuing north on CR 29 as the road leaves the reservoir.

12.1   Turn left onto CR 27/Buckhorn Road.

14.4   Back at Masonville.

Bike Shops

Brave New Wheel. 105 E. Myrtle, Fort Collins; (970) 416-0417; www.bravenewwheel.com.

Drake Cyclery. 2100 W. Drake Rd., Fort Collins; (970) 631-8326; drakecyclery.com.

Fort Collins Bike Co-op. 331 N. College Ave., Fort Collins; (970) 484-3804; fcbikecoop.org.

Lee's Cyclery. Two locations: 931 E. Harmony Dr., Fort Collins; (970) 226-6006; 202 W. Laurel St., Fort Collins; (970) 482-6006; leescyclery.com.

Peloton Cycles. 3027 E. Harmony Rd., Fort Collins; (970) 449-5595; peloton-cycles.com.

The Phoenix Cyclery. 152 E. Mulberry St., Fort Collins; (970) 493-4517; thephoenixcyclery .com.

ProVelo Bicycles. 4612 S. Mason St. #110, Fort Collins; (970) 204-9935; provelobikes .com.

REI. 4025 S. College Ave., Fort Collins; (970) 223-0123; REI.com.

Breakaway Cycles. 2237 W. Eisenhower Blvd., Loveland; (970) 663-1726; breakaway-cycles .com.

Rocky Mountain Cyclery. 504 N. Garfield Ave., Loveland; (970) 669-2361.

Food

Lupita's Mexican Restaurant. 1720 W. Mulberry St., Fort Collins; (970) 568-8363.

Maza Kabob. 2427 S. College Ave., Fort Collins; (970) 484-6292; mazakabob.com. For years I bought *bolani* from Sayed's cart in downtown Denver. Now he's got his own restaurant! Excellent.

Paninos. 310 W. Prospect Rd., Fort Collins; (970) 498-8292; paninos.com. Cheap Italian.

Restaurant 415. 415 S. Mason St., Fort Collins; (970) 407-0415; thefourfifteen.com.

Next Door Food & Drink. 222 E. 4th St. #100, Loveland; (970) 541-3020; nextdoorloveland .com.

Lodging

Fort Collins and Loveland both have the full complement of chain hotels.

Armstrong Hotel. 259 S. College Ave., Fort Collins; (970) 484-3883; thearmstronghotel .com. Refurbished old hotel.

Wilder-Nest Retreats Bed & Breakfast. 9144 N. Glade Rd., Loveland (closer to Masonville); (970) 481-2563; retreatsatwildernest.com.

OTHER RIDES AROUND FORT COLLINS AND LOVELAND

Big Thompson Canyon. Theoretically a top road ride, this long, steady-climbing canyon route between Loveland and Estes Park was known for close passes, high speeds, semi trucks, and other sketchy traffic situations. Interestingly, recent flooding may have been the catalyst for improvements on that front, giving the highway department a chance to redo the road. We have hope, because otherwise it's a very cool ride. For the brave, try a super-climbing 75-mile loop using the Big T, Peak to Peak Highway, and South Saint Vrain Canyon into Lyons. Note that the toughest climb on this loop doesn't begin until you roll through Estes Park. Alternatively, ascend South Saint Vrain Canyon first and descend Big Thompson. Start early, bring stuff.

Carter Lake. Another reservoir created after World War II and poised above the plains, Carter Lake is a beautiful destination accompanied by a fantastic and challenging road. There might not be enough pavement here to justify driving up to Carter Lake from Denver for a road ride, but it does make a great addition to a ride out of Fort Collins, Masonville, Loveland, Lyons, or Longmont (the L's). Boulder to Carter Lake and back is a crosswind classic—100 miles give or take a few.

Fort Collins Bike Path Loop. One of the marvelous features of the Fort is its system of off-street paths. Not that the Fort's streets are hard to ride, but these paths make things even easier. Two main paths, the Poudre Trail and Spring Creek Trail, run through the town diagonally, forming a big V. Both paths are hard surfaced and run in their own rights-of-way, totally separated from the street system, passing beneath all the streets and intersections. The Poudre path skirts the town to the north and spends much of its time among ponds, fields, and cottonwoods; Spring Creek runs right through town. The paths come together among the tall grasses north of Prospect Road. (Check out the extension to the nature center on the east side.) Use one of the nicely accommodated north–south avenues on the west side of town to form a long, flat loop. There are parking areas and trailheads at pleasant little parks all along the paths. Download the Fort Collins bike map here: fcgov.com/bicycling/pdf/bike-map-front.pdf.

Pole Hill Road. This little zinger lies in wait just north of Carter Lake. Like a mini Lookout Mountain or Flagstaff, it's a twisting guardrail-laced climb up the side of a steep little mountain. Works great for hill repeat training, if you're into that sort of thing. Some people know this climb as "Rattlesnake."

Poudre Canyon. The climb to Cameron Pass is one of the longest continuous climbs anywhere in Colorado. Anywhere, anywhere. Thirty-six miles or so of fighting gravity, with a raging river as a companion much of the way. The ride is not beloved by area cyclists, primarily due to its incredible length—nobody likes having to turn around before reaching the top—but also because the traffic can be uncomfortable. The payoff at the top is huge, however. Cameron Pass is a stunner, and it's moderate in slope. Beyond lie the mysteries of North Park.

Rist Canyon–Poudre Canyon Loop. A cousin of the Big Masonville Loop, this one starts with a climb of Rist Canyon, then takes a right at Stove Prairie after the infamous face-ripper descent off the top. More descending on Stove Prairie Road brings you to the Catch the Pooder River. Wide, shallow canyon turns ease you back to the flats, but not in time to prevent a good glute burning.

3 Bear Lake

This is a moderate climb to a popular tourist attraction in Rocky Mountain National Park. The scenery is gorgeous and the road lovable. But don't feed the tourists!

Start: Moraine Park Discovery Center, Rocky Mountain National Park
Length: 16.3 miles out-and-back
Terrain: You're definitely in the big mountains, but the road isn't very steep.

Traffic and hazards: Moderate, steady tourist traffic
Things to see: Rocky Mountain National Park
Fee alert: It costs 20 bucks per car to enter Rocky Mountain National Park, or 10 bucks per bike (see below).

Getting there: From Denver, take I-25 north to Loveland and go west on US 34 to Estes Park. From Estes Park, go west on US 36 (Park Entrance Road) through the southern entrance to Rocky Mountain National Park. Take the first left after entering the park onto Bear Lake Road. Turn left into the parking lot of the Moraine Park Discovery Center. **GPS:** N 40 21'32.00" / W 105 35'9.23"

Ride Description

Rocky Mountain National Park was created only through the work of diligent and devoted conservationists more than one hundred years ago. Not that the mountains would crumble down without that National Park designation, but the area would have become something quite different without it. So appreciate the park in its relatively pristine state while you still can. Arguably, biking on roads that are bumper-to-bumper with looky-loos is a poor way to do that. Plan a little extra time to get off the road and into the woods. Go sit on some rocks and hug some trees.

Fee alert: As of 2015, it costs 20 bucks to get into Rocky Mountain National Park by car, or 10 by bike. (That's 10 bucks per person, so two on a tandem will pay 20.) For that you get a seven-day pass. There are also several fee-free days throughout the year. Check the park's website for more details: nps.gov/romo/planyourvisit/fees .htm. To save 10 dollars and lengthen the ride, start from somewhere outside the gate. Riding from Estes itself adds a bit of difficulty and traffic discomfort.

The first leg of this simple out-and-back to Bear Lake is a moderately tough climb, but it's not super relentless and sadistic. There are some nicely placed flat portions along the way, and only a few short stretches that would be described as steep by a reasonable human. It makes a nice, chilled-out alternative to the much more extreme Trail Ridge Road, which looms above.

The start is one of the prettiest in the book, overlooking Moraine Park, the famous moose-viewing area. As you climb out of the watery, glacier-sculpted valley, several rocky peaks poke their way into view: Otis Peak, the Sharkstooth, Taylor Peak, and McHenry's Peak are all thirteeners trailing off northwest of Long's Peak, the park's grandaddy mountain.

Blue sky, smooth road, and jagged peaks

Unfortunately Bear Lake, with its easy hiking trail, is one of the most popular attractions in the vicinity. On busy days you'll be passed by a steady drip of vehicles for the duration of the climb. And once you get up there you might be alarmed to find a huge and chaotic parking lot, with so many tourists vying for position that park rangers are pressed into service as parking attendants.

Even the apocalyptic crowds can't wreck this ride, however. The road is too sweet, and the views are just too . . . too much.

Miles and Directions

0.0 Start from the parking area at the Moraine Park Discovery Center.

8.2 Arrive at the Bear Lake parking area. Turn around or do some hiking.

16.3 Back at the Moraine Park Discovery Center.

Attractions

Rocky Mountain National Park. A beautiful parcel filled with tall, jagged peaks, pristine forests, and about 150 lakes. Lousy with tourists! No mountain biking allowed (as of now), but road biking is encouraged. Several campgrounds. (970) 586-1206; nps.gov/romo/index.htm.

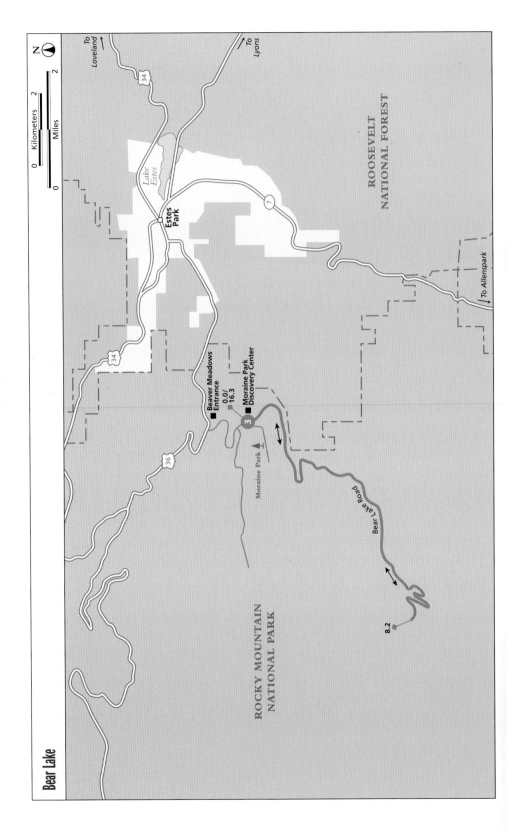

Bear Lake

Bike Shops

Estes Park Mountain Shop. 2050 Big Thompson Ave., Estes Park; (970) 586-6548; estesparkmountainshop.com.

Food

Big Horn Restaurant. 401 W. Elkhorn Ave., Estes Park; (970) 586-2792; estesparkbighorn.com.

Smokin' Dave's BBQ & Taphouse. 820 Moraine Ave., Estes Park; (970) 577-7427; smokindavesq.com.

Lodging

Saddle & Surrey Motel. 1341 S. Saint Vrain Ave., Estes Park; (970) 586-3326; saddleandsurrey.com.

The Stanley Hotel. 333 E. Wonderview Ave., Estes Park; (970) 586-3371; stanleyhotel.com.

OTHER ROCKY MOUNTAIN NATIONAL PARK RIDES

Old Fall River Road. This was the Rocky Mountain National Park ride I was most looking forward to doing. I mean, Bear Lake is a nice ride. But Old Fall River Road is one of the *best* rides. In short, it's a challenging climb to the Alpine Visitor Center near the high point of Trail Ridge. The road is unpaved but well maintained and rarely poses much extra trouble for a road bike (unless it's soupy with rain or snowmelt). It's an amazing alternate route to Trail Ridge Road. It's not devoid of tourist traffic, but compared to Trail Ridge Road, it might seem like it.

The floods of September 2013 thwarted this dream ride along with some others. For the duration of my work on this book, Old Fall River Road was closed for repairs. Efforts to sneak past the barriers were just not sneaky enough. It is slated to reopen in July 2015. Don't miss it.

Trail Ridge Road. This road, snaking up to an alpine pass with almost unbelievable views, provides one of the most challenging rides in the entire West: high altitude, harsh weather (two people were killed by separate lightning strikes off this road in 2014), long miles,

Trail Ridge will destroy you or be the best ride you've ever done—maybe both.

relentless grades, and oppressive traffic. You could punish yourself real good on this thing. But if it all comes together with clear skies, light traffic—maybe a helpful tailwind—you'll never have a better ride. Don't forget the foul-weather gear, extra calories and water, and a camera.

Most of the auto-tourists, and cycle-tourists as well, ride up from the Estes Park side, then turn around at the top (actually at the Alpine Visitor Center, just below the summit on the other side). So naturally the east side of the pass is super crowded compared to the west side. But the west side happens to have spectacular riding as well. The scenery is maybe a notch lower, but the traffic isn't nearly as bad. West-siders take note—Milner Pass may seem like a promising waypoint on the map, but there is no summit of any kind there. The hill chugs right on by, onward and upward to Trail Ridge. Descending the west side, US 34 is relatively comfortable for biking all the way to Granby.

4 Lyons-Lefthand Canyon Loop

A variation of a classic loop, this ride is one of the most difficult and beautiful rides in the book. Lefthand Canyon is a proving ground for power and endurance, and the Peak to Peak Highway is an end in itself.

Start: The parking lot at the Lyons Whitewater Park along CO 66 on the east edge of Lyons
Length: 48.4 miles
Terrain: Rolling hills, long canyon climb, high-altitude rollers, and long canyon descent
Traffic and hazards: Heavy traffic along the first stretch (CO 66 and US 36/North Foothills Highway). Moderate traffic the rest of the way. The descent of South Saint Vrain Canyon (CO

7) was badly compromised by the 2013 floods and has been under construction. While open to bikes, the descent requires some extra care and may not be enjoyable for some riders. Improvements are being made, and the road should be back to its former condition within a year or so.
Things to see: Lefthand Canyon, Peak to Peak Highway, Ward, South Saint Vrain Canyon, Lyons

Getting there: From Denver, head north on I-25 to the CO 66 exit. Go west on CO 66 to Lyons. From Boulder, go north on US 36/North Foothills Highway to CO 66, then turn left toward Lyons. There is public parking on the east end of town on the south side of the highway at the Lyons Whitewater Park, and usually plenty of parking around central Lyons. **GPS:** N 40 13'16.00" / W 105 15'49.12"

Ride Description

Traditionally, local riders start a big Lefthand Canyon loop from Boulder, which makes a lot of sense as most of them live there. Today we decided to give some love to Lyons and stage the ride from this plucky little town to the north. Starting and ending here instead of Boulder also happens to shorten the Lefthand–South Saint Vrain loop by about 15 miles—not an unwelcome abbreviation. You might find yourself agreeing to that somewhere just east of Ward.

Lefthand is the crown jewel of Front Range canyon climbs. It's a very long climb (17 miles) that begins easy and steadily ramps up, with maddening consistency, all the way to the top, where it achieves a nearly wall-like attitude through the town of Ward.

The canyon can be used in a number of different loops, each awesome in its own way. Instead of descending South Saint Vrain, for instance, you could loop back via Estes Park, using either North Saint Vrain or Big Thompson Canyon. You could just as easily head south and descend Sugarloaf, Boulder Canyon, Magnolia Road, Coal Creek Canyon, or Golden Gate Canyon. Sugarloaf and Magnolia connect to the Peak to Peak on dirt. Those who seek out and enjoy dirt roads can combine Lefthand with Sunshine Canyon via Lickskillet Road (CR 89) and Gold Hill; they can drop into Fourmile Canyon from Gold Hill as well. And any of those loop options can be turned around. Reverse it and ride down Lefthand. It's hard to go wrong.

The top of the loop

As you climb Lefthand, you can consider all the greats that have used the canyon as their personal training ground over the decades. Lefthand is one of the most heavily utilized training hills in the nation, without a doubt, decorated almost year-round with kitted-up pros. The list of champions who have graced this hill is fairly mind-blowing and now spans generations.

At Ward you'll probably want to stop. You'll probably want to lie down for a bit. But services are pretty minimal here, and that's just the way the residents like it. There is a small general store in Ward—last time I checked. The establishment does not exude permanence. There was a "For Sale" sign out front in 2014. Bring some cash along because this store (which may or may not exist when you get there) provides the route's only chance to restock, and it doesn't take credit cards. The bathroom consists of a Port-o-Let out back.

If you're among the elite who barely break a sweat on this 17-mile incline, flagellate yourself even more on Brainard Lake Road, which continues up to the base of the gray thirteeners west of the highway. The start of Brainard Lake Road is right there off the Peak to Peak Highway near Ward.

The rest of you will be happy to start cruising downhill immediately on the Peak to Peak. Except for a few climbs thrown in to keep you honest, this 10-mile section of road requires no pedaling, and the shoulder is relatively smooth and luxuriously wide. It's about as close to road-bike bliss as we get around here. Views are so nice from the Peak to Peak that many of the highway's users are here for sightseeing purposes alone.

The descent of South Saint Vrain Canyon was always fun but usually straightforward and uneventful. After the deluge of 2013 reworked the canyon, the post-flood road was narrowed with concrete barriers, and riding it was transformed into a totally different experience. Let's just say not for the faint of heart. (One day while riding *up* the canyon I noticed a small cardboard sign propped up next to the road. It said simply, "Hwy 7 not safe for bikes." I could see their point, although I didn't completely

Let gravity do the work on the Peak to Peak.

agree, obviously.) But the restoration of the road is ongoing as I write. It's a work in progress. Chances are that things will be fixed up nicely by the time you read this, but check with CDOT to make sure.

Lefthand, of course, did not escape the floods either. It was in bad-enough shape that it was closed to bicyclists until the summer of 2014. Except for some unpaved sections and ragged edges, Lefthand Canyon Drive was back to its former state by late 2014.

South Saint Vrain Canyon spills out into Lyons, the unassumingly awesome village of the northern hogbacks, sitting quietly in the cultural shadows of the two bustling college towns that flank it to the north and south. Lyons has had a rough go recently. The big flood was particularly horrific in Lyons, at the business end of two big canyons. Lyons will be just fine without us, but I'm sure the folks wouldn't complain if you stayed awhile and started throwing some money around.

Miles and Directions

0.0 Start from the parking lot off CO 66/US 36/CO 7 at the Lyons Whitewater Park on the east end of town, and begin riding east.

1.0 Turn right onto US 36 (Foothills Highway).

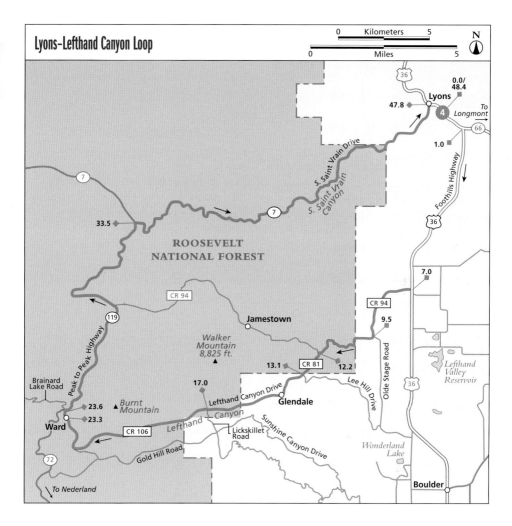

Lyons–Lefthand Canyon Loop

7.0 Turn right onto Lefthand Canyon Drive. The climb starts easy and goes out like a lion.

23.3 Arrive at Ward. The road has become Utica Street. General store is (hopefully) ahead on the right.

23.6 Turn right onto Nelson Street.

23.8 Turn right onto the Peak to Peak Highway.

33.5 Veer right onto CO7/South Saint Vrain Canyon.

47.8. Turn right onto CO 7/US 36 in Lyons. (**Note:** The 2013 flood wiped out the bike path that used to follow the river directly back to Whitewater Park. Ongoing reconstruction implies that this option will be available again in the future.)

48.4 Back at the parking area.

Bike Shops

Redstone Cyclery. 355 Main St., Lyons; (303) 823-5810; redstonecyclery.com. A mountain-bike-oriented shop.

Food

Barking Dog Cafe. 447 Main St., Lyons; (303) 823-9600. Coffee and food.

Oskar Blues Brewery. 303 Main St., Lyons; (303) 823-6685; oskarblues.com. Not known for their food, unless you count beer as food.

Smokin' Dave's BBQ & Taphouse. 228 Main St., Lyons; (303) 823-0993; smokindavesq .com.

St. Vrain Market, Deli & Bakery. 455 Main St., Lyons; (303) 823-5225; stvrainmarket .com. Deli sandwiches to go, plus groceries.

Steamboat Mountain Natural Food. 454 Main St., Lyons; (303) 823-9444. Small grocery.

The Stone Cup. 442 High St., Lyons; (303) 823-2345; thestonecup.com. Breakfast and lunch.

Lodging

Aspen Leaf Antiques and Motel. 338 Main St., Lyons; (303) 823-6181. Humble, right in town.

Stone Mountain Lodge and Cabins. 18055 N. Saint Vrain Dr., Lyons; (303) 823-6091; stonemountainlodge.com. Located a few miles up US 36.

5 Sunshine Canyon

There's nothing fancy about this simple out-and-back route, but the setting is sweet, and the hill's a crusher. Sunshine Canyon is one of the reasons Boulder is so great.

Start: Centennial/Mt. Sanitas Trailhead parking lot on Mapleton Avenue/Sunshine Canyon Drive
Length: 10.8 miles out-and-back
Terrain: Challenging climb; fast descent

Traffic and hazards: Moderate traffic. High-speed descent on curvy mountain road. Watch for other cyclists descending the road at speed. Sunburn.
Things to see: Sunshine Canyon, Bald Mountain Scenic Area

Getting there: From Denver, head north on I-25 to US 36 and take US 36 to Boulder. Exit at Baseline Road and go west up the hill to 9th Street. Take 9th Street north to Mapleton Avenue. Turn left and take Mapleton past the hospital, and park in the Centennial Trailhead lot on the left (across the street from Mount Sanitas). **GPS:** N 40 1'13.00" / W 105 17'51.88"

Ride Description

If you like climbing hills on your bike, and you're in the vicinity of Boulder, Colorado, give this one a try. Rarely will you find a more conveniently crushing hill climb, poised and ready to accept your challenge at all hours of the day. Got a crazy whim to ride up a hill after dinner? What's stopping you—Sunshine is ready. Need to sweat out last night's overindulgence before breakfast? Sunshine Canyon will get the nasty out . . . and fast.

Sunshine Canyon is the most accessible of all the climbs near town. To find it, simply get on Mapleton Avenue—the grand divided residential street at the top of the hill north of Pearl Street—and head toward the mountains. Mapleton continues west past a hospital and a few hikers' trailheads and becomes Sunshine Canyon Drive. The climbing begins immediately and continues more or less unabated for 7.5 miles or so, before the road drops into Gold Hill, improbably, from above.

For this particular out-and-back, I've got you turning around where the pavement ends—a nod to the gravel avoiders—which gives you about 5.5 miles of solid, asphalt-plated climbing from the Centennial Trailhead parking lot. If you happen to be driving in from a remote location, you can park along the road at the bottom of the hill, or use one of these trailhead lots. The mileage cues begin as the road passes the entrance of the Centennial Trailhead lot. Of course if you're based in or around Boulder, it makes more sense to ride to the hill.

The entirety of the climb hovers between the moderate and difficult range, with spates of relatively easy road bookended by long, steep stretches. On a hot day, when you've got that not-so-fresh feeling, those steep stretches are particularly cruel. The hardest bit is the half-mile pitch that starts about 2.5 miles into the climb and

Stand and deliver: the steepest section of Sunshine

maintains a solid 12 percent incline for just under half a mile. Total elevation gain for the paved portion of Sunshine is about 1,800 feet.

If you're just looking for a quick, incredibly effective workout, this little out-and-back will do the trick. It's more than enough. If you're looking to get somewhere via Sunshine Canyon or put together one of those classic Boulder loops, your best bet is to continue after the pavement ends, up and over the top to the little village called Gold Hill. At the crossroads in Gold Hill you can turn left and bomb down to Fourmile Canyon, turn right and descend on Lickskillet Road to Lefthand Canyon, or continue straight to the Peak to Peak Highway. All on gravel, however.

Another gravel route connecting to Sunshine is Poorman Road, off to the left 2.3 miles up the hill. Poorman Road winds around a bit, then drops steeply and without pavement to Fourmile Canyon. It's a well-traveled connector for the local riders, although most of the folks on Poorman will be using knobby tires. See the Poorman Loop ride for a Fourmile-to-Sunshine excursion via Poorman.

Miles and Directions

0.0 Start from the Centennial/Mt. Sanitas Trailhead parking lot and begin riding up Sunshine Canyon Drive.

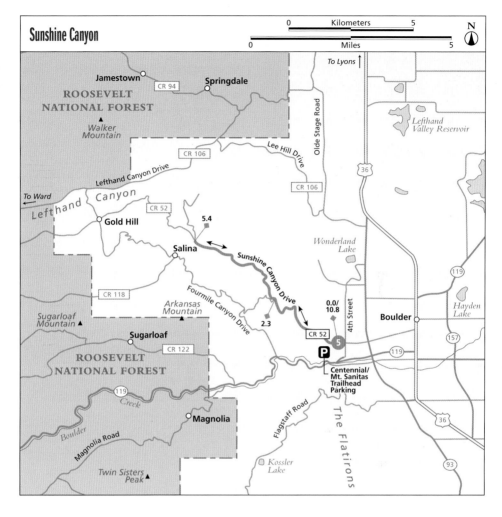

Sunshine Canyon

2.3 Pass the intersection with Poorman Road.

5.4 Pavement ends. Turn around here or . . . (**Option:** Continue to Gold Hill.)

10.8 Back at the parking lot.

Bike Shops

Behold this *partial* list of Boulder's favorite bike shops:

Boulder Cycle Sport. 4580 Broadway St., Boulder; (303) 444-2453; bouldercyclesport .com. They have another location on South Broadway.

Excel Sports. 2045 32nd St., Boulder; (303) 444-6737; excelsports.com.

Fat Kitty Cycles. 3380 Arapahoe Ave., Boulder; (720) 982-4120; fatkittycycles.com.

Full Cycle. 1795 Pearl St., Boulder; (303) 440-1002; fullcyclebikes.com.

LTD Cycleworx. 5360 Arapahoe Ave., Boulder; (303) 442-3283; ltdcycleworx.com.

Pro Peloton Cyclery. 2615 13th St., Boulder; (303) 415-1292; propeloton.com.

The Pro's Closet. 4939 N. Broadway St. #58, Boulder; (303) 993-7776; theproscloset.com.
REI. 1789 28th St., Boulder; (303) 583-9970; REI.com.
The Sports Garage. 2705 Spruce St., Boulder; (303) 473-0033; sportsgarage.net.
Standard Bike Repair. 1823 Marine St., Boulder; (720) 837-8984. standardbikerepair.com.
University Bicycles. 839 Pearl St., Boulder; (303) 444-4196; ubikes.com.
Vecchio's. 1833 Pearl St., Boulder; (303) 440-3535; vecchios.com.

Food

Chautauqua Dining Hall. 900 W. Baseline Rd., Boulder; (303) 440-3776; chautauqua.com. Overpriced food but great location, views, and historical ambience.
Il Pastaio. 3075 B Arapahoe Ave., Boulder; (303) 447-9572; ilpastaioboulder.com. Italian.
Mountain Sun Pub & Brewery. 1535 Pearl St., Boulder; (303) 546-0886; mountainsunpub .com.
Ras Kassa's Ethiopian Restaurant. 2111 30th St., Boulder; (303) 447-2919; raskassas .com.
Rincon Argentino. Village Boulder Shopping Center, 2525 Arapahoe Ave., Boulder; (303) 442-4133; rinconargentinoboulder.com. Argentinean food in a strip mall.

Rio Grande Mexican Restaurant. 1101 Walnut St., Boulder; (303) 444-3690; riogrande mexican.com. People go here for margaritas and don't expect too much from the food.

Lodging

Alps Boulder Canyon Inn. 38619 Boulder Canyon Dr., Boulder; (303) 444-5445; alpsinn .com. Upscale, located on the route in Boulder Canyon.
Boulder University Inn. 1632 Broadway, Boulder; (303) 417-1700; boulderuniversityinn .com. Motel on Broadway.
Briar Rose Bed & Breakfast. 2151 Arapahoe Ave., Boulder; (303) 442-3007; briarosebb .com.
Foot of the Mountain Motel. 200 Arapahoe Ave., Boulder; (303) 442-5688; footofthe mountainmotel.com. Right by Eben G. Fine Park.
Quality Inn & Suites Boulder Creek. 2020 Arapahoe Ave., Boulder; (303) 449-7550; qualityinn.com.
Silver Saddle Motel. 90 Arapahoe Ave., Boulder; (303) 442-8022; silversaddlemotel.com. Also right there by Eben G. Fine Park.

6 Poorman Loop

This short loop, a traditional outing for local riders, dishes out a lot of hurt as it climbs between Fourmile and Sunshine Canyons on a dirt road. The route is suitable for mountain bikes or road bikes, but neither type of bike would be totally at home.

Start: Eben G. Fine Park in west Boulder
Length: 8.9 miles
Terrain: An easy, shallow climb up Fourmile Canyon leads to a difficult, steep climb on dirt Poorman Road.

Traffic and hazards: Moderate traffic in Fourmile Canyon and Sunshine Canyon. Requires crossing CO 119.
Things to see: Boulder Canyon, Fourmile Canyon, Sunshine Canyon

Getting there: From Denver, head north on I-25 to US 36 and take US 36 to Boulder. Exit at Baseline Road and go west up the hill to 9th Street. Take 9th Street north to Arapahoe Avenue. Turn left and take Arapahoe until you reach Eben G. Fine Park. **GPS:** N 40 0'46.40" / W 105 17'48.31'

Ride Description

Start this spicy loop by heading up Boulder Canyon to Fourmile Canyon. Fourmile is a real gem, with mellow slopes and traffic. One of the best sections of road in the vicinity, a true joy to ride when the truck traffic is on a low boil, Fourmile Canyon makes a legit out-and-back in its own right. But it's another one of those pavement structures that doesn't connect to any other pavement structures, and it requires forays onto dirt in order to make a loop.

Dirt roads sprouting from Fourmile Canyon provide a few very interesting options for hearty loopers. Taking a right at Salina, the obvious fork in the road way up the canyon, puts travelers on a very steep course toward Gold Hill. To the south, Logan Mill Road climbs to the top of the hill and, with a little luck or ninja navigation skills or both, can be connected to Sugarloaf Road on the other side. To the north, Poorman Road provides a connection to Sunshine Canyon. Poorman's no walk in the park, but it's the most accessible and by far the shortest of these three loop options.

Boulderites express themselves at Eben G. Fine Park.

A Flatiron viewed from Boulder Creek

(Note that the Switzerland Trail, a four-wheel-drive road connecting to the top of Fourmile Canyon at Sunset, is just too rough for a road bike.)

After pedaling 2 miles up winding, leafy Fourmile Canyon Drive, take a right onto Poorman Road.

Poorman doesn't mess around. The pavement disappears. Gone as well are the mellow slopes. The most notorious section of Poorman Road is steep enough (15 percent or so) to cause traction problems for road bikers. That's a deal breaker for a lot of people; for others, it's the prime attraction. The dirt-surfaced climb is certainly more suitable for mountain bikes; however, the dirt section is only about 1 mile long, and road bikes are much more appropriate for the remainder of the loop. In other words, the Poorman Loop is a pretty good excuse to break out the cyclocross bike.

The reward for the climb is a fast descent of lower Sunshine Canyon, and the satisfied afterglow of a good workout.

Miles and Directions

0.0 Start from Eben G. Fine Park and begin riding west up Boulder Canyon on the bike path.

2.1 The path, having turned to dirt, ends at CO 119. Carefully cross and begin riding up Fourmile Canyon Drive. The intersection is directly across the road from the path's terminus.

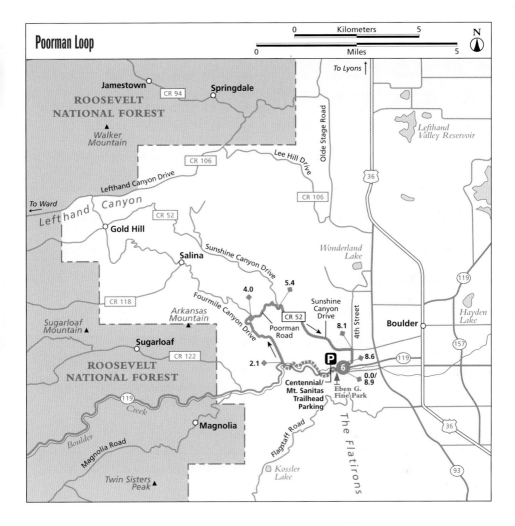

Poorman Loop

4.0 Turn right onto Poorman Road.

5.4 Turn right onto Sunshine Canyon Drive.

8.1 Turn right onto 4th Street.

8.4 Turn right onto Spruce Street, briefly, and then turn left onto a concrete bike path.

8.5 Turn right onto Pearl Street.

8.6 Veer right onto the bike path.

8.9 Back at Eben G. Fine Park.

Bike Shops

Behold this *partial* list of Boulder's favorite bike shops:

Boulder Cycle Sport. 4580 Broadway St., Boulder; (303) 444-2453; bouldercyclesport.com. They have another location on South Broadway.

Excel Sports. 2045 32nd St., Boulder; (303) 444-6737; excelsports.com.

Fat Kitty Cycles. 3380 Arapahoe Ave., Boulder; (720) 982-4120; fatkittycycles.com.
Full Cycle. 1795 Pearl St., Boulder; (303) 440-1002; fullcyclebikes.com.
LTD Cycleworx. 5360 Arapahoe Ave., Boulder; (303) 442-3283; ltdcycleworx.com.
Pro Peloton Cyclery. 2615 13th St., Boulder; (303) 415-1292; propeloton.com.
The Pro's Closet. 4939 N. Broadway St. #58, Boulder; (303) 993-7776; theproscloset.com.
REI. 1789 28th St., Boulder; (303) 583-9970; REI.com.
The Sports Garage. 2705 Spruce St., Boulder; (303) 473-0033; sportsgarage.net.
Standard Bike Repair. 1823 Marine St., Boulder; (720) 837-8984; standardbikerepair.com.
University Bicycles. 839 Pearl St., Boulder; (303) 444-4196; ubikes.com.
Vecchio's. 1833 Pearl St., Boulder; (303) 440-3535; vecchios.com.

Food

Chautauqua Dining Hall. 900 W. Baseline Rd., Boulder; (303) 440-3776; chautauqua.com. Overpriced food but great location, views, and historical ambience.
Il Pastaio. 3075 B Arapahoe Ave., Boulder; (303) 447-9572; ilpastaioboulder.com. Italian.
The Kitchen. 1039 Pearl St., Boulder; (303) 544-5973; thekitchen.com.
Mountain Sun Pub & Brewery. 1535 Pearl St., Boulder; (303) 546-0886; mountainsunpub.com.

Ras Kassa's Ethiopian Restaurant. 2111 30th St., Boulder; (303) 447-2919; raskassas.com.
Rincon Argentino. Village Boulder Shopping Center, 2525 Arapahoe Ave., Boulder; (303) 442-4133; rinconargentinoboulder.com. Argentinean food in a strip mall.
Rio Grande Mexican Restaurant. 1101 Walnut St., Boulder; (303) 444-3690; riogrande mexican.com. People go here for margaritas and don't expect too much from the food.

Lodging

Alps Boulder Canyon Inn. 38619 Boulder Canyon Dr., Boulder; (303) 444-5445; alpsinn.com. Upscale, located on the route in Boulder Canyon.
Boulder University Inn. 1632 Broadway, Boulder; (303) 417-1700; boulderuniversityinn.com. Motel on Broadway.
Briar Rose Bed & Breakfast. 2151 Arapahoe Ave., Boulder; (303) 442-3007; briarosebb.com.
Foot of the Mountain Motel. 200 Arapahoe Ave., Boulder; (303) 442-5688; footofthe mountainmotel.com. Right by Eben G. Fine Park.
Quality Inn & Suites Boulder Creek. 2020 Arapahoe Ave., Boulder; (303) 449-7550; qualityinn.com.
Silver Saddle Motel. 90 Arapahoe Ave., Boulder; (303) 442-8022; silversaddlemotel.com. Also right there by Eben G. Fine Park.

7 Boulder Creek Path Loop

Relax with this chilled-out loop through and around Boulder, primarily on off-street paths.

Start: Eben G. Fine Park in west Boulder
Length: 14.4 miles
Terrain: Slightly downhill path by Boulder Creek as it transforms from a mountain to a prairie river; slightly uphill on the way back into town
Traffic and hazards: Busy paths with sharp curves require you to stay on high alert even without motor traffic. Some on-street riding with light traffic and one short stretch with heavy traffic on Table Mesa Drive.
Things to see: Boulder, inside and out; Boulder Creek; University of Colorado; National Institute of Standards

Getting there: From Denver, head north on I-25 to US 36 and take US 36 to Boulder. Exit at Baseline Road and go west up the hill to 9th Street. Take 9th Street north to Arapahoe Avenue. Turn left and take Arapahoe until you reach Eben G. Fine Park. **GPS:** N 40 0'46.40" / W 105 17'48.31"

Ride Description

Even Boulder's pro racers like to cruise on the bike path now and then. The path might be crowded with walkers and relatively slow pedalers, but there's something about riding there that is truly delightful—the complete lack of cars, of course.

As a true fully separated cycling facility, the Boulder Creek Path passes under all the roads and intersections, providing nonstop—if often slower than you'd like—passage all the way through the city. You couldn't call it carefree by any means, but riding has a totally different feel to it when cars aren't involved. The path literally and figuratively exists on a different plane than the traffic grid.

This loop starts with a tour of nearly the entire length of the Boulder Creek Path, from the west edge of town against the mountains all the way to the hinterlands to the east. You'll pass, in order of appearance, the Boulder County Justice Center, Boulder Public Library, and Boulder High School. This is central Boulder in all its glory, and the path through here is usually pretty clogged with many different types of users, from strolling students and homeless guys to aero-tucked triathletes and everything in between. Don't expect to ride fast through town.

Pretty soon the path busts out into semi-open country. East Boulder is a patchwork of research and industrial parks crisscrossed by mini highways. There is substantial green space surrounding the creek, and the path rolls right through it.

The route is pretty easy to follow, though there are several intersecting paths along the way. Boulder has done a nice job of building out its off-street path network, and there are a ton of options for different loops. (See *Best Bike Rides Denver and Boulder* [FalconGuides] for more path rides around town.) For this route, stick to the main path that follows Boulder Creek, ignoring all the spurs, until mile 4.5. After crossing

South Boulder Creek Trail

55th, Boulder Creek veers off to the north. Turn right here onto the South Boulder Creek Path, continuing east around the bottom of a tooth-shaped reservoir. This path turns due south, following a different creek and greenway.

The South Boulder Creek Path is not continuous but spills out onto quiet residential streets along the way. At South Boulder Road, turn west and roll in the bike lane. South Boulder Road (becoming Table Mesa Drive) passes a series of highway ramps, the most harrowing portion of the ride.

Use Moorhead Avenue to cut up to another section of bike path through Martin Park, just to add some interest and another pleasant park cruise to the mix, as described below and shown on the map; alternatively, continue straight west on Table Mesa Drive and rejoin the route at Broadway. Here the route passes right in front of the National Institute of Standards, a real point of interest for science geeks. Ask for a tour of the atomic clock.

Passing the University of Colorado–Boulder campus and "The Hill," the route follows a very different kind of bike path. This path, though helpful in its own way, is more like a big sidewalk. It's separated from traffic between intersections but requires riders to cross busy streets, in sharp contrast to the Boulder Creek Path.

Leaving the campus behind, the side path follows Broadway down a steep hill to the creek. Find the Boulder Creek Path there and turn left to head back to Eben G.

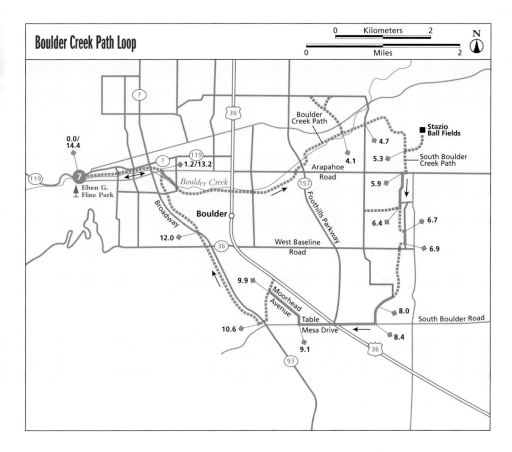

Boulder Creek Path Loop

Fine Park. There are several interesting ways to return to the start from the southeast corner of Boulder, so keep an open mind, and if possible check the Boulder County bike map (bouldercounty.org/doc/transportation/bikemap.pdf) to get some more ideas. There is no obvious bike-path route from there, but there are countless funky ones.

Miles and Directions

0.0 Start from Eben G. Fine Park and begin riding east on the Boulder Creek Path.

1.2 Veer left at the fork, following the creek.

2.4 Continue straight at the path intersection.

3.0 Continue straight as another path intersects on the right.

3.3 After crossing under Foothills Parkway (CO 157), continue east-northeast on the Boulder Creek Path.

4.1 Continue straight as other paths intersect on the left. (The second of these leads north to Valmont Bike Park.)

4.5 Cross under 55th Street and continue due east.

Looking southwest from South Boulder Creek

4.7 Veer right at the fork onto the South Boulder Creek Path. You should find yourself on the south shore of a small, tooth-shaped lake.

4.9 Continue straight as a path intersects on the right.

5.3 Continue due south at a path intersection. (The path to the left goes to Stazio Softball Fields.)

5.9 After crossing under Arapahoe Avenue, the path ends at Old Tale Road. Turn south on Old Tale Road.

6.4 Continue due south on the South Boulder Creek Path at the end of the road. Continue straight as another path intersects on the right.

6.7 The path turns east and spills out onto Dimmitt Drive. Take the first right onto Gapter Road, due south again.

6.9 Turn right, back onto bike path. The path turns south and crosses under West Baseline Road, then enters open space.

7.7 The path crosses a road. On the other side, turn south, passing several path intersections. The path will hug the road (55th Street) and curve around to the west.

8.0 The path spills out onto 55th Street. Continue on the street.

8.2 Continue south on 55th Street as it crosses Ontario Place.

8.4 Turn right onto South Boulder Road.

8.8 South Boulder Road crosses under Foothills Parkway (CO 157) and becomes Table Mesa Drive. Carefully continue through an intersection and past a few on- and off-ramps.

9.1 Turn right onto Moorhead Avenue. (**Option:** Continue straight on Table Mesa Drive, rejoining the route at mile 10.6, for a more direct option.)

9.9 Turn right onto the bike path. Take a sharp left immediately at the first intersection and cross under Moorhead Avenue. You are now headed southwest.

10.6 After cruising through Martin Park, the path crosses under South Broadway near its intersection with Table Mesa Drive. Turn right onto Harvard Lane, next to South Broadway.

11.0 Crossing Dartmouth Avenue, the route continues on bike path.

11.7 Continue as the path spills out onto Sunnyside Lane after passing the National Institute of Standards.

11.8 Cross West Baseline Road.

12.0 Turn right, dive under Broadway, and continue following Broadway via a path on the other side.

12.2 Cross Regent Drive and continue on the path past the campus.

12.3 Cross 18th Street.

12.4 Cross Euclid Avenue.

12.8 Cross Pleasant Street.

12.9 Cross University Avenue.

13.0 Cross Grandview Avenue and 13th Street.

13.2 At the bottom of the hill, continue around the athletic field and turn left to cross the creek on a bridge.

13.2 On the other side of the creek, turn left onto the Boulder Creek Path.

14.4 Back at Eben G. Fine Park.

Attractions

National Institute of Standards (NIST). 325 Broadway St., Boulder; (301) 975-6478; nist .gov. Get calibrated!

Bike Shops

Behold this *partial* list of Boulder's favorite bike shops:

Boulder Cycle Sport. 4580 Broadway St., Boulder; (303) 444-2453; bouldercyclesport .com. They have another location on South Broadway.

Excel Sports. 2045 32nd St., Boulder; (303) 444-6737; excelsports.com.

Fat Kitty Cycles. 3380 Arapahoe Ave., Boulder; (720) 982-4120; fatkittycycles.com.

Full Cycle. 1795 Pearl St., Boulder; (303) 440-1002; fullcyclebikes.com.

LTD Cycleworx. 5360 Arapahoe Ave., Boulder; (303) 442-3283; ltdcycleworx.com.

Pro Peloton Cyclery. 2615 13th St., Boulder; (303) 415-1292; propeloton.com.

The Pro's Closet. 4939 N. Broadway St. #58, Boulder; (303) 993-7776; theproscloset.com.

REI. 1789 28th St., Boulder; (303) 583-9970; REI.com.

The Sports Garage. 2705 Spruce St., Boulder; (303) 473-0033; sportsgarage.net.

Standard Bike Repair. 1823 Marine St., Boulder; (720) 837-8984; standardbikerepair.com.

University Bicycles. 839 Pearl St., Boulder; (303) 444-4196; ubikes.com.

Vecchio's. 1833 Pearl St., Boulder; (303) 440-3535; vecchios.com.

Food

Chautauqua Dining Hall. 900 W. Baseline Rd., Boulder; (303) 440-3776; chautauqua.com. Overpriced food but great location, views, and historical ambience.

Il Pastaio. 3075 B Arapahoe Ave., Boulder; (303) 447-9572; ilpastaioboulder.com. Italian.

The Kitchen. 1039 Pearl St., Boulder; (303) 544-5973; thekitchen.com.

Mountain Sun Pub & Brewery. 1535 Pearl St., Boulder; (303) 546-0886; mountainsunpub .com.

Ras Kassa's Ethiopian Restaurant. 2111 30th St., Boulder; (303) 447-2919; raskassas .com.

Rincon Argentino. Village Boulder Shopping Center, 2525 Arapahoe Ave., Boulder; (303) 442-4133; rinconargentinoboulder.com. Argentinean food in a strip mall.

Rio Grande Mexican Restaurant. 1101 Walnut St., Boulder; (303) 444-3690; riogrande mexican.com. People go here for margaritas and don't expect too much from the food.

Lodging

Alps Boulder Canyon Inn. 38619 Boulder Canyon Dr., Boulder; (303) 444-5445; alpsinn .com. Upscale, located on the route in Boulder Canyon.

Boulder University Inn. 1632 Broadway, Boulder; (303) 417-1700; boulderuniversityinn .com. Motel on Broadway.

Briar Rose Bed & Breakfast. 2151 Arapahoe Ave., Boulder; (303) 442-3007; briarosebb .com.

Foot of the Mountain Motel. 200 Arapahoe Ave., Boulder; (303) 442-5688; footofthe mountainmotel.com. Right by Eben G. Fine Park.

Quality Inn & Suites Boulder Creek. 2020 Arapahoe Ave., Boulder; (303) 449-7550; qualityinn.com.

Silver Saddle Motel. 90 Arapahoe Ave., Boulder; (303) 442-8022. silversaddlemotel.com. Also right there by Eben G. Fine Park.

8 Sugarloaf Loop

This ride is for hard-core road bikers who crave endless steep climbs and who don't mind a little dirt. Sugarloaf Road is an interesting, less-crowded alternative to the big canyons. It's also a much steeper alternative to the big canyons.

Start: Eben G. Fine Park in west Boulder
Length: 43.5 miles
Terrain: Mountains: tough climbing, fast descending
Traffic and hazards: Heavy traffic in Boulder Canyon and US 36 (North Foothills Highway). Some dirt-road mileage. One short tunnel to deal with in Boulder Canyon. Lefthand Canyon was affected by the floods of 2013, and the road was in less-than-perfect shape throughout 2014. Some of the road's width was washed away in spots, and the surface was unpaved and fairly rough here and there in late 2014. Restoration projects are ongoing.
Things to see: Boulder Canyon, Sugarloaf Mountain, Peak to Peak Highway, Ward, Lefthand Canyon, Wonderland Lake

Getting there: From Denver, head north on I-25 to US 36. Take US 36 to Boulder. Exit at Baseline Road and go west up the hill. Turn right at 9th Street. Take 9th back down the hill and turn left on Arapahoe Avenue. Take Arapahoe Avenue west until it ends at Eben G. Fine Park. **GPS:** N 40 0'46.40" / W 105 17'48.31"

Ride Description

As the 1960s came to a close, a Denver band called Chocolate Hair finished recording its first album. The album included a groovy tune called "Green-Eyed Lady," which would go on to be a big hit. The band's record company had just one request before publishing the album and unleashing "Green-Eyed Lady" on the masses: Change the band's name. Anything but Chocolate Hair, they said. So the members of Chocolate Hair looked around their environs and tried to come up with a new name.

There are gazillions of Sugarloaf Mountains around the country, but the band formerly known as Chocolate Hair, the band behind the international radio superhit "Green-Eyed Lady," named itself after *this* one. This one right here, looming over Boulder County. They can never take that away from us!

Save that info for the trivia-contest semifinals, and save this ride for a day when you're feeling particularly badass. Featuring some sketchy traffic, super-steep climbs, dirt roads, and flood-ravaged canyons, this loop is not only strenuous but adventurous. It's a serious challenge best suited to experienced riders. It's also an amazing and beautiful ride.

Start by heading west out of Boulder on the Boulder Creek Path, which turns to dirt as it snakes up the canyon in the roar of the creek. This crunchy, slippery stretch of rusticated path is your taxiway to some classic road rides.

When the path hits CO 119 (Boulder Canyon Drive), carefully get on the highway and head uphill by angry Boulder Creek. The traffic here can be annoying—harrowing

Unpaved road connects Sugarloaf to the Peak to Peak Highway.

even—especially when the road goes through a short tunnel. (After working half my life as a bike messenger, I still sprint like a freaked-out bunny through tunnels like this.) But if all the drivers happen to have their wits about them, you'll make it past this snaky 2.3-mile section. And if you don't think the traffic is that bad, you might even decide to come back and ride the whole canyon, all the way to Nederland and beyond.

Just beyond the turnoff for Magnolia Road (to your left, file that one away for later), find the sharp right turn—generally unmarked—onto Sugarloaf Road (CR 122). The early climbing could be described as moderate. Not too steep for too long. After this initial bit of manageable climbing, the road even flattens out for a spell. This could give you the very false impression that Sugarloaf is a mellow, forgiving climb.

Starting about 6.5 miles into the ride (and about 2 miles up Sugarloaf Road), you round a corner and run into a wall. For the next 2.5 miles, the grade hovers in the 10 to 15 percent range, displaying an alarming lack of switchbacks and a complete lack of respect for your well-being. You'll be hallucinating giant green-eyed ladies up there. Sugarloaf is a true test of a cyclist's love for climbing.

There is actually quite a bit going on up here on the hill. Off to your left is Dream Canyon. This hidden gorge carved by Boulder Creek is one of the area's most stunning natural attractions, if you can find it. Don't go poking around over there, however, if you'd be hugely disturbed to run across some of the male nudists who have been known to gather around the canyon's swimming holes. So there's that. Notice also the huge burn scar still visible up here from a 1989 forest fire that destroyed forty-four homes on the mountain and filled Boulder with heavy smoke, but claimed no lives. That, too, was caused by male nudists. (Seriously, that one was caused by a fully clothed guy tossing a cigarette down in Boulder Canyon.) Near the top of the hill, there's a connector on the right to the Switzerland Trail, an old railbed that now serves as an awesome route for all-terrain bikes. Come back and make a big loop out of that someday, too, but don't try it on a regular road bike (too rocky).

Something else notable happens up here: The climb actually ends. Sort of. For a while. In fact the road points *downhill* for a while, if you can believe that. Then it turns to dirt. Don't feel ashamed to turn around right here if you're not happy with the idea of pedaling through 3 to 4 miles of choppy, mostly uphill dirt road. Nothing to be ashamed of after climbing that hill. And the descent back down Sugarloaf Road is among the best.

Turn around at the "Pavement Ends" sign if you want, but some really fine riding lies beyond the dirt. Persevere and you'll be able to turn onto the Peak to Peak Highway to start one of the nicer road segments available to mankind. The climb continues on the Peak to Peak at a point in the ride when many will be struggling big time, already spent. But the road is undeniably sweet.

Eight miles on the smooth Peak to Peak, with the steel-gray peaks poking up over the sea of pine trees, brings you to Ward, the town that always sleeps. You were charmed by Ward when you climbed to it on the Lyons–Lefthand Canyon Loop ride, but you'll love it when coasting into it from above. Pull over at the general store (cash only) to shore up for the home stretch. In 2014, I noticed the store was for sale, so let's just hope it still exists in the coming years.

The descent of Lefthand Canyon is no walk in the park. The flood of 2013 ate much of the road, and not all of it had been replaced by late 2014. There were still big sections of washed-out road and lots of dirt sections that had yet to be repaved, making for an exciting ride. No doubt the situation will be improved as time goes on, but, then, no doubt the canyon will see more floods, too. In any case, watch carefully for road damage when descending Lefthand.

At this point you're probably thinking, boy, all this descending is starting to piss me off! I could use another

Local riders are hoping this store in Ward continues to exist.

seriously steep and painful climb! Just in time, turn right onto Lee Hill Drive, another classic. It is steep and painful, but it doesn't last too long. The little summit here marks the last of the ride's 5,000-plus feet of climbing. Soon you're dropping into North Boulder like an eagle onto a prairie mouse. (You could avoid the Lee Hill climb by descending all the way down Lefthand to US 36, but that's longer and has enough climbing that it probably wouldn't save you an ounce of exertion to take that route.)

Finish the ride by joining the path system of northwest Boulder. Skirt Wonderland Lake as you roll southbound, and find the path on the other side of Linden that connects to 4th Street, the quiet street that provides most of the final leg of the loop.

Miles and Directions

0.0 Start from Eben G. Fine Park and pedal up Boulder Canyon Drive on the bike path.

0.9 The path surface turns to crushed gravel. Watch out for the pinch-flat-causing lip of the bridge.

2.1 The path climbs to the highway and ends. Carefully turn left and begin to ride up CO 119 (not Fourmile Canyon Drive).

3.3 Ride through a short tunnel.

4.5 Turn right onto Sugarloaf Road (CR 122).

9.2 Begin a surprising descent after a very long, tough climb.

11.2 Sugarloaf Road turns to dirt.

14.8 Turn right onto the Peak to Peak Highway (CO 72).

23.2 Turn right onto Nelson Street at Ward.

23.5 The road goes around a switchback and becomes Utica Street.

23.6 Little grocery store on the left.

34.0 Take a right onto Lee Hill Drive.

35.3 Top of the Lee Hill climb.

38.4 Stay right on Lee Hill Drive as Olde Stage Road intersects on the left.

39.5 Take a right onto 8th Street.

39.6 8th Street ends. Continue straight on the bike path for one block, jog left briefly on Yellow Pine Lane, then continue straight south on the bike path.

39.8 Turn right and continue south on 9th Street.

40.0 Cross Cherry Avenue and continue due south on the bike path.

40.1 The path ends at Locust Avenue. Continue straight on 9th Street again.

40.2 Turn right onto Utica Avenue.

40.3 Turn left, back onto the gravel bike path skirting the east shore of Wonderland Lake.

40.6 After passing the lake, find a path continuing south briefly between some houses and condos. Cross Quince Avenue and continue south on Wonderland Hill Avenue.

41.3 Zig west briefly, cross Linden Avenue, and continue south on a path.

41.5 The path spills out onto 4th Street. Continue straight.

43.1 Take a right onto Spruce Street, then within a block take a left onto a concrete bike path by some tennis courts.

Sugarloaf Loop

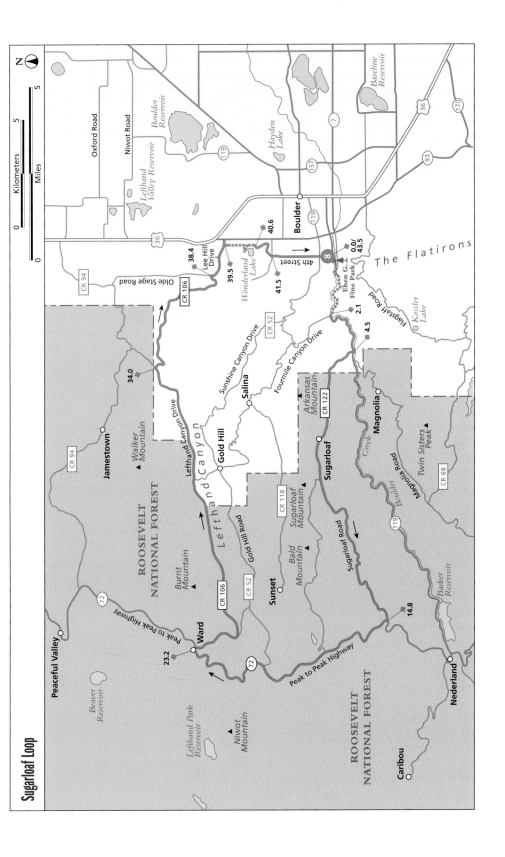

N

Kilometers
0   5

Miles
0   5

Oxford Road

Niwot Road

Boulder Reservoir

Lefthand Valley Reservoir

CR 94

Olde Stage Road

38.4

Lee Hill Drive

39.5

Wonderland Lake

40.6

Hayden Lake

119

157

Boulder

119

7

Baseline Reservoir

36

93

170

CR 106

41.5

4th Street

8

0.0/ 43.5

Eben G. I Fine Park

Flagstaff Road

Kossler Lake

The Flatirons

2.1

4.5

Sunshine Canyon Drive

CR 52

Salina

Fourmile Canyon Drive

Arkansas Mountain

CR 122

Sugarloaf

34.0

Lefthand Canyon Drive

Walker Mountain

Gold Hill

Jamestown

CR 94

ROOSEVELT NATIONAL FOREST

Lefthand Canyon

Gold Hill Road

CR 118

Sugarloaf Mountain

Magnolia

Boulder Creek

Magnolia Road

Twin Sisters Peak

CR 68

119

Burnt Mountain

CR 106

CR 52

Sunset

Bald Mountain

Sugarloaf Road

72

Peak to Peak Highway

Ward

23.2

14.8

Baker Reservoir

Nederland

Peaceful Valley

Beaver Reservoir

Lefthand Park Reservoir

Niwot Mountain

72

Peak to Peak Highway

ROOSEVELT NATIONAL FOREST

Caribou

43.2 Take a right onto Pearl Street.

43.3 Get on the bike path on the right side of Pearl Street.

43.5 The path deposits you back at Eben G. Fine Park.

Bike Shops

Behold this *partial* list of Boulder's favorite bike shops:

Boulder Cycle Sport. 4580 Broadway St., Boulder; (303) 444-2453; bouldercyclesport .com. They have another location on South Broadway.

Excel Sports. 2045 32nd St., Boulder; (303) 444-6737; excelsports.com.

Fat Kitty Cycles. 3380 Arapahoe Ave., Boulder; (720) 982-4120; fatkittycycles.com.

Full Cycle. 1795 Pearl St., Boulder; (303) 440-1002; fullcyclebikes.com.

LTD Cycleworx. 5360 Arapahoe Ave., Boulder; (303) 442-3283; ltdcycleworx.com.

Pro Peloton Cyclery. 2615 13th St., Boulder; (303) 415-1292; propeloton.com.

The Pro's Closet. 4939 N. Broadway St. #58, Boulder; (303) 993-7776; theproscloset.com.

REI. 1789 28th St., Boulder; (303) 583-9970; REI.com.

The Sports Garage. 2705 Spruce St., Boulder; (303) 473-0033; sportsgarage.net.

Standard Bike Repair. 1823 Marine St., Boulder; (720) 837-8984; standardbikerepair.com.

University Bicycles. 839 Pearl St., Boulder; (303) 444-4196; ubikes.com.

Vecchio's. 1833 Pearl St., Boulder; (303) 440-3535; vecchios.com.

Food

Chautauqua Dining Hall. 900 W. Baseline Rd., Boulder; (303) 440-3776; chautauqua.com. Overpriced food but great location, views and historical ambience.

Il Pastaio. 3075 B Arapahoe Ave., Boulder; (303) 447-9572; ilpastaioboulder.com. Italian.

The Kitchen. 1039 Pearl St., Boulder; (303) 544-5973; thekitchen.com.

Mountain Sun Pub & Brewery. 1535 Pearl St., Boulder; (303) 546-0886; mountainsunpub .com.

Ras Kassa's Ethiopian Restaurant. 2111 30th St., Boulder; (303) 447-2919; raskassas .com.

Rincon Argentino. Village Boulder Shopping Center, 2525 Arapahoe Ave., Boulder; (303) 442-4133; rinconargentinoboulder.com. Argentinean food in a strip mall.

Rio Grande Mexican Restaurant. 1101 Walnut St., Boulder; (303) 444-3690; riogrande mexican.com. People go here for margaritas and don't expect too much from the food.

Lodging

Alps Boulder Canyon Inn. 38619 Boulder Canyon Dr., Boulder; (303) 444-5445; alpsinn .com. Upscale, located on the route in Boulder Canyon.

Boulder University Inn. 1632 Broadway, Boulder; (303) 417-1700; boulderuniversityinn .com. Motel on Broadway.

Briar Rose Bed & Breakfast. 2151 Arapahoe Ave., Boulder; (303) 442-3007; briarosebb .com.

Foot of the Mountain Motel. 200 Arapahoe Ave., Boulder; (303) 442-5688; footofthe mountainmotel.com. Right by Eben G. Fine Park.

Quality Inn & Suites Boulder Creek. 2020 Arapahoe Ave., Boulder; (303) 449-7550; qualityinn.com.

Silver Saddle Motel. 90 Arapahoe Ave., Boulder; (303) 442-8022; silversaddlemotel.com. Also right there by Eben G. Fine Park.

9 Chapman Cyclocross Loop

This short loop is not really a road-bike ride at all. But if you're enthusiastic, somewhat skilled, and at least a little bit weird, you can do it on your road bike and have a great time.

Start: Eben G. Fine Park in west Boulder
Length: 11.1 miles
Terrain: Flagstaff Mountain back to front. Very rustic dirt-road climb—more like a singletrack trail in 2014—and serpentine descent down (paved) Flagstaff Road.
Traffic and hazards: Moderate motor and bike traffic. Technical descending on pavement, technical climbing on dirt. Requires riding on CO 119 (Boulder Canyon Drive) for a short stretch.

Things to see: Boulder Canyon, Flagstaff Mountain summit, Boulder from above
Note: Do not attempt this ride if you don't enjoy the extra challenge of riding off-road terrain on skinny tires. Those who read this warning, decide to ride Chapman anyway, and then complain about it later will be fired immediately and escorted to the state line with their personal belongings. It's an obscure section of the traffic code.

Getting there: From Denver, head north on I-25 to US 36 and take US 36 to Boulder. Exit at Baseline Road and go west up the hill to 9th Street. Take 9th Street north to Arapahoe Avenue. Turn left and take Arapahoe until you reach Eben G. Fine Park. **GPS:** N 40 0'46.40" / W 105 17'48.31"

Ride Description

Chapman Road sprouts from Boulder Canyon and zigzags up the back side of the iconic Flagstaff Mountain. The little dirt road was off-limits to the public for as long as I can remember, and there was widespread rejoicing when it was finally opened in 2013. The recently liberated route proved to be a fantastic recreational ride and a great little training ground for local racers, especially the cyclocrossers, the number of whom is growing rapidly.

For a time Chapman was a fairly tame dirt road, thoughtfully routed up the mountain. After a series of flash floods and brutal downpours in 2013, the road morphed into a singletrack trail—more or less—that dips and dives along the culvert where the road used to be. Even on a mountain bike it can be a little tricky here and there. So why, in the name of all that is holy, is it included in a road-biking guide?

Consider it a bonus for those who want a bit *more* out of their ride. More challenge, more pain, more craziness. More fun. Flood-ravaged Chapman on a road bike is like the secret menu at your favorite restaurant, or that crazy uncle who brings illegal fireworks to the family picnic.

I had so much fun riding this loop on a standard steel-racing bike with skinny tires that I had to do it a few more times just to make sure I wasn't fooling myself. Without a doubt it is one of my top favorites. I brought some other folks up here, also

We don't know if Chapman will ever "recover" from the 2013 floods—and we don't care.

on standard road bikes, and they loved it, too. So what the heck, it went in the book. But not everybody will love it, that's for sure. If you don't like dirt, you'll absolutely hate Chapman.

The descent of Flagstaff Road begins wide open and straight on mellow slopes. Soon the road goes through a series of slow looping switchbacks, then, below the Flagstaff House restaurant, it gets really steep, fast, and dangerous. Be extra careful with it.

Miles and Directions

0.0 Start from Eben G. Fine Park and begin riding west on the bike path up Boulder Canyon, next to Boulder Creek and CO 119.

0.9 The path surface turns to crushed gravel. Watch out for the pinch-flat-causing lip of the bridge.

2.1 The path climbs to the highway and ends. Carefully turn left and ride up CO 119 (not Fourmile Canyon Drive).

2.7 Turn left (carefully crossing the busy road) to the Chapman Road Trailhead. Begin riding up Chapman Road. The term "road" is used loosely here.

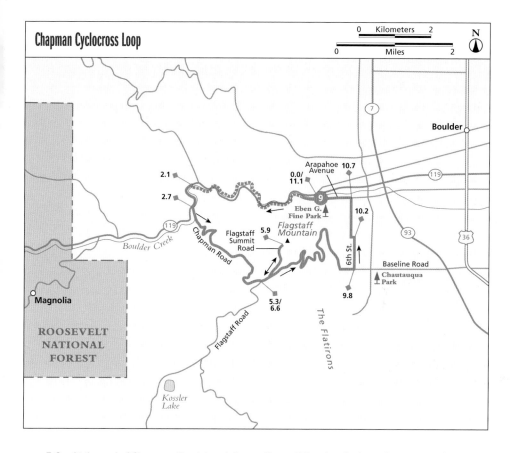

Chapman Cyclocross Loop

5.3 At the end of Chapman Road, turn left onto Flagstaff Road and take an immediate left onto the Flagstaff Summit Road. (**Option:** If you're not up for a little more climbing, simply ride down Flagstaff Road from here.)

5.9 Flagstaff summit. The benches there are great for gazing out over the city and eastern Colorado. When you're done meditating, head back down Flagstaff Summit Road.

6.6 Turn left onto Flagstaff Road and continue descending.

9.5 Flagstaff Road passes Gregory Canyon, swoops left, and becomes Baseline Road.

9.8 Turn left onto 6th Street.

10.2 Jog left for a half block on Euclid Avenue, then turn right and continue descending on 6th Street.

10.7 Turn left onto Arapahoe Avenue. (**Option:** Continue for another block, cross Boulder Creek, and turn left onto the Boulder Creek Path. Take the path to Eben G. Fine Park.)

11.1 Back at Eben G. Fine Park.

Bike Shops

Behold this *partial* list of Boulder's favorite bike shops:

Boulder Cycle Sport. 4580 Broadway St., Boulder; (303) 444-2453; bouldercyclesport .com. They have another location on South Broadway.

Excel Sports. 2045 32nd St., Boulder; (303) 444-6737; excelsports.com.

Fat Kitty Cycles. 3380 Arapahoe Ave., Boulder; (720) 982-4120; fatkittycycles.com.

Full Cycle. 1795 Pearl St., Boulder; (303) 440-1002; fullcyclebikes.com.

LTD Cycleworx. 5360 Arapahoe Ave., Boulder; (303) 442-3283; ltdcycleworx.com.

Pro Peloton Cyclery. 2615 13th St., Boulder; (303) 415-1292; propeloton.com.

The Pro's Closet. 4939 N. Broadway St. #58, Boulder; (303) 993-7776; theproscloset.com.

REI. 1789 28th St., Boulder; (303) 583-9970; REI.com.

The Sports Garage. 2705 Spruce St., Boulder; (303) 473-0033; sportsgarage.net.

Standard Bike Repair. 1823 Marine St., Boulder; (720) 837-8984; standardbikerepair.com.

University Bicycles. 839 Pearl St., Boulder; (303) 444-4196; ubikes.com.

Vecchio's. 1833 Pearl St., Boulder; (303) 440-3535; vecchios.com.

Food

Chautauqua Dining Hall. 900 W. Baseline Rd., Boulder; (303) 440-3776; chautauqua.com. Overpriced food but great location, views and historical ambience.

Il Pastaio. 3075 B Arapahoe Ave., Boulder; (303) 447-9572; ilpastaioboulder.com. Italian.

The Kitchen. 1039 Pearl St., Boulder; (303) 544-5973; thekitchen.com.

Mountain Sun Pub & Brewery. 1535 Pearl St., Boulder; (303) 546-0886; mountainsunpub .com.

Ras Kassa's Ethiopian Restaurant. 2111 30th St., Boulder; (303) 447-2919; raskassas .com.

Rincon Argentino. Village Boulder Shopping Center, 2525 Arapahoe Ave., Boulder; (303) 442-4133; rinconargentinoboulder.com. Argentinean food in a strip mall.

Rio Grande Mexican Restaurant. 1101 Walnut St., Boulder; (303) 444-3690; riogrande mexican.com. People go here for margaritas and don't expect too much from the food.

Lodging

Alps Boulder Canyon Inn. 38619 Boulder Canyon Dr., Boulder; (303) 444-5445; alpsinn .com. Upscale, located on the route in Boulder Canyon.

Boulder University Inn. 1632 Broadway, Boulder; (303) 417-1700; boulderuniversityinn .com. Motel on Broadway.

Briar Rose Bed & Breakfast. 2151 Arapahoe Ave., Boulder; (303) 442-3007; briarosebb .com.

Foot of the Mountain Motel. 200 Arapahoe Ave., Boulder; (303) 442-5688; footofthe mountainmotel.com. Right by Eben G. Fine Park.

Quality Inn & Suites Boulder Creek. 2020 Arapahoe Ave., Boulder; (303) 449-7550; qualityinn.com.

Silver Saddle Motel. 90 Arapahoe Ave., Boulder; (303) 442-8022; silversaddlemotel.com. Also right there by Eben G. Fine Park.

10 Big Flagstaff

A very tough tour of Flagstaff Road—all of Flagstaff Road, not just the popular lower section—leads to Gross Reservoir. Getting home involves more strenuous climbing.

Start: Chautauqua Park, west Boulder
Length: 18.7 miles out-and-back
Terrain: Steep, rugged mountains west of Boulder; lots of climbing
Traffic and hazards: Narrow roads and moderate traffic lead to occasional uncomfortable situations. The lower steep slopes of Flagstaff Road can be especially problematic. Traffic thins out a lot above Flagstaff Mountain.
Things to see: Chautauqua Park, Flagstaff Mountain, Boulder from above, Gross Reservoir

Getting there: From Denver, head north on I-25 to US 36 and take US 36 to Boulder. Exit at Baseline Road and go west on Baseline and up the hill to Chautauqua Park. Park in the lot on the left by the park or on the street. **GPS:** N 40 0'0" / W 105 16'59"

Ride Description

This is a pretty route, but sightseeing is not what this ride is all about. Gross Reservoir, sitting at the end of the line, is an impressive location, but this isn't one of those destination rides. This ride is about getting there, and cyclists would ride the route

Gross Reservoir

Above the Flagstaff summit, the road gets real serious.

even if there were no reservoir on the other end. This ride is all about the hill, one of the toughest available around Boulder.

The ascent of Flagstaff Mountain is a traditional favorite for Boulder bikers. It's a nice, strenuous little climb. (See *Best Bike Rides Denver and Boulder* [FalconGuides] for more on that ride.) But this extend-o-rama Flagstaff climb is much more difficult. This route climbs Flagstaff, then continues to climb. In fact, as all the local wheelers know very well, the "real" climbing doesn't begin until the Flagstaff summit is in the rearview mirror. Beyond Flagstaff Mountain is an even bigger mountain, and the road chugs right on up the thing.

Unlike the lower portion of the road that snakes all over the side of Flagstaff Mountain, the upper portion isn't too concerned about keeping the incline reasonably moderate for travelers. It gets right to business gaining elevation. Right at the intersection with the Summit Road, Flagstaff Road takes it up a notch, ramping up from 5 to 10 percent slopes to 10 to 15-plus.

The popular lower portion and the heinously steep upper section together make a sustained 5.1-mile climb that gains a little over 2,000 feet before releasing its grip. The road then descends briefly, climbs a little more, descends, climbs . . . and finally tops out at 7,850 feet above sea level after 6.1 miles. It's a hill.

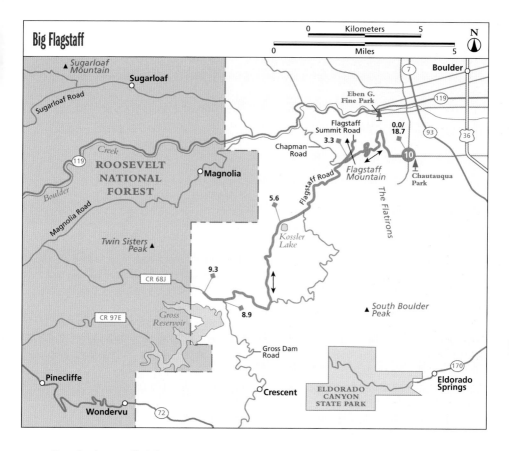

Big Flagstaff

	Kilometers	
0		5
0	Miles	5

N

Sugarloaf
Mountain

Sugarloaf

Sugarloaf Road

Boulder

7

119

Eben G.
Fine Park

Flagstaff
Summit Road

0.0/
18.7

93

36

3.3

Chapman
Road

10

Creek

ROOSEVELT
NATIONAL
FOREST

119

Magnolia

Flagstaff
Mountain

Chautauqua
Park

Boulder

Flagstaff Road

Magnolia Road

5.6

The Flatirons

Kossler
Lake

Twin Sisters
Peak

CR 68J

9.3

South Boulder
Peak

CR 97E

Gross
Reservoir

8.9

Gross Dam
Road

Pinecliffe

Crescent

ELDORADO
CANYON
STATE PARK

170

Eldorado
Springs

Wondervu

72

But that's not all. The route continues over the back of the mountain, descending 700 feet. Then it climbs another 400 feet or so before reaching the reservoir and turnaround point. In other words, there are two climbs on the way out, one whopper of about 2,200 feet and a bonus 400-footer, while a significant 700-foot climb awaits on the way back. It's a three-climber! Total gain for the entire route is over 3,300 feet, making it one of the more vertical rides in the book.

Gross Dam was completed in 1954, making a huge lake out of much of South Boulder Canyon. The 440-acre reservoir is gaze-worthy, although there isn't really an obvious place to take a siesta there other than some picnic spots. Some of the picnic spots are covered, and there are a few toilets. But that's about it for services at the turnaround.

Returning via the same road is the only *paved* option from here. If you're feeling adventurous, consider a loop that finds its way south into Coal Creek Canyon; to get there, use the dirt road that passes the reservoir to the east (Gross Dam Road). Expect washboard and additional climbing on the dirt. Coal Creek Canyon spills out onto the flats, and the remainder of the loop is on a somewhat sketchy high-speed two-lane highway back to Boulder. (For a detailed description of the Flagstaff–Coal Creek loop, see *Road Biking Colorado's Front Range* [FalconGuides].)

Miles and Directions

0.0 Start from Chautauqua Park and begin riding up West Baseline Road toward the mountain.

0.4 Turning right and sharply up, the road passes Gregory Canyon and becomes Flagstaff Road.

3.3 Pass the intersection with Flagstaff Summit Road. (**Option:** Take a side trip up to the top; no outlet.)

4.1 The steepest part of the climb is here.

5.6 Pass little Kossler Lake.

8.9 Pass the intersection with Gross Dam Road.

9.3 Turn around at the intersection with Lakeshore Park Road.

18.7 Back at Chautauqua Park.

Bike Shops

Behold this *partial* list of Boulder's favorite bike shops:

Boulder Cycle Sport. 4580 Broadway St., Boulder; (303) 444-2453; bouldercyclesport .com. They have another location on South Broadway.

Excel Sports. 2045 32nd St., Boulder; (303) 444-6737; excelsports.com.

Fat Kitty Cycles. 3380 Arapahoe Ave., Boulder; (720) 982-4120; fatkittycycles.com.

Full Cycle. 1795 Pearl St., Boulder; (303) 440-1002; fullcyclebikes.com.

LTD Cycleworx. 5360 Arapahoe Ave., Boulder; (303) 442-3283; ltdcycleworx.com.

Pro Peloton Cyclery. 2615 13th St., Boulder; (303) 415-1292; propeloton.com.

The Pro's Closet. 4939 N. Broadway St. #58, Boulder; (303) 993-7776; theproscloset.com.

REI. 1789 28th St., Boulder; (303) 583-9970; REI.com.

The Sports Garage. 2705 Spruce St., Boulder; (303) 473-0033; sportsgarage.net.

Standard Bike Repair. 1823 Marine St., Boulder; (720) 837-8984; standardbikerepair.com.

University Bicycles. 839 Pearl St., Boulder; (303) 444-4196; ubikes.com.

Vecchio's. 1833 Pearl St., Boulder; (303) 440-3535; vecchios.com.

Food

Chautauqua Dining Hall. 900 W. Baseline Rd., Boulder; (303) 440-3776; chautauqua.com. Overpriced food but great location, views, and historical ambience.

Il Pastaio. 3075 B Arapahoe Ave., Boulder; (303) 447-9572; ilpastaioboulder.com. Italian.

The Kitchen. 1039 Pearl St., Boulder; (303) 544-5973; thekitchen.com.

Mountain Sun Pub & Brewery. 1535 Pearl St., Boulder; (303) 546-0886; mountainsunpub .com.

Ras Kassa's Ethiopian Restaurant. 2111 30th St., Boulder; (303) 447-2919. raskassas .com.

Rincon Argentino. Village Boulder Shopping Center, 2525 Arapahoe Ave., Boulder; (303) 442-4133; rinconargentinoboulder.com. Argentinean food in a strip mall.

Rio Grande Mexican Restaurant. 1101 Walnut St., Boulder; (303) 444-3690; riogrande mexican.com. People go here for margaritas and don't expect too much from the food.

Lodging

Alps Boulder Canyon Inn. 38619 Boulder Canyon Dr., Boulder; (303) 444-5445; alpsinn .com. Upscale, located on the route in Boulder Canyon.

Boulder University Inn. 1632 Broadway, Boulder; (303) 417-1700; boulderuniversityinn.com. Motel on Broadway.

Briar Rose Bed & Breakfast. 2151 Arapahoe Ave., Boulder; (303) 442-3007; briarosebb.com.

Foot of the Mountain Motel. 200 Arapahoe Ave., Boulder; (303) 442-5688; footofthemountainmotel.com. Right by Eben G. Fine Park.

Quality Inn & Suites Boulder Creek. 2020 Arapahoe Ave., Boulder; (303) 449-7550; qualityinn.com.

Silver Saddle Motel. 90 Arapahoe Ave., Boulder; (303) 442-8022; silversaddlemotel.com. Also right there by Eben G. Fine Park.

OTHER RIDES AROUND BOULDER

Coal Creek Trail. This sweet gravel bike path starts in Superior, one of the old coal-mining towns that was absorbed into the ring of development around Boulder's open space buffer, and squiggles northeast into the rolling prairie along with Coal Creek. Recently it's been extended to the Rock Creek Trail, which can be looped back around. It's a good family biking option, although following the route is a little messy.

Hygiene Loop. Looping mini tours of the farmland northeast of Boulder are super popular with locals because the roads are often dry in the off-season and because they provide some of the only flat (at least flatish) riding in the vicinity. Almost all the variations on this theme begin with a northbound leg on rolling US 36, snugged up next to the hogback. Turn right onto Hygiene Road and roll fast eastbound. Another right at the tiny town of Hygiene puts you on North 75th Street, headed south. Turn right on Monarch Road, then left on 55th Street. A final westbound leg on Jay Road gets you back to Boulder. There are a ton of possible variants. Watch for vindictive anti-bike sheriffs out there near Hygiene.

Magnolia Road. This is probably the steepest of all roads around Boulder. It rises from Boulder Canyon, west of the tunnel, and goes up to the Peak to Peak Highway near Nederland. It turns to dirt about halfway up, but the super-steep stuff is paved. The descent is notorious for overwhelming mechanical braking systems. Burn your brakes, not your bridges!

NCAR. That's the National Center for Atmospheric Research, which happens to be housed in a complex (designed by I. M. Pei, no less) on top of a hill in southwest Boulder, at the end of a really sweet road. The ride isn't much all by itself, but it works great as an add-on to other rides or a quickie staged from just about anywhere in town. The NCAR road is the top of Table Mesa Drive, but don't ride up Table Mesa to get to it. It's better to use the sneaky bike paths that approach the road from the north, through the neighborhood. You can pick up the path behind the NIST building on Broadway.

NCAR is at the end of a really sweet road.

11 Lookout Mountain-Grapevine Loop

While only 23 miles long, this loop through the hills west of Denver packs a punch, with over 2,500 feet of climbing.

Start: Beverly Heights Park near Golden
Length: 23 miles
Terrain: Climb, climb, climb. Descend. Climb. Descend. Climb.
Traffic and hazards: Descent of Bear Creek Canyon on CO 74 can be stressful and dangerous; it's best suited to experienced riders.

Sharp curves and fairly busy roads. Keep eyes open for drivers, motorcyclists, and other bicyclists on Lookout Mountain. Grapevine Road is partially dirt-surfaced with rougher patches.
Things to see: Bird's-eye view of Golden, Lookout Mountain, Bear Creek Canyon

Getting there: From Denver, take the 6th Avenue Freeway west to where it curves to the north around Golden. Turn left onto 19th Street/Lookout Mountain Road, drive up around the first curve, and park on the left in the large parking area at Beverly Heights Park. **GPS:** N 39 44'27" / W 105 13'40"

Ride Description

It's easy to turn the classic and curvy Lookout Mountain climb, one of the most popular cycling routes in North America, into an even more rewarding ride. Just

The curves of Lookout

drop off the back of the antennae-spiked mountain and cross I-70 to reach the web of roads on the other side of the interstate. By doing so, you can climb your legs off all over the Genesee development south of I-70, or climb over the lump and drop into Bear Creek Canyon, which unlocks another set of opportunities. Cruising the big curves of Bear Creek Canyon's CO 74, you can roll to Kittredge, Evergreen, or the Kerr Gulch spur, or head up and over Myers Gulch Road to Indian Hills, the top of Mount Falcon, Turkey Creek Canyon, and other lovely stuff. (Also see the Myers Gulch–Evergreen Loop ride.) For this ride, however, we'll hit Bear Creek Canyon and drop down to Red Rocks before looping back to Golden.

Rough and lovable Grapevine Road provides passage between the I-70 corridor and Bear Creek. If Grapevine has a catch, it's probably the road surface, which alternates between smooth gravel and choppy pavement most of the way. A little extra tire width is helpful here, but not necessary. Even a superlight racing bike can handle Grapevine, as long as its pilot uses a reasonably light touch. Notice how the gravel sections are smoother than the deteriorating pavement, a fairly common situation in these hills.

There's a definite Euro feel as Grapevine thins and twists into the tiny village called Idledale, straddling Bear Creek and CO 74. (Don't be too alarmed when Grapevine Road branches into about a thousand mini-Grapevines near the bottom—just keep going downhill and you'll get there.) You won't find much in the way of refreshments or services here, but Morrison is just 3.5 quick miles down the canyon. Even with a decent shoulder, CO 74 can be a little oppressive at times. Account for the probability of slippery gravel on the road.

Just before Morrison, turn left into Red Rocks Park, home to one of the most incredible rock gardens you'll ever see, as well as the best outdoor concert venue in the world. Note that there are a few different ways to navigate through the park. The route described here follows the lower road, but all the park's roads are fun to ride. Some of them go up especially steep hills, so be aware of that. Our route is probably the easiest, but it's still a bit hilly.

If you're new to the area, you'll enjoy lingering here. To see the amphitheater itself, you'll have to climb to the tip-top, although there are many fine spots throughout the park where you can sit on a red sandstone rock and ponder the mysteries of life, such as, what is the precise melting point of a turkey sandwich?

Unfortunately the rest of the route is less than spectacular. Leaving Red Rocks, climb the remainder of the well-known road west of Dakota Ridge (Hogback Road). With the boring straight climb, speeding traffic, and the sweet-hot stank of road death, this is the least pleasant portion of the ride. It doesn't last long, topping out as it crosses under I-70.

Veer left onto Heritage Road on the other side of the hill, roll down toward "the Taj Mahal"—the ostentatious building that holds Jefferson County's courts and government offices—and get on the bike path that follows the 6th Avenue Freeway. (**Option:** Instead of using Heritage Road, you can use the Kinney Run Trail, a bike

Rough and lovable Grapevine Road

path that starts from one of the big lower lots at Heritage Square. The path cuts through the neighborhood, crosses under the 6th Avenue Freeway, and joins the bike path on the other side, although the route is a bit fiddly the first time.) The path next to the freeway will take you back to 19th Street and the final, painful climb back to the lot.

For a serious challenge, try this ride from downtown Denver; ride up to the west side and get on 32nd for a direct route between Denver and Golden, or head north on the Platte Trail and use the Clear Creek Path for a much longer off-street route (see West Denver Path Loop ride).

Miles and Directions

0.0 Start riding up Lookout Mountain Road from the large parking lot just below Beverly Heights Park.

4.8 Continue straight past the turnoff for the Buffalo Bill Memorial Museum and Grave—not quite at the top of the hill yet.

6.0 After passing several intersections, turn left onto Paradise Road.

6.6 At the stop sign, turn right and continue on Paradise Road.

7.0 Turn left at the intersection with Charros Drive and continue descending.

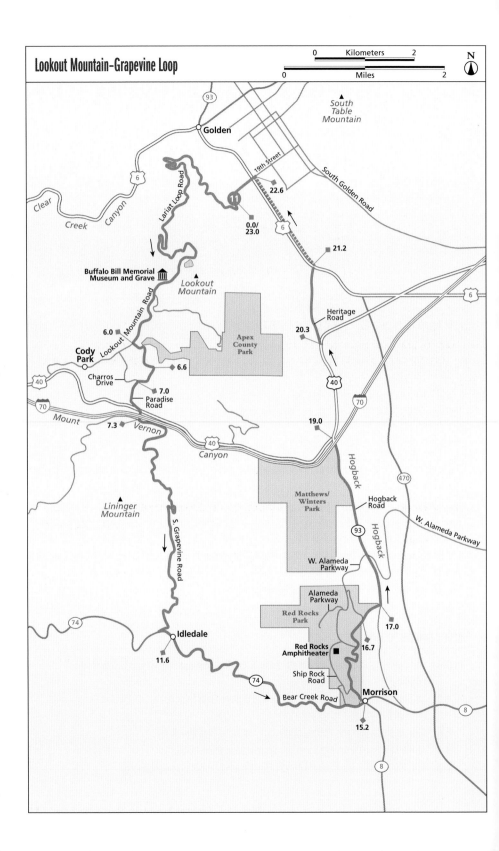

Lookout Mountain-Grapevine Loop

0   Kilometers   2

0   Miles   2

N

93
Golden

▲ South Table Mountain

19th Street

South Golden Road

6

Lariat Loop Road

Clear Creek Canyon

11

22.6

0.0/ 23.0

6

21.2

Buffalo Bill Memorial Museum and Grave

▲ Lookout Mountain

6

Lookout Mountain Road

Heritage Road

6.0

Cody Park

6.6

Apex County Park

20.3

Charros Drive

40

7.0
Paradise Road

40

70

70

Mount

7.3

Vernon

40

Canyon

19.0

470

▲ Lininger Mountain

S. Grapevine Road

Matthews/ Winters Park

Hogback

Hogback Road

93

Hogback

W. Alameda Parkway

W. Alameda Parkway

Alameda Parkway

74

Idledale

11.6

Red Rocks Park

17.0

Red Rocks Amphitheater

16.7

Ship Rock Road

74

Bear Creek Road

Morrison

8

15.2

8

7.3 At the bottom of the hill, turn left onto US 40. Careful! Ack!

7.4 Take a right and cross I-70 on South Grapevine Road.

7.5 Take an immediate left and continue on South Grapevine Road. Be especially careful here; cars don't stop.

8.4 Pavement ends!

11.0 Continue straight here on Southwest Grapevine Road, instead of turning *left* onto South East Grapevine Road. (Yes, South Grapevine splits into several separate roads with the same name, or nearly the same name. It's not quite as complicated as it sounds.)

11.6 Southwest Grapevine Road drops into the tiny town of Idledale. Turn left onto CO 74.

15.2 Turn left onto Red Rocks Park Road. "Hey this is Red Rocks!"

15.5 Veer right, continuing on Red Rocks Park Road.

16.3 Continue past the intersection with Trading Post Road.

16.7 Continue past the intersection with Red Rocks Trail Road.

17.0 Turn left onto Hogback Road/CR 93.

19.0 Cross beneath I-70 near the top of the hill.

19.2 Continue through the signalized intersection. The route is now called US 40.

20.0 Continue past the turnoff to Heritage Square. (**Option:** Turn left and find the Kinney Run Trail on the far side of the upper of the two big parking lots. After some tricky route-finding, the trail pops out near mile 21.5.)

20.3 Veer left onto Heritage Road.

21.2 Cross 6th Avenue and get on the bike path, which starts on the northwest corner. Follow the 6th Avenue Freeway.

22.6 Turn left onto 19th Street.

23.0 Back at the parking area. Whew.

Bike Shops

Big Ring Cycles. 600 12th St. #170, Golden; (303) 216-2000; bigringcycles.com.

Peak Cycles. 1224 Washington Ave. #145, Golden; (303) 216-1616; bikeparts.com.

Pedal Pushers Cyclery. 710 Golden Ridge Rd., Golden; (303) 365-2453; pedalpusherscyclery .com.

Rise Above Cycles. 111 Rubey Dr. #1, Golden; (720) 541-6115.

Red Rocks Cyclery. 300 Bear Creek Ave., Morrison; (303) 697-8833; redrockscyclery.com.

Food

Golden Diner. 700 12th St., Golden; (303) 279-5959; thegoldendiner.com. Open 'til 2 p.m.

Sherpa House. 1518 Washington Ave., Golden; (303) 278-7939; ussherpahouse.com.

Lodging

Dove Inn Bed & Breakfast. 711 14th St., Golden; (303) 278-2209; doveinn.com.

The Golden Hotel. 800 11th St., Golden; (303) 279-0100; ascendcollection.com.

12 Denver to Golden

Although not exactly like a hot knife through butter, on this route you'll be able to cut through multiple layers of Denver and finally break free before arriving in Golden, in the shadow of the Coors plant. Golden is like a different world. See the brewery, have a bite to eat, and ride home—or rev up and make a run at Lookout Mountain.

Start: Confluence Park

Length: 12.3 miles one way

Terrain: Surprisingly unflat; you'll realize that downtown Denver sits in a valley.

Traffic and hazards: An urban route with lots of side parking, intersections, pedestrians, and the rest. For an urban route, traffic is moderate. West 32nd Avenue has some tight, busy sections. Watch for truck traffic on approach to the Coors plant.

Things to see: Highlands, Crown Hill Park, Coors Brewery, Golden

Getting there: Take I-25 to downtown Denver and exit onto Water Street (exit 211), northeast toward downtown. Water Street turns into Platte Street and goes directly past the REI. Free public parking is scarce, but there is a lot with about 25 spaces on the right side of Water Street before it goes under Speer Boulevard at Fishback Park. REI has an overflow lot on the west side of Platte Street. It may also be possible to park on the street along Platte Street. If at all possible, leave the car at home and ride to the start. **GPS:** N 39 45'17.11" / W 105 0'32.44"

Ride Description

There are other ways to get to Golden from downtown Denver, but none so direct; see the West Denver Path Loop for a much longer all-path route along Clear Creek.

This route is easy to follow once you get out of central Denver. Basically, from downtown you cross the highway (I-25) on the bike-ped bridge and head straight up the hill on 16th, which curves to the right and runs smack into 32nd at the first stoplight. Take a left, and you're off to the races. After a brief finagle around a semi-circular park and a crossing of diagonal Speer Boulevard, it's a straight shot for miles. Stick to 32nd as it crosses the four big boulevards along the way: Federal, Sheridan, Wadsworth, and Kipling. Then stay on it some more as you cross Youngfield. The road travels through tree-ring-like layers of suburban development almost all the way to Golden.

Traffic on 32nd is moderate (could be a lot worse). Close to downtown the street travels through some commercial pockets and is likely to be packed with parked cars, narrowing the roadway. As you get out of town, the road opens up a bit, but so do vehicle speeds. The section between Wadsworth and Kipling can feel both narrow and fast, but there is a bike-path-like structure next to the road if you want to escape.

Another thing you'll notice about 32nd is that it isn't exactly flat. Getting out of downtown is a bit of a grunt, and even after you gain the top of the Highlands, there

Lookout Mountain looms over Golden.

are a few smaller humps along the way. The little ramp prior to Youngfield and I-70 is the most annoying. There is traffic to contend with there, which doesn't help matters.

A mile or so before the Coors plant, the suburbs relent, and 32nd meanders past a small farm. South Table Mountain looms above. For a block or two, it feels like a country ride. Then the sights, sounds, and smells of a massive industrial operation begin to make themselves apparent. Semi trucks turn on and off the road. Finally, the route cozies up to the hulking concrete structures of the brewery and then goes right under it before running smack into downtown Golden.

Miles and Directions

0.0 From Confluence Park, head north on the Platte River bike path located down the ramp and under 15th Street. (**Option:** Take 15th Street west to Platte Street, take a right onto Platte, and rejoin the route at mile 0.3.)

0.2 Exit the path and ride west through the plaza between apartment buildings.

0.3 Cross Platte Street, then cross I-25 on the bike-ped bridge.

0.4 Cross Central Street and begin riding up the hill on 16th Street.

0.5 The street curves around to the north and becomes Tejon Street.

0.7 Take a left onto West 32nd Avenue.

Denver to Golden

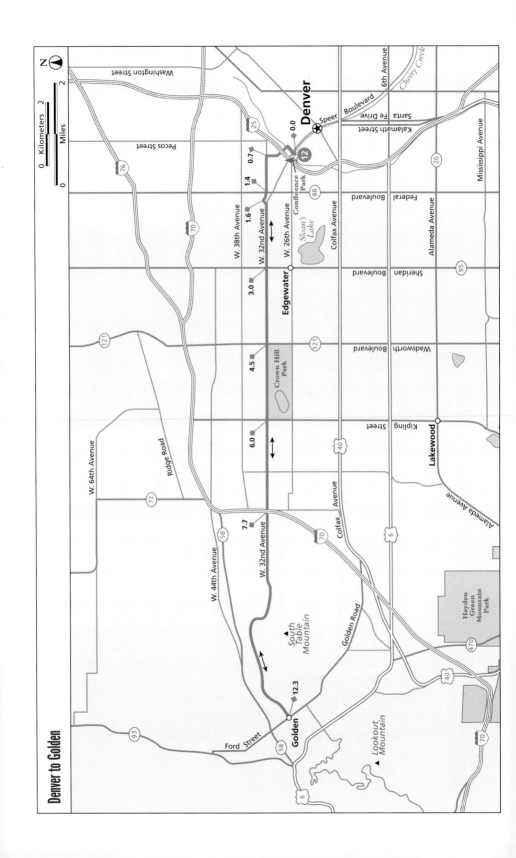

1.4 Cross Federal Boulevard.

1.6 Turn left onto Green Court.

1.7 Cross Speer Boulevard and continue west on West 32nd Avenue.

3.0 Cross Sheridan Boulevard.

4.5 Cross Wadsworth Boulevard. (You can ride on the side path between Wadsworth and Kipling if preferred.)

6.0 Cross Kipling Street.

7.7 Cross Youngfield Street.

12.3 Arrive at the intersection of 13th Street and Ford Street in Golden.

Attractions

Coors Brewery. 13th and Ford Streets, Golden; (303) 277-2337; millercoors.com/golden-brewery-tour.aspx. Now "MillerCoors," but there's still free beer at the end of the brewery tour.

Bike Shops

C3 Bike Shop. 3316 Tejon St., Denver; (303) 953-8720; c3bikeshop.com.

Jinji Cycles. 2538 W. 32nd Ave., Denver; (303) 433-3474; jinjicycles.com.

REI. 1416 Platte St., Denver; (303) 756-3100; REI.com. Located at the start of the ride.

Salvagetti Bicycle Workshop. 3800 Irving St., Denver; (303) 691-5595; salvagetti.com.

Big Ring Cycles. 600 12th St. #170, Golden; (303) 216-2000; bigringcycles.com.

Peak Cycles. 1224 Washington Ave. #145, Golden; (303) 216-1616; bikeparts.com.

Pedal Pushers Cyclery. 710 Golden Ridge Rd., Golden; (303) 365-2453; pedalpusherscyclery.com.

Rise Above Cycles. 111 Rubey Dr. #1, Golden; (720) 541-6115.

Wheat Ridge Cyclery. 7085 W. 38th Ave., Wheat Ridge. (303) 424-3221; ridewrc.com.

Food

D'Corazon. 1530 Blake St., Suite C, Denver; (720) 904-8226. Mexican food.

My Brother's Bar. 2376 15th St. (corner of 15th and Platte), Denver; (303) 455-9991; mybrothersbar.com. Homey bar/burger place that's been there forever.

Proto's Pizza. 2401 15th St., Denver; (720) 855-9400; protospizza.com.

Golden Diner. 700 12th St., Golden; (303) 279-5959; thegoldendiner.com. Open 'til 2 p.m.

Lodging

Castle Marne Bed & Breakfast. 1572 Race St., Denver; (303) 331-0621; castlemarne.com.

Oxford Hotel. 1600 17th St., Denver; (303) 628-5400; theoxfordhotel.com. Historic Denver landmark.

Warwick Hotel. 1776 Grant St., Denver; (303) 861-2000; warwickhotels.com. A little bit cheaper than the others downtown.

OTHER RIDES AROUND GOLDEN

Golden Gate Canyon. The road is wickedly curved and wickedly sloped, leading from CR 93 north of Golden into the mountains. Golden Gate may not become your go-to ride, but it's definitely worth doing once. It terminates at the Peak to Peak Highway. Try an epic loop using Golden Gate, Peak to Peak, and Coal Creek Canyon. Most imagine a solid climb to the Peak to Peak and a solid descent down Coal Creek; that's way off the mark. Paradoxically, there are big descents on the way up and painful climbs on the way down.

13 West Denver Path Loop

This loop on the west side rolls almost 60 miles from downtown Denver to Golden and Morrison, and back to the Platte, mostly on off-street paths.

Start: Confluence Park
Length: 56.7 miles
Terrain: Fairly flat until you start getting close to Golden.
Traffic and hazards: Route follows a busy road for 4.6 miles, between Heritage Square and Morrison, with a few busy intersections. This ride has relatively few street crossings, but pay careful attention on the paths. Watch for other bicyclists!
Things to see: Golden, Coors Brewery from above, Bear Creek Lake State Park, Platte River Greenway

Getting there: Take I-25 to downtown Denver and exit onto Water Street (exit 211), northeast toward downtown. Water Street turns into Platte Street and goes directly past the REI. Free public parking is scarce, but there is a lot with about 25 spaces on the right side of Water Street before it goes under Speer Boulevard at Fishback Park. REI has an overflow lot on the west side of Platte Street. It may also be possible to park on the street along Platte Street. If it's workable, leave the car at home and ride to the start. **GPS:** N 39 45'17.11" / W 105 0'32.44"

Ride Description

This isn't a garden-party, country-club, Sunday-stroll sort of outing. This ride takes you way out west, via the gritty and unglamorous north side, tracing the city's most important industrial arteries: the Platte River and Clear Creek. The loop reaches all the way to Golden, then returns by way of scenic Bear Creek Lake Park. Not a simple or casual outing, this hefty ride requires plenty of climbing (too much?) as it loops around Golden. By the time you get back downtown, your legs most likely will be feeling the distance.

Start this one at Confluence Park in lower downtown Denver, where the Platte and Cherry Creek come together. After stocking up on provisions, head north along the west bank of the Platte, across from Commons Park (still known to many as River Front Park). There are paths on both sides of the river, but cross one of the bridges and continue on the east bank, as the path on the west side currently ends at a park just north of downtown (City of Cuernavaca Park).

The Platte River Trail northbound provides a smooth concrete surface, completely unbroken by street crossings. Hazards and annoyances still exist up here, ranging from sour industrial stank to wandering geese. The path also hosts moderate levels of hooliganism—love that word—and other shadiness, but generally at a manageable level. Don't let fear of crime keep you from riding the Platte River Trail, but definitely stay awake to the possibility, and maybe avoid riding on the path after dark. Racers and racer wannabes will love the invitingly fast surface; just be aware of a few tight curves and blind corners along the way.

Clear Creek Trail

As you head north, away from downtown, through what used to be known as "the bottoms," you'll pass the historic Riverside Cemetery, the leaky Suncor refinery blowing thick orange smoke, the city's water treatment plant, junkyards, stockyards, and other industrial sites. Freight trains rumble across bridges and blow their horns. Still, this remains a river ride. River birds, clouds of gnats, huge shady cottonwoods, and plenty of interesting natural features abound. It's easy to imagine the whole deal—the path, the overpasses, factories and smokestacks—all swallowed back into nature in some not-so-distant future.

Watch for signs to help with tricky route-finding along the Clear Creek Trail.

At mile 7.1 the second phase of the ride begins with a left turn onto the Clear Creek Trail. Like the Platte trail, this westbound route is nearly flat and flanked by an interesting combo of riverside greenery and gritty industrial yards. The Clear Creek path requires a little more work to stay on route, with a few tricky turns and detours here and there, and the surface is less consistent as it rolls through the middle-class suburbs of Wheat Ridge and Arvada. Watch for some street crossings and a few other places where the route dumps out onto residential streets for short stretches.

Before too long the path escapes Wheat Ridge and heads toward the lumpy topography of the foothills, aiming for the gap between North and South Table Mountains. The concrete ribbon, here firmly established, spills into the open fields around the Coors complex east of Golden, then hugs the freeway (CO 58) as it chugs up and over some relatively obnoxious little hills. This is the first real gravity of the ride. If you're new to the area, the view from the high point along this stretch, looking down on the massive bunker-like structures of the Coors plant while the chunky volcanic cliffs loom overhead, will impress on many levels. This is definitely an interesting spot in the universe.

Our route hangs a (very) sharp left at a path intersection near mile 25.3 and dives into central Golden, with its inviting riverside parks and many eateries. If you need it, this is your best opportunity to rest and refuel for the remainder of the loop, as it starts by heading up, up, and up.

Without actually reaching into the mountains, the far western portion of the route dishes out plenty of pain as it rolls north to south away from Golden, gaining about 700 feet in one swell foop. I've got you veering right (due south) onto the Kinney Run Trail to the Heritage Square parking lot, then chugging over the top of the hill on US 40 and descending past Red Rocks into Morrison and Bear Creek

Approaching the Coors complex

Lake Park, but there are a few different ways you can get to that spot from Golden, all similarly bike-friendly.

The climbing portion of US 40 is the worst part of this ride, in my opinion. The traffic is not horrible but not great either; the grade is moderate but relentless. After crossing under I-70, the road bombs straight into Morrison between Dakota Ridge and Red Rocks.

Morrison is another stand-alone small town on the edge of the Denver metro area, eager to provide just about anything your tired little heart desires, including bike shop services, ice cream, burritos, and trinkets. But, feeling recharged from that descent, you'll probably just sweep on through and head into Bear Creek Lake Park for the sweetest section of the loop.

Bear Creek Lake Park is a relatively massive parcel of open land flanked by dense housing developments on three sides and CO 470 on the other. A really nice bike-pedestrian path begins at the northwest corner of the park, near CO 470 and Morrison Road, and rolls southeast through tall grasses, making its way toward the big lump in the distance known as Mount Carbon. Watch for some minor road crossings within the park.

After cruising about 3 delightful miles (delightful unless a headwind happens to be sandblasting you), arrive at the bottom of the aforementioned hill, the last notable climb along the entire route. Zigzag to the very top and continue east—if you find yourself headed southbound before reaching the top and either crossing or riding near US 285, you took a wrong turn. Soon the path points down, diving through Fox Hollow Golf Course in a tight and winding descent off the back of Mount Carbon. The trail dumps out onto the golf course service road at the bottom of the hill; the road twists past the clubhouse and ends at the very northeast corner of the park, where the Bear Creek Trail resumes.

You ain't home yet!

The Bear Creek Trail (or BCT, as it is called on signs marking the route) continues as a fun, shady concrete path slicing through Englewood. Like the other paths that make up this loop, it crosses beneath major streets and allows bicyclists to roll unimpeded for mile after mile. The BCT has seen some serious improvements in recent years and now ranks among the best paths on the Front Range. With a few minor exceptions, finding the route is easy and obvious (look for the BCT signs when in doubt) and the surface is good. Late-ride jitters can be assuaged at a very nicely located convenience store, right next to the path at mile 44. If you need it, it's right there after the path crosses beneath Wadsworth Boulevard, just east of the Bear Creek Greenbelt.

At about mile 47 the path runs rudely into South Lowell Boulevard and appears to end. If you happen to arrive at this point around rush hour, as I often do, you'll find a stream of cars cranking aggressive turns off nearby US 285, a sharp contrast to the path experience. Cross South Lowell *very* carefully—totally without signals here—and find the BCT continuing east on the north side of the creek.

A few more sharp turns and you'll see Bear Creek tumbling into the South Platte. Hang a left at the junction and begin the final phase. Watch for ducks, geese, shockingly huge turtles, large bike-flipping sticks, deep puddles, many other cyclists, and the occasional homeless individual stretched out on the path as you cruise next to the Platte all the way home. It's not a garden party, this ride, but it sure is an adventure.

Miles and Directions

0.0 Start by the REI at Confluence Park and begin riding north on the Platte River Trail. (Go down the ramp just east of the bike racks and bike-share station, and find the path headed northeast beneath 15th Street.)

0.5 Cross to the other side of the river and continue. The path will cross the river a few times as it rolls northeast.

6.1 Continue straight at the intersection with the Sand Creek Trail.

7.1 Continue straight at the intersection with the Fernald Trail.

7.1 Cross Clear Creek and turn left onto the Clear Creek Trail.

10.6 The path crosses under Pecos Street, jogs due north, then continues next to 64th Avenue westbound.

11.0 The path crosses under 64th and heads northwest along Little Dry Creek.

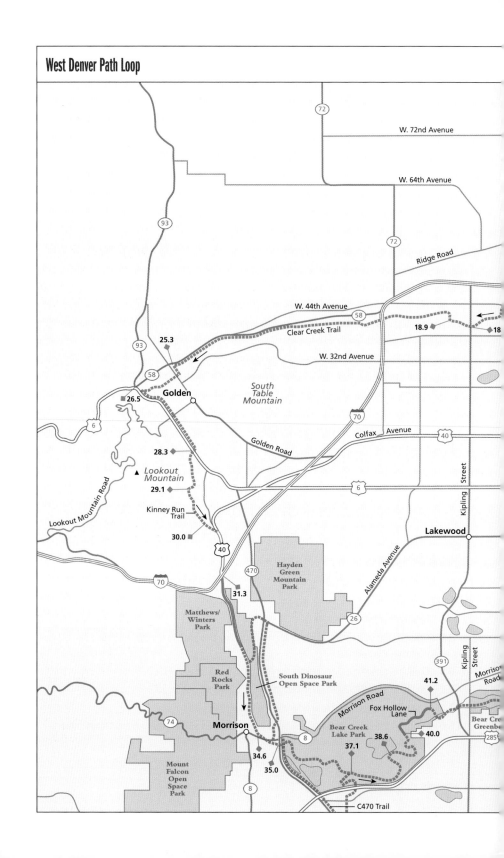

W. 72nd Avenue

W. 64th Avenue

72

Ridge Road

93

W. 44th Avenue
58
Clear Creek Trail
18.9
18

93
25.3
W. 32nd Avenue

58
South
Table
Mountain

26.5
Golden
70

6
Colfax Avenue
40
Golden Road

28.3
6

▲ Lookout
Mountain
29.1

Kinney Run
Trail

Lookout Mountain Road

30.0

Lakewood

40

470

Kipling Street

31.3

Hayden
Green
Mountain
Park

26

Alameda Avenue

Matthews/
Winters
Park

70

Kipling Street

391

Morrison Road

41.2

Red
Rocks
Park

South Dinosaur
Open Space Park

Morrison Road
Fox Hollow
Lane

40.0

Bear Cre
Greenbe

285

74

Morrison

8

Bear Creek
Lake Park
38.6
37.1

34.6
35.0

Mount
Falcon
Open
Space
Park

8

C470 Trail

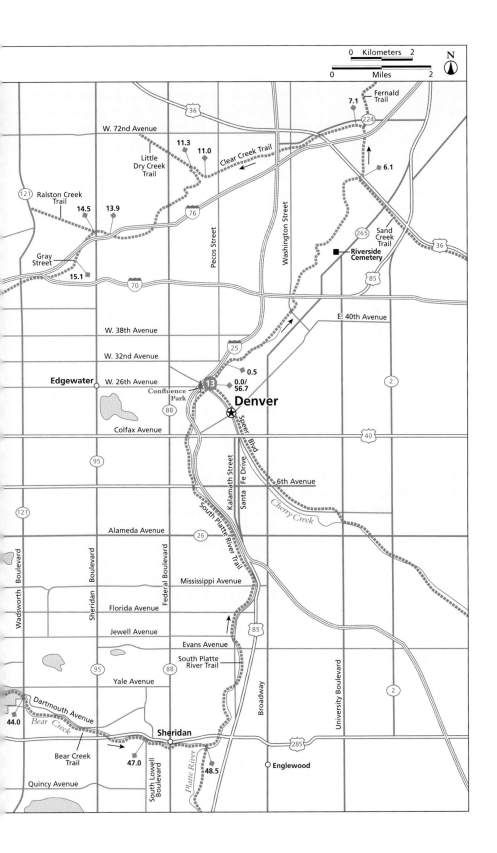

0   Kilometers   2

0   Miles   2

N

7.1   Fernald Trail

36

224

W. 72nd Avenue

11.3

11.0

Clear Creek Trail

6.1

Little Dry Creek Trail

Washington Street

121   Ralston Creek Trail

14.5   13.9

76

Pecos Street

265   Sand Creek Trail

36

Riverside Cemetery

Gray Street

85

15.1

70

E. 40th Avenue

W. 38th Avenue

W. 32nd Avenue

25

0.5

Edgewater   W. 26th Avenue   0.0/ 56.7

Confluence Park

13

2

88   Denver

Colfax Avenue   40

95

Kalamath Street   Santa Fe Drive   6th Avenue

121   Cherry Creek

Alameda Avenue   26

Wadsworth Boulevard   Sheridan Boulevard   Federal Boulevard   South Platte River Trail   Mississippi Avenue

Florida Avenue

Jewell Avenue   85

Evans Avenue

95   88   South Platte River Trail

Yale Avenue

Broadway   University Boulevard   2

Dartmouth Avenue

44.0   Bear Creek   Sheridan

Bear Creek Trail   47.0   South Lowell Boulevard   Platte River   48.5   285   Englewood

Quincy Avenue

11.3 Take a sharp left! (If you were to continue northwest here, you'd be on the Little Dry Creek Trail.)

11.6 Back under 64th . . . the Clear Creek Trail rolls around the edge of an unnamed lagoon.

13.9 Cross Tennyson Street.

14.5 Continue past the intersection with the Ralston Creek Trail.

15.1 The path ends at West 52nd Avenue. Continue directly across on Gray Street.

15.2 As Gray Street intersects Clear Creek Drive, find the continuation of the Clear Creek Trail on your right.

18.2 The trail spills out onto a residential street (Independence Place). Take an immediate right onto West 41st Avenue.

18.3 Turn left, back onto the Clear Creek Trail.

18.6 After passing under Kipling Street, follow the path through the parking lot of the Arvada Rec Center.

18.7 Turn left onto West 41st Avenue.

18.9 Continue on West 41st as it turns to dirt and heads downhill toward Prospect Park.

19.0 Continue westbound on the Clear Creek Trail. There are trails on both sides of the creek for a while.

25.3 Take a sharp left at a path intersection and roll down toward downtown Golden.

25.6 Continue on the path as it dives under Ford Street and continues southwest through downtown Golden.

26.0 Take a right as the path crosses Clear Creek. (Or continue straight: There are paths on both sides of the creek; the routes come together at 26.8 miles.)

26.5 Take a left and cross Clear Creek. (The Clear Creek Trail continues straight up the canyon here.)

26.8 Turn right at a path intersection and begin a tough climb.

27.5 Cross 19th Street and continue on the path.

28.3 Take a right onto the Kinney Run Trail (sometimes called Kenny Run Trail) and go through a tunnel under the 6th Avenue Freeway.

28.6 Go under Eagle Ridge Drive, continue south on the path.

29.1 The path spills onto Tripp Road. Climb the hill and turn left onto Crawford Street.

29.2 Turn left onto Tripp Drive.

29.3 Find the trail continuing at the end of Tripp Drive.

29.5 Continue straight through a path intersection, climbing up and around a little playground.

29.6 Continue straight at another path intersection.

29.7 Cross Kimball Avenue.

30.0 The trail ends at the upper Heritage Square parking lot. Continue straight across the lot, toward the exit.

30.3 Exit Heritage Square, taking a right onto US 40 (uphill).

31.1 As US 40 goes hard right at a light, continue straight (your route now called Route 93/ Hogback Road/Mount Vernon Avenue).

31.3 Cross under I-70. Top of the hill!

34.6 Take a left onto Morrison Road and get onto the roadside bike path.

35.0 Continue on the path as it veers right into the trees and crosses under C-470.

35.4 Take a sharp right and continue on the path, entering Bear Creek Lake Park. Stay on the main path, ignoring all the off-shoots.

35.8 Cross a minor road.

36.1 Cross a minor road.

37.1 Continue straight at a major path intersection.

38.5 Continue climbing on the path—don't turn right at an inviting path intersection.

38.6 At the top of the hill, take a right.

40.0 After a fast descent off the back of Mount Carbon, through the golf course, the trail spits you out onto the golf course service road (Fox Hollow Lane). Follow this road all the way past the clubhouse to the northeast corner of the park.

41.2 Where Fox Hollow Lane ends, turn right onto the Bear Creek Trail.

42.0 Go under Kipling Street and jog right before continuing east on the Bear Creek Trail.

43.4 Continue straight at a path intersection.

44.0 Cross under Wadsworth Boulevard. Notice the convenience store on your right, if needed. Continue on the path, passing many minor intersections.

46.5 Take a right across a bridge and continue on the path.

47.0 Carefully cross South Lowell Boulevard.

48.5 Veer left onto the South Platte River Trail, headed northeast. Stay on this path until the finish.

56.7 Arrive back at Confluence Park.

Bike Shops

Big Ring Cycles. 600 12th St. #170, Golden; (303) 216-2000; bigringcycles.com.

Peak Cycles. 1224 Washington Ave. #145, Golden; (303) 216-1616; bikeparts.com.

Pedal Pushers Cyclery. 710 Golden Ridge Rd., Golden; (303) 365-2453; pedalpusherscyclery.com.

Rise Above Cycles. 111 Rubey Dr. #1, Golden; (720) 541-6115.

Wheat Ridge Cyclery. 7085 W. 38th Ave., Wheat Ridge; (303) 424-3221; ridewrc.com.

Food

D'Corazon. 1530 Blake St., Suite C, Denver; (720) 904-8226. Mexican food.

My Brother's Bar. 2376 15th St., corner of 15th and Platte, Denver; (303) 455-9991; mybrothersbar.com. Homey bar/burger place that's been there forever.

Proto's Pizza. 2401 15th St., Denver; (720) 855-9400; protospizza.com.

Golden Diner. 700 12th St., Golden; (303) 279-5959; thegoldendiner.com. Open 'til 2 p.m.

Lodging

Castle Marne Bed & Breakfast. 1572 Race St., Denver; (303) 331-0621; castlemarne.com.

Oxford Hotel. 1600 17th St., Denver; (303) 628-5400; theoxfordhotel.com. Historic Denver landmark.

Warwick Hotel. 1776 Grant St., Denver; (303) 861-2000; warwickhotels.com. A little bit cheaper than the others downtown.

14 Big South Denver Path Loop

This long loop through and around metro Denver uses a network of off-street paths. The ride heads out of downtown to Cherry Creek Reservoir and beyond, traces an arc of the C-470 Trail to Bear Creek Lake Park, and comes back to downtown on the Platte.

Start: Confluence Park
Length: 72.2 miles
Terrain: Most of the ride is quite flat. There is some noticeable climbing on the approach to Cherry Creek Reservoir and rolling hills on the back side of the loop, along C-470.

Traffic and hazards: Other bicyclists! This ride has very few street crossings or interactions with motor traffic.
Things to see: Cherry Creek, Cherry Creek State Park, Bear Creek Lake Park, South Platte River

Getting there: Take I-25 to downtown Denver and exit onto Water Street (exit 211), northeast toward downtown. Water Street turns into Platte Street and goes directly past the REI. Free public parking is scarce, but there is a lot with about 25 spaces on the right side of Water Street before it goes under Speer Boulevard at Fishback Park. REI has an overflow lot on the west side of Platte Street. It may also be possible to park on the street along Platte Street. If at all possible, leave the car at home and ride to the start. **GPS:** N 39 45'17.11" / W 105 0'32.44"

Ride Description

Sometimes it seems like a dream, all these paths around the city. They are like freeways for bikes, diving under the roads, rolling unbroken mile after mile.

Strangely, there is a distinct lack of rejoicing about these concrete ribbons from the local bike crowd. Focused primarily on bike lanes these days, advocates and beginning riders seem like they take Denver's paths for granted. Do they even understand what they have here? Maybe not. The path network stretches so far and wide that few local riders have seen it all. Most of us have only vague notions of what lies beyond our favorite routes.

If I said you could ride 70 miles, even 100 miles, around Denver, entirely on paths, without crossing more than a handful of roads the entire trip, would you believe it? Go see for yourself!

Start this big loop where the Platte River and Cherry Creek, as well as their bike paths, come together, down in Lodo by the REI store (the current iteration of the giant brick building on the west bank of the Platte at the confluence, originally the powerhouse for the city's urban railways). Of course, you can jump onto this loop from anywhere around it. Cherry Creek State Park is another obvious staging area, but only one of many. If you're already way down south or out west, there's no compelling reason to drive downtown just for this ride.

Leaving the downtown area, the Cherry Creek Trail goes under University Boulevard, Colorado Boulevard, Cherry Street, Holly Street, Monaco, Quebec, Iliff—any

Concrete put to good use

of those intersections would likely cost several minutes of waiting if you were at street level. By the time you get that far away from downtown, your body might be yearning to sit at an intersection. This sort of unbroken false-flat pedaling causes its own brand of pain after a while, if you're not used to it. First World problems, am I right? The best remedy is to switch position frequently, even stand up on occasion.

The terrain starts to get bumpy as it approaches the Cherry Creek Reservoir. At a fork in the path near the dam, you can go either direction around the lake. The route described below goes around the west side. There is a road around the lake that is a traditional training and racing route for time trialers. Traffic on the road is usually light to moderate. The path also continues through the park, crossing the road a few times. Road or path, get to the south end of the reservoir and find the Cherry Creek Trail headed south across open land. Keep an eye open for coyotes, unusual waterfowl, and raptors in the cottonwoods.

South of the open space the trail spills out into suburbia, and an underpass below Arapahoe Avenue leads to the hinterlands of Parker—or at least we hope it does. The connection, an unfulfilled dream of local riders for decades, was still under construction when I wrote this in early 2015. But it's pretty clear that it's being built. Finally! On the other side the trail meanders south along with the creek, through several parcels of dedicated open space, lined by tan houses.

Cherry Creek Reservoir, created to stop periodic flooding of central Denver

Turning onto the E-470 Trail at mile 24.8, the ride enters a distinctly different phase. Instead of meandering through open space with birds chirping, the path follows the freeway, cars humming. It's not particularly close to the freeway, but it's in the same corridor. Instead of diving under the street intersections at water level, the path now sits at street level and runs smack into several street intersections as it rolls west. You'll find a street crossing every mile or two. And the path is no longer nearly flat. Now it rolls relentlessly over big humps. The rolling terrain gets taller and tougher as the path and highway proceed toward the hogbacks, curving to the north before they get there.

This does not really qualify as a hilly ride. Compared to other rides in the book, it's among the flattest. But these big rollers along C-470, the long run-up along the creek, the little climbs around Cherry Creek Reservoir, and Mount Carbon in Bear Creek Lake Park add up to some serious elevation gain. You'll climb over 2,000 feet around this loop.

The most painful and tedious part of the ride is the section along C-470, say from Wadsworth up to Bowles, especially if there's a headwind. If you're feeling spent down there along the highway or you need services, the best bet is to turn north and follow the South Platte into town using the Mary Carter Greenway (see mile 40.7). This cuts some mileage and is arguably more scenic than the C-470 corridor, but you'll miss out on the Bear Creek Trail (or BCT). The BCT is a fun leg of the journey, starting in wide-open Bear Creek Lake Park and cutting through shady Englewood back to the Platte.

If you want even more miles, consider continuing straight up C-470 to Golden, and using the Clear Creek–Platte route to get home. I think that would get you close to 90 miles.

Miles and Directions

0.0 Start from Confluence Park, in front of the bike rack on the west side of the confluence. Cross the bridge over the Platte and begin riding east-southeast on the Cherry Creek Trail.

3.7 Cross the driveway of the Denver Country Club (signaled intersection).

4.4 The path splits as it approaches the Cherry Creek Mall. The left fork takes you directly past the mall; the right fork follows the creek. Either way will work; they come together just beyond the mall.

9.0 The path goes under East Iliff Avenue then loops up to road level before continuing southbound.

10.3 Turn right at an intersection with the Highline Canal Trail.

10.4 Turn left as the Highline Canal Trail heads off to the right. Follow signs to Cherry Creek Reservoir.

12.1 After diving under I-225, take a right at a fork in the path near the dam. (**Option:** Go around the reservoir on the east side and rejoin the Cherry Creek Trail on the south side.)

13.6 Continue straight at an intersection with the Village Greens North Trail.

14.2 The path arrives at an intersection with Dam Road and South Dayton Street, near Cherry Creek High School. Turn left and cross Dam Road. This is the first Dam Road we've had to deal with on this ride so far. . . .

14.4 Turn left and enter Cherry Creek State Park, either on the road or path next to it.

17.3 The path crosses the road. If you're not already on it, get on the Cherry Creek Trail and head south.

19.2 The path ends at East Caley Avenue. Turn right and follow the street or the sidewalk/path along it.

19.3 Turn left (south) onto the path that runs along the left side of Jordan Road. This is the continuation of the Cherry Creek Trail.

19.6 The trail diverges from Jordan Road.

20.2 The path goes under Arapahoe Road.

22.1 Continue south as another path (Happy Canyon Trail) intersects on the right.

24.8 Go under E-470 and take a right (west) onto the E-470 Trail/Cherokee Trail.

26.4 Cross South Chambers Road and continue west.

26.7 Continue west as the Happy Canyon Trail joins from the right.

28.2 Cross South Peoria Street.

29.5 Cross South Jamaica Street and turn right onto the sidewalk on the other side, headed north. This is the continuation of the E-470 Trail/Cherokee Trail.

29.6 Take a left as the trail continues westbound, now on the north side of E-470.

Big South Denver Path Loop

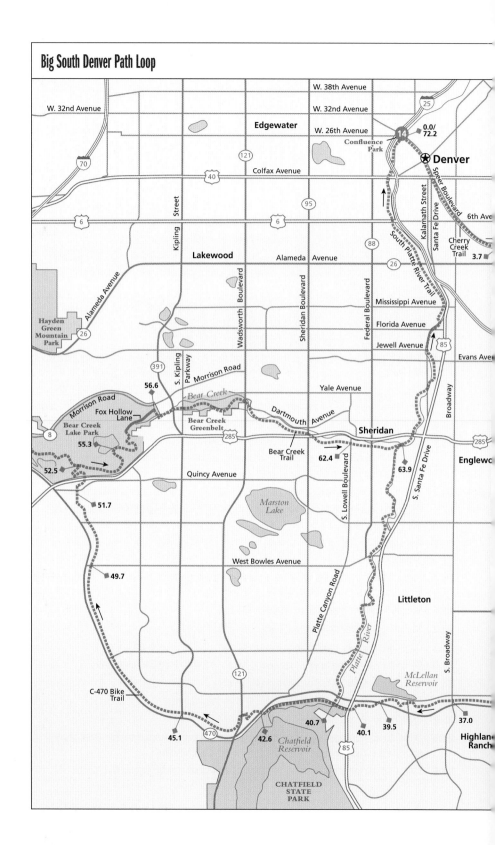

Kilometers

0   5

Miles

0   5

N

Colorado Boulevard

Monaco Parkway

225

Colfax Avenue

40

6th Avenue

6th Avenue

Alameda Avenue

Cherry Creek

University Boulevard

Mississippi Avenue

2

Parker Road

Havana Street

Peoria Street

S. Chambers Road

Aurora

Jewell Avenue

E. Iliff Avenue

2

25

9.0

83

S. Buckley Road

Tower Road

10.3

Hampden Avenue

Hampden Avenue

12.1

CHERRY CREEK STATE PARK

225

Cherry Creek Reservoir

Quincy Avenue

Cherry Hills Village

17.3

Quincy Reservoir

Belleview Avenue

14.2

Smoky Hill Road

Greenwood Village

Arapahoe Road

19.6

19.2

Arapahoe Road

88

Foxfield

S. Colorado Boulevard

S. Quebec Street

S. Yosemite Street

Parker Road

Jordan Road

470

County Line Road

35.5

34.5

32.4

30.9

29.5

Peoria Street

E-470 Bike Path

26.4

24.8

83

Lone Tree

25

Lincoln Avenue

30.1 The path goes under I-25 and several flyovers.

30.9 The path arrives at South Yosemite Street. Turn right and cross South Park Meadows Center Drive, then turn left, cross South Yosemite, and continue west on the path.

32.0 Cross Acres Green Drive.

32.4 Cross South Quebec Street.

34.5 Cross South Colorado Boulevard.

35.5 Cross South University Boulevard.

37.0 Cross South Broadway.

37.7 Continue west as the Centennial Trail becomes the Highline Canal Trail.

39.5 The trail goes under C-470 and continues west; now called the C-470 Bikeway.

40.1 Cross South Santa Fe Drive.

40.7 Turn right as another path intersects on the left. Cross the South Platte River and continue on the C-470 Bikeway. (**Option:** Turn right on the other side of the river and head north on the South Platte River Trail/Mary Carter Greenway Trail, and rejoin the route at mile 63.9.)

42.6 Continue on the C-470 Bikeway past another path intersection and dive under C-470. On the other side, the trail does a little curlicue and continues west by the highway. (There is a cool resting spot here by the creek.)

43.5 After crossing under South Wadsworth Boulevard, the C-470 Bikeway spills out into a small parking lot. Continue straight through and find the path on the other side.

45.1 Cross South Kipling Parkway. The trail steadily curves to the north.

47.4 Cross West Ken Caryl Avenue.

49.7 Cross West Bowles Avenue.

50.7 Cross West Belleview Avenue.

51.7 Cross West Quincy Avenue, and continue north on South Eldridge Street for a block, then find the C-470 Bikeway continuing at the end.

52.5 Veer right (east) onto the Bear Creek Trail, in Bear Creek Lake Park.

53.8 Ignore the path intersecting on the right and continue up the hill.

54.1 At the top of the hill, turn right.

55.3 The trail pops out onto a road (Fox Hollow Lane). Continue straight.

56.6 Fox Hollow Lane comes to an end. Find the Bear Creek Trail headed south.

57.5 After the trail goes under South Kipling Parkway, take a right then a left, following the signs for the Bear Creek Trail (BCT), headed due east by the creek.

58.7 As the path enters open space, continue straight as another path intersects on the right.

59.5 After passing under Wadsworth Boulevard, the trail goes right by a little convenience store, if you're in need.

62.4 Carefully cross South Lowell Boulevard, then cross the creek on the sidewalk and continue on the path. This is probably the most dangerous crossing along the route.

63.9 The Bear Creek Trail ends at the intersection with the South Platte River Trail. Continue north on the South Platte River Trail.

70.7 Cross West 13th Avenue. Continue north on the South Platte River Trail, following the river, passing all intersections with other paths along the way.

72.2 Back at Confluence Park.

Attractions

Four Mile Historic Park. 715 S. Forest St., Denver; (720) 865-0800; fourmilepark.org. Right along the Cherry Creek Path.

Bike Shops

These shops are located in Central Denver:

C3 Bike Shop. 3316 Tejon St., Denver; (303) 953-8720; c3bikeshop.com.

Jinji Cycles. 2538 W. 32nd Ave., Denver; (303) 433-3474; jinjicycles.com.

Joe's Bicycle Shop. 86 Pennsylvania St., Denver; (720) 292-7218; joesbikeshop.weebly.com.

REI. 1416 Platte St., Denver; (303) 756-3100; REI.com. Located at the start of the ride.

Salvagetti Bicycle Workshop. 3800 Irving St., Denver; (303) 691-5595; salvagetti.com.

Track Shack. 1338 Tremont Place, Denver; (303) 629-9267; trackshackdenver.com. Cool little shop specializing in track bikes and fixed-wheel action.

Turin Bicycles. 700 Lincoln St., Denver; (303) 837-1857; turinbikes.com.

Velosoul Cyclery. 1109 S. Pearl St., Denver; (720) 570-5039; velosoul.com.

Food

D'Corazon. 1530 Blake St., Suite C, Denver; (720) 904-8226. Mexican food.

My Brother's Bar. 2376 15th St., corner of 15th and Platte, Denver; (303) 455-9991; mybrothersbar.com. Homey bar/burger place, been there forever.

Proto's Pizza. 2401 15th St., Denver; (720) 855-9400; protospizza.com.

The Bicycle Cafe. 1308 E. 17th Ave., Denver; (720) 446-8029; denverbicyclecafe.com. Part bike shop, part cafe. Why isn't every cafe part bike shop, and every bike shop part cafe? Not very close to the start/finish.

Lodging

Castle Marne Bed & Breakfast. 1572 Race St., Denver; (303) 331-0621; castlemarne.com.

Oxford Hotel. 1600 17th St., Denver; (303) 628-5400; theoxfordhotel.com. Historic Denver landmark.

Warwick Hotel. 1776 Grant St., Denver; (303) 861-2000; warwickhotels.com. A little bit cheaper than the others downtown.

15 Deer Creek Canyon

Enjoy one of the most popular climbs in the state, possibly the world. Then loop back via a nifty route through the mountain suburbs.

Start: South Valley Park parking area on Deer Creek Canyon Road
Length: 27.0-mile lollipop loop
Terrain: Lots and lots of climbing. A long canyon climb, increasingly difficult, leads to a twisting climb through the exurbs. At the far side of the loop, you find yourself in Turkey Creek Canyon, with one more small climb to get

over before hitting the laundry chute descent back to the start.
Traffic and hazards: Plenty of car and truck traffic in Deer Creek Canyon, thinning out as the climb progresses. Conflicts and road-rage incidents are part of the route's history, but things have improved greatly.
Things to see: Deer Creek Canyon, the High Grade Road, South Turkey Creek Canyon

Getting there: Deer Creek Canyon Road can be accessed on extreme South Wadsworth Boulevard, just south of C-470, a freeway curving all the way around the edge of the southwest quarter of the city, from I-25 to Golden. To get to Deer Creek Canyon, get on C-470 and drive to South Wadsworth Boulevard, go south on Wadsworth for a few blocks, and turn right onto West Deer Creek Canyon Road (CR 124). Take West Deer Creek Canyon west for about 3 miles and park on the right at the South Valley Park trailhead. **GPS:** N 39 33'4.24" / W 105 8'22.29"

Ride Description

Most cyclists approach the Deer Creek Canyon ride the same way—in a car from a home somewhere in the Denver metro area. So, as this is an extremely popular ride, there are a lot of cars and trucks belonging to bicyclists parked around the bottom of this canyon.

It should be noted that you don't *have* to drive to Deer Creek, which begins just south of C-470 and Wadsworth. The start is actually very well placed near the area's bike-path network, which means you could pedal there all the way from downtown Denver without crossing more than a few roads and make one heck of an epic ride. So if this sub–30-mile route looks too tame for you, try it from downtown and see how it feels with those extra 35 miles or so tacked on. Fierce!

The rest of us will be adequately challenged by the more traditional route described here. If you drive, there are several places you can start the ride. Most folks leave their cars down on the flats near Wadsworth. You can also park in the often-empty Hildebrand Ranch Open Space lot, the South Valley Park lot, or some other places along the road. We'll start a few miles up the canyon at the parking lot of the South Valley Park, which has a toilet.

You might feel a little cheated out of those few miles beginning here, but trust me, you'll still get your fill of climbing. There's more than enough to go around. When it's all said and done, this ride includes about 3,400 feet of climbing, which puts it squarely in the difficult column despite its moderate distance.

How's the car traffic in Deer Creek Canyon? That's a loaded question! Actual risk of collision is difficult to gauge. Traffic-related annoyance seems moderate. Individual riders or small groups riding courteously (that is, singling up when cars approach) almost never run into hassles up here. However, there has been a significant amount of conflict over the years between the residents of Deer Creek Canyon and cyclists on *group rides*, riding in packs up the road.

Local residents are beginning to appreciate bicyclists.

There was one particularly nasty incident in early November 2012, in which a 70-year-old retired engineer named Andrew Hoover drove up behind a group of about a dozen riders and, though the group was riding single file on the right side, started laying on his horn. Hoover was returning to the site of his recently burned-out Deer Creek Canyon home, so he was probably in a very sour mood to begin with, even before he rounded that curve and saw that long line of Lycra. He admitted later that he had a history of conflicts and road rage with cyclists on the road.

Seemingly on purpose, Hoover rammed his Ford Ranger into a rider at the back of the group, Byron Nix. The collision crushed his bike and dropped him injured in the road. Hoover, the grandson of President Herbert Hoover, managed to convince the police that the whole thing was unintentional and drove away with a careless-driving citation.

Hoover's behavior wasn't exactly typical, but it didn't come out of the blue either. Tension had been building for a long time before this, and things were bad enough that angry residents, voicing "concern for cyclists' safety," were blowing up in public meetings and demanding that bicycling be banned outright from Deer Creek Canyon. The bad outcome of Hoover's apparent outburst seems to have led to realizations on both sides, then a softening of positions, and ultimately the defusing of tensions. Cyclists and residents have learned to coexist. But it can't hurt to know the ugly history as you interact with the locals.

The climb begins modestly, warming you up nicely for a few miles. Shallow slopes and big round turns lead to a few short "jumper" climbs by the creek. Right away you'll notice the landscape starting to change, as you emerge from the red rocks and rattlesnake dens and climb toward the mountains. After about 3 miles, take a left at the crossroads.

Near the bottom, headed up

The south branch of Deer Creek Canyon climbs easily past charming little homes, then twists up some switchbacks to begin one of the most well-known sections on the Front Range: the steep guardrail-flanked climb known to many as "the High Grade." Nothing but air on the other side of the guardrail as you ascend, with sublime views down the valley. This is what it's all about.

The slope does mellow out eventually, with a series of rollers and then long stretches of false flat at the top of the canyon. Watch for a "Cyclist's Rest Stop" up there, near the top on the right side. Here you'll find coolers full of water and Gatorade, picnic tables, and a Port-o-Let in the shade of the pines, helpfully provided by a local organization. Not bad, eh? Sure is preferable to getting run over by Hoover's grandson! All they ask in exchange for partaking in the cold beverages is a small donation, if you've got a buck stuffed into your jersey pocket.

You can take this road (now called Pleasant Park Road) all the way to US 285 at Conifer, but to avoid the highway use residential roads (Oehlmann Park Road/City View) to cut north through this mountain suburbia to Turkey Creek Canyon. The route through the neighborhood looks complicated on the map, winding all over the place with several street name changes and intersections, but it's actually pretty easy to follow. Just stay on the main *paved* route as it switches names from Oehlmann to

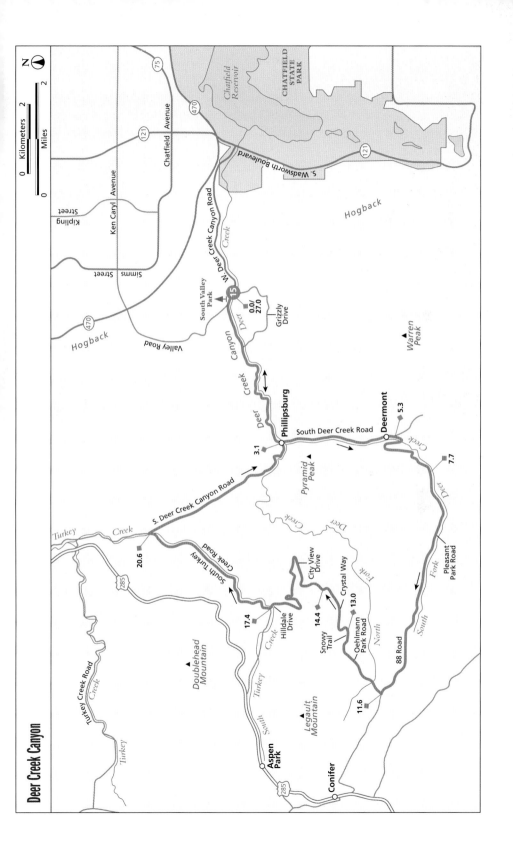

Deer Creek Canyon

Turkey Creek Road

Turkey Creek

Turkey

South Turkey Creek

Turkey Creek

Aspen Park

285

Conifer

285

Doublehead Mountain

Legault Mountain

South Turkey Creek Road

S. Deer Creek Canyon Road

20.6

17.4

Hilldale Drive

City View Drive

Crystal Way

Snowy Trail

14.4

13.0

Oehlmann Park Road

11.6

88 Road

North Fork

Deer Creek

Deer Creek

South Fork

Pleasant Park Road

Deer Creek

Pyramid Peak

Phillipsburg

3.1

South Deer Creek Road

Deermont

5.3

7.7

Warren Peak

Deer Canyon Creek

Deer Creek

Grizzly Drive

0.0/ 27.0

15

South Valley Park

Valley Road

Hogback

470

W. Deer Creek Canyon Road

Deer Creek

Hogback

Simms Street

Kipling Street

Ken Caryl Avenue

Chatfield Avenue

75

121

470

Chatfield Reservoir

CHATFIELD STATE PARK

S. Wadsworth Boulevard

121

Crystal Way to City View, and some other names in between. Basically, it's the same road all the way through.

Be sure to eat enough food and save some energy for this middle portion of the ride, which is not flat at all. Along with face-ripper descents, there are many steep climbs and at least one serious switchback climb lying in wait between Pleasant Park and Turkey Creek.

South Turkey Creek Canyon is truly great for bicycling. The easy-breezy descent through the shady turns is a delightful reward after all the huffing and puffing you did earlier. You could cruise this canyon all day long. Unfortunately the canyon is relatively short, and you're going to see just a portion of it. Take a right onto the north branch of Deer Creek Canyon at mile 20.6 and begin the final phase of the ride.

You will notice that you're fighting gravity again. Yes, one more hill. But it's no biggie, a 200-foot hump. Soon you'll be flying downhill (in a responsible fashion) all the way back to the car.

Miles and Directions

0.0 Start riding up West Deer Creek Canyon Road from the parking area at South Valley Park.

0.1 Pass the intersection with Valley Road.

3.1 Turn left onto South Deer Creek Road, along the South Fork of Deer Creek.

5.3 Continue up as the road turns into High Grade Road.

7.7 Continue as the road turns to Pleasant Park Road.

11.6 Turn right onto Oehlmann Park Road. Stay on the paved road, passing all dirt spurs.

13.0 Oehlmann Park Road becomes Snowy Trail. Stay on pavement.

13.2 Snowy Trail becomes Crystal Way. Continue and stay on the paved route.

14.0 Crystal Way becomes South Crystal Drive.

14.4 Turn right at the T intersection and continue on City View Drive.

17.3 City View becomes Hilldale Drive.

17.4 Turn right onto South Turkey Creek Road.

20.6 Turn right onto South Deer Creek Canyon Road.

27.0 Back at the South Valley Park lot.

Bike Shops

Here are some shops in the southern Denver metro area:

Alpha Bicycle Company. 8006 E. Arapahoe Rd., Centennial; (303) 220-9799; alphabicycle.com.

Elevation Cycles. 2030 E. County Line Rd., Highlands Ranch; (303) 730-8038; elevationcycles.com.

Big Kahuna Bicycles. 10201 W. Bowles Ave., Littleton; (720) 981-5199; bigkahunabicycles.com.

Pedal. 2640 W. Belleview Ave. #100, Littleton; (303) 798-5033; pedalonline.com.

Performance Bicycle. 5066 S. Wadsworth Blvd., Unit 124, Littleton; (303) 987-1376; performancebike.com.

Food

If you're looking for something other than chain restaurants, the C-470 corridor is pretty tricky.

Luigi's Italian Restaurant. 8130 S. University Blvd., Festival Shopping Center, Centennial; (303) 694-9357; luigisitalian.net.

Mi Cocina Express. 137 W. County Line Rd., Littleton; (303) 795-3552. Counter-service Mexican food.

Virgilio's Pizzeria & Wine Bar. 10025 W. San Juan Way, Littleton; (303) 972-1011; ilovepizza pie.com.

Lodging

TownePlace Suites. 10902 W. Toller Dr., Littleton; (303) 972-0555; www.marriott.com/hotels/travel/dentp-towneplace-suites-denver-southwest-littleton. Close to Deer Creek Canyon.

16 Myers Gulch–Evergreen Loop

A compact but vertical loop in the mountains west of Denver, this fun outing takes you from creek to creek, canyon to canyon, with some minor mountains in between.

Start: Corwina Park in Bear Creek Canyon near Kittredge
Length: 20.9 miles
Terrain: Moderate mountains; two tough climbs, two winding descents
Traffic and hazards: Moderate traffic on well-used roads. Semi-technical descending. Route requires riding on US 285 very briefly, then it must be crossed. The crossing is not as bad as it sounds, but it could be dangerous if botched. Consider avoiding this route during rush hour.
Things to see: Bear Creek Canyon, Indian Hills, Turkey Creek Canyon, Evergreen, Kittredge

Getting there: From Denver, take the 6th Avenue Freeway west to I-70, then I-70 west briefly to C-470. Head south on C-470 to the Morrison exit. Go west through Morrison and up Bear Creek Canyon (CO 74). About 7.5 miles up the canyon, park in the Corwina Park parking area on the left side of the road and across a little bridge. (There is another parking area about a mile down the canyon, also part of Corwina Park.) **GPS:** N 39 39'41.44" / W 105 17'4.93"

Ride Description

This is a personal favorite that just might become one of yours. Quick but satisfying, painful but relaxing, pretty and mountainous, and not too far from the Big City.

Starting from down in Bear Creek Canyon, the first order of business is climbing up and over Myers Gulch Road. It's a nice little wake-up call, nothing too severe. It climbs about 600 feet in 2.5 miles. When you see the Pence Park lot and sign, you're at the top. On the other side is a flowing area dotted with houses, Parmalee or Indian Hills, depending on whom you ask.

The road drops into Parmalee Gulch and is now fittingly named Parmalee Gulch Road. It's very curvy and narrow in spots, with plenty of traffic. I personally try to avoid all these bedroom-community roads during the afternoon rush home, but it doesn't always work out that way. Expect a wandering SUV around every turn.

At the bottom of Parmalee Gulch, you'll have to get on US 285 just for a smidge in order to access Turkey Creek Canyon. The shoulder of US 285 is super wide but also strewn with debris. Ride 0.3 mile on US 285 and cross when the coast is clear. With a little patience, the crossing is pretty benign.

South Turkey Creek Road is an easy, slightly uphill cruise. Just 1.5 miles or so on this lovely road brings you to the next turn, at North Turkey Creek Canyon. North Turkey Creek is also a great little road with mellow inclines and, unfortunately, lots of traffic during the evening rush.

Turn right onto High Drive, the main course of this multicourse meal. High Drive starts off pretty chill, as they say around here, then loses its cool multiple times, zigzagging up some switchbacks and kissing 15 percent repeatedly. It tops out at about

The woefully under-biked Cub Creek Road

8,000 feet, a surprisingly low high point for a mountain ride. The climb isn't lose-control-of-your-bowels difficult, but it'll burn some calories. It's a solid 1,000-footer from North Turkey Creek Canyon, making it the larger of the loop's two big climbs.

High Drive finally gives up the ghost at a T intersection with Stanley Park Road. Turn left and descend, pausing if you can to enjoy the view of Mount Evans. The route changes names on the way down, becoming Lower Cub Creek Road.

Cub Creek/Stanley Park Road is world-class cool in either direction. In fact the whole loop is composed of very interesting, challenging sections of road. If only they were all closed to motor traffic.

This 20-mile loop might not be enough for an enthusiast craving a big day in the saddle, but the route can be

Whenever you see this sign, you know the top of the hill is near.

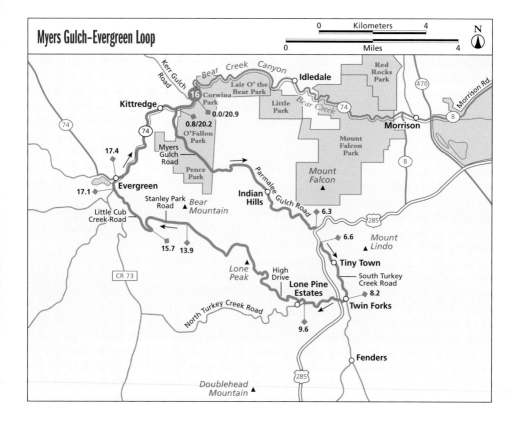

Myers Gulch-Evergreen Loop

spiked with additional climbs in several spots. The best opportunity could be the road to Mount Falcon, which can be found over the top of the first climb; watch for signs pointing the way to the Mount Falcon Park. Kerr Gulch, sprouting from Bear Creek Canyon not far from the start, is another great, highly recommended side trip. There are also a few nice climbs out of South Turkey Creek, potentially connecting to the Deer Creek loop (see Deer Creek Canyon ride) and more great roads emanating from the main arteries around Evergreen.

Miles and Directions

0.0   Start from Corwina Park and begin riding up Bear Creek Road (CO 74), west.

0.8   Turn left onto Myers Gulch Road.

6.3   Turn right onto US 285.

6.6   Turn left onto South Turkey Creek Road.

8.2   Turn right onto North Turkey Creek Road. Continue past US 285 and associated ramps.

9.6   Turn right onto High Drive. Continue on High Drive past numerous intersecting streets.

13.9   Turn left onto Stanley Park Road.

15.7   Go around a sharp right-hand turn and continue downhill on the road that becomes Little Cub Creek Road.

17.1 Turn right onto CR 73.

17.4 Turn right onto CO 74 (Bear Creek Road).

20.2 Continue past the intersection with Myers Gulch Road in Kittredge.

20.9 Arrive back at Corwina Park.

Bike Shops

Evergreen Bicycle Outfitters. 29017 Hotel Way #101c, Evergreen; (303) 674-6737; velocolorado.com.

Red Rocks Cyclery. 300 Bear Creek Ave., Morrison; (303) 697-8833; redrockscyclery.com.

Food

One World Cafe. 28275 CO 74, Evergreen; (303) 670-1114.

Wildflower Café. 28035 CO 74, Evergreen; (303) 674-3323; wildflowerevergreen.com.

Bear Creek Restaurant. 25940 CO 74, Kittredge; (303) 674-9929; thebearcreek restaurant.com.

Lodging

Alpen Way Chalet Inn. 4980 CR 73, Evergreen; (303) 674-7467; alpenwaychalet.net.

Bear Creek Cabins. 27400 CO 74, Evergreen; (303) 674-3442; bearcreekcabinsco.com.

17   Squaw Pass-Mount Evans

Approach Mount Evans from the east for a change, climbing Squaw Pass Road to reach Echo Lake. See a new side of the mountain and a new side of yourself on this formidable super epic.

Start: Bergen Park, near the intersection of Evergreen Parkway and Squaw Pass Road
Length: 64.5 miles out-and-back
Terrain: A big mountain-pass climb followed by one of the toughest and most well-known cycling roads in the world. Huge.
Traffic and hazards: Moderate traffic on curvy mountain roads. Road damage is a serious issue up here. So is weather and, potentially, altitude sickness. Save this one for a day with stable weather conditions.
Things to see: Squaw Pass, Mount Evans
Fee alert: It costs 3 bucks to ride past the guard shack at the bottom of Mount Evans Road near Echo Lake.

Getting there: From Denver, take I-70 west to the Evergreen Parkway (CO 74), and Evergreen Parkway to Bergen Park. Turn left onto Ellingwood Trail (Squaw Pass Road) and park on the left in the Buchanan Park parking lot. **GPS:** N 39' 41'6.91" / W 105 21'52.22"

Ride Description

The traditional route up 14,200-foot Mount Evans (and the route of the famous race) begins just outside Idaho Springs. That's a beautiful section of road, from Idaho

Evening descends on Squaw Pass Road near Juniper Pass.

Squaw Pass Road

Springs to Echo Lake, and you should definitely ride it even if you have no intention of turning at Echo Lake and conquering Evans. However, if you're looking for something a little different, have a go at Evans from the other side, via Squaw Pass Road. Start from Bergen Park, the commercial development on Evergreen Parkway, and climb, climb, climb.

Squaw Pass (Juniper Pass to be more precise) is a brutal ride all by itself. If you don't have time or motivation for the full monty, try an ethereal out-and-back to Echo Lake. (Adding Evans, another 15 miles and over 3,000 feet of climbing, probably triples the overall difficulty.) Squaw Pass Road (CO 103) descends a few hundred feet to Echo Lake from the top of Juniper Pass, which adds a little jolt to the return trip. Adventure lovers take note: You can ride to the Squaw Pass Road from Evergreen via Bear Creek Road and (steep) dirt-road connectors.

People basically laugh at Mount Evans these days. During the summer of 2014, a group of smart alecks summited on B-cycle bikes—the three-speed bike-share tanks equipped with dynamo hubs, front baskets, and barstool-like seats. That won't make you feel any better if you have to turn back while riding a $7,000 rig that weighs less than a B-cycle bike's rear wheel.

The Evans road's been eclipsed by the recently opened Pikes Peak Highway, which is clearly more extreme, but it's still one of the more ridiculously strenuous

Squaw Pass–Mount Evans

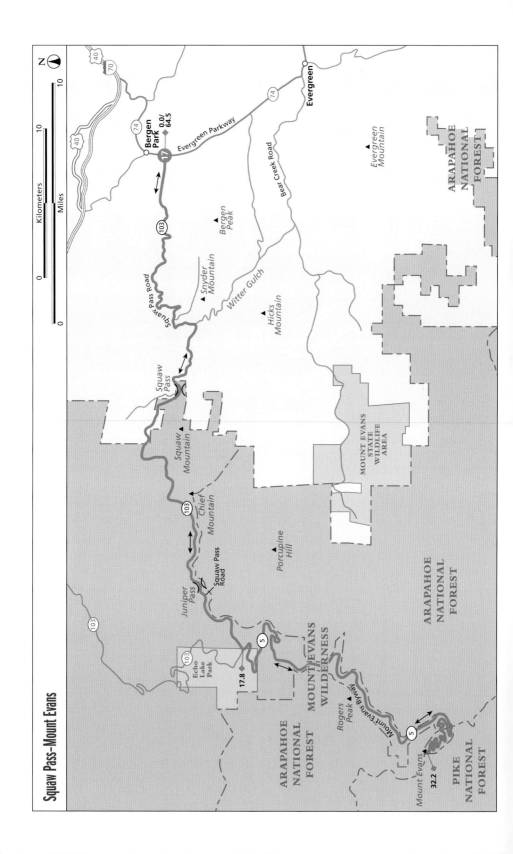

climbs that can be attempted by a human on a bicycle. And it always will be. Consider attempting the ride during a warm spell in the weeks after the road is closed to auto traffic in the fall. As you progress up the majestic peak, ponder whether it should be renamed, and if the speed records set on the mountain by admitted dopers should be erased from the books. And give my regards to the goats.

Miles and Directions

0.0 From the intersection of Evergreen Parkway and Squaw Pass Road, begin riding up Squaw Pass Road.

17.8 At Echo Lake, turn left onto the Mount Evans Road. (Echo Lake has a restaurant, gift shop, and bathrooms.)

32.2 Evans summit. Retrace your tire tracks back toward Evergreen.

64.5 Back at the start.

Bike Shops

Evergreen Bicycle Outfitters. 29017 Hotel Way #101c, Evergreen; (303) 674-6737; velo colorado.com.

Food

One World Cafe. 28275 CO 74, Evergreen; (303) 670-1114.
Wildflower Café. 28035 CO 74, Evergreen; (303) 674-3323; wildflowerevergreen.com.

Lodging

Alpen Way Chalet Inn. 4980 CR 73, Evergreen; (303) 674-7467; alpenwaychalet.net.
Bear Creek Cabins. 27400 CO 74, Evergreen; (303) 674-3442; bearcreekcabinsco.com.

18 Jarre Canyon

There's not much actual canyon going on here. Twelve miles of false flats, sharp climbs, and twisting descents separate the little town of Sedalia from the collection of cabins known as Sprucewood, where the pavement of CO 67 ends. This out-and-back is a scenic and interesting challenge.

Start: The intersection of Perry Park Road (CO 105) and Jarre Canyon Road south of Sedalia
Length: 25.4 miles out-and-back
Terrain: Rolling hills lead to steep climbs. Lots of vertical: 3,000-plus feet.

Traffic and hazards: Fast car traffic on curvy roads. Motocrossers pulling their bikes on trailers. Semi-tricky descents with a fair bit of road damage.
Things to see: The Rampart Range

Getting there: From Denver, go south on South Santa Fe Drive/US 85 to Sedalia. Take a right onto CO 67 and drive through town to the intersection with CO 105 (Perry Park Road). Park off to the side of US 105 near the intersection. **GPS:** N 39 25'51.98" / W 104 57'54.92"

Ride Description

Sedalia is like a wormhole between two universes: the modern Denver metropolitan area on one side and Civil War–era rural Colorado on the other.

South of the town the landscape opens up into beautiful green hills that were very familiar to local Native American tribes for centuries. Beginning in the 1850s,

A portion of Douglas County that continues to defy the spread of development

Phase Two on CO 67

white settlers fenced off and claimed the land, carving irrigation ditches as high in the canyons as they could. Working around the rock formations, the settlers grew hay, fruit, and potatoes; raised cattle; and sold timber, sending produce to Denver and fresh milk to the local creameries.

The low-grade warfare and massacres of the 1860s chased the outnumbered Cheyenne and Arapahoe bands to the northern plains, and the Utes were marched west toward Utah not long after. This left the settlers to contend only with each other (which they did regularly in fierce feuds and court battles), the too-dry climate, and the shift from agrarian to industrial society that was slowly crushing their chosen lifestyle. This shift was illustrated most painfully here by the advent of fake butter ("oleo") in the 1880s.

The farms and ranches along West Plum Creek managed to adapt and survive, for the most part, although few would think of their domain as prime dairy land any more. For whatever reason, the area appears substantially the same today as it did 150 years ago. Something around here managed to repel the long arm of suburban development through the next century and beyond.

From a bicyclist's perspective, CO 67 is composed of three sections. First is a long, false-flat run-up to the mountains, across the tall grass– and scrub oak–covered slopes, with red-rock formations dotting the landscape. Classic Front Range stuff. Second, a

The establishment in Sprucewood caters primarily to ATV and moto riders.

steep, tough climb as the road attacks the mountain. Third, a long section of sharp climbs and descents and crazy curves that really defines the ride. The pavement ends at a crossroads called Sprucewood. (Or maybe that is just the name of the little restaurant there. But lots of us around here have been under the impression that Sprucewood is a place.)

Don't burn all your matches on the deceivingly difficult first few miles, or the initial appearance of the big climb will throw you into a state of shock. At mile 4.5 you encounter the first shocking ramp. The pavement was in a notably sorry state when I last rode this. Don't despair; the steepness doesn't persist much farther than your line of sight, and the relentless climb turns to a rollicking roller coaster behind the mountain. The route doesn't suddenly get easy, but it does become much more agreeable.

Traffic can be a big issue on otherwise beautiful little CO 67. On weekends the road serves as the preferred runway for dirt bikers headed to the trails along the Rampart Range Road. They're in big pickups, often pulling trailers and often driving way too fast. In my opinion, this makes the road a no-go for weekend riding. On weekdays, you'll still experience a few uncomfortable passes by trucks or trailers, just a sample of the weekend action.

Miles and Directions

0.0 Start from the intersection of CO 67 (Jarre Canyon Road/Manhart Avenue) and CO 105 (Perry Park Road) and begin riding southwest.

9.4 Pass the intersection with Rampart Range Road.

12.7 Turn around at Sprucewood, at the Y intersection with West Pine Creek Road. (**Option:** Continue and explore some rugged dirt roads. Both roads eventually make their way down to the Platte River. The road on the right—West Pine Creek Road—is much more direct and roller-coaster steep on the way to the river. The left branch—CO 67—also goes to the river but takes much longer to get there, connecting much farther south. I can't vouch for either surface. I know they've been fairly rough in the past.)

25.4 Back at the intersection of CO 105 and CO 67.

Bike Shops

Country Pedaler Bikes and Skis. 203 5th St., Castle Rock; (303) 688-6775; countrypedaler .com.

Some shops in the southern Denver metro area:

Big Kahuna Bicycles. 10201 W. Bowles Ave., Littleton; (720) 981-5199; bigkahunabicycles .com.

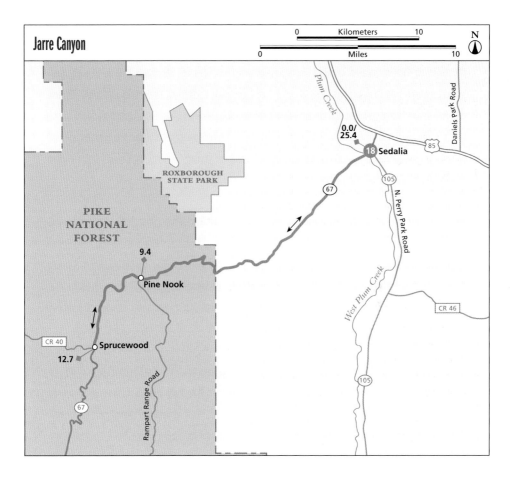

Pedal. 2640 W. Belleview Ave. #100, Littleton; (303) 798-5033; pedalonline.com.

Performance Bicycle. 5066 S. Wadsworth Blvd., Unit 124, Littleton; (303) 987-1376; performancebike.com.

Alpha Bicycle Company. 8006 E. Arapahoe Rd., Centennial; (303) 220-9799; alpha bicycle.com.

Elevation Cycles. 2030 E. County Line Rd., Highlands Ranch; (303) 730-8038; elevation cycles.com.

Food

Services are few and far between.

Gabriel's Northern Italian. 5450 Manhart Ave., Sedalia; (303) 688-2323. Pricey by most hungry cyclists' standards.

Jarre Mart. 5466 Manhart Ave. (CO 67), Sedalia; (303) 688-8555. Convenience store/ gas station. Bathroom available for paying customers.

Sprucewood Inn Restaurant. 491 S. CO 67, Sedalia; (303) 688-3231. The little place at the far end of the pavement caters primarily to motocrossers and ATV riders.

SOME OTHER RIDES AROUND DOUGLAS COUNTY

Greenland Open Space Trail. A crushed-gravel trail looping through the strikingly gorgeous grasslands around Greenland, south of Larkspur. To find it, take exit 167 off I-25 and picture what this area was like before the highway. Thankfully they're keeping at least some of the land as open space. According to the papers, my great-grandfather once grew a giant radish here that had a 17-inch circumference. Imagine trying to farm this land! Better have some irrigation skills, buddy boy.

Perry Park/Larkspur. Try an excellent loop using Perry Park Road (CO 105), Spruce Mountain Road, and Larkspur Road. Ruggedly beautiful, rolling terrain. Take a side trip into Perry Park itself to meander among the incredible rock formations. The route goes to Palmer Lake and also Larkspur. Start from up in Sedalia to complete the small-town trifecta and maximize the mileage of fun roads. All three towns were important stops on the Denver & Rio Grande narrow-gauge route completed in 1871.

Upper Lake Gulch Road. A rolling gravel road meandering northeast from Spruce Mountain Road near Larkspur, this road crosses I-25 and quickly turns to dirt. Works as a cool out-and-back or a loop connecting to Lake Gulch Road, Wolfensburger Road out of Castle Rock, Perry Park Road and West Perry Park Avenue, or Fox Farm Road back to Larkspur. Getting through Castle Rock these days feels about as . . . suboptimal . . . as negotiating the busiest places in Denver or Colorado Springs. And I think that is what they are shooting for.

19 North Cheyenne Canyon Loop

A relatively short but very adventurous loop. While just 10 miles, this rough and gorgeous canyon-climbing ride is not for the faint of heart or weak of leg.

Start: Stratton Open Space trailhead parking area on Ridgeway Avenue in Cheyenne Canyon
Length: 10.4 miles
Terrain: A beautiful, challenging climb up North Cheyenne Canyon, flanked by steep mountains and rock formations, and a traverse of rough-surfaced Gold Camp Road followed by a steep drop through the city's southwestern suburbs
Traffic and hazards: Tourist traffic can be heavy in the canyon, but speeds tend to be low. Gold Camp Road is a dirt road that can be quite rough with washboard and potholes, as well as sloshy with gravel. There are two dark tunnels along Gold Camp Road. The descent is steep and slippery with gravel.
Things to see: Helen Hunt Falls, beautiful Cheyenne Canyon, Colorado Springs from above

Getting there: From downtown Colorado Springs, go south on Tejon Street to Cheyenne Boulevard. Go west on Cheyenne Boulevard to Ridgeway Avenue. Turn right on Ridgeway and then right into the Stratton Open Space parking lot. From I-25, take exit 140 and go south on South Tejon Street, then west on Cheyenne Boulevard to Ridgeway Avenue and the Stratton Open Space parking lot. **GPS:** N 38 47'43.52" / W 104 51'28.79"

Ride Description

North Cheyenne Canyon is one of the coolest and nastiest little climbs you'll ever ride. Unfortunately there are challenges along the way that could ruin the experience for some. The road is crawling with tourists, picnickers, and dudes looking for places to dump bodies (only a slight exaggeration there). The pavement is so narrow that any car traffic gets bottled up behind a climbing bicyclist. Then, when you reach the top, the pavement disappears entirely, replaced by a moderately rough and sloshy gravel road that most road bikers will find difficult to navigate with skinny tires. And then there are tunnels. Two of them, known to have some salad-spinner-size potholes hidden in their cold darkness. It's an adventurous ride for those who are looking for a little something *extra*, which is not often said of 10-mile road rides.

To mitigate the traffic aspect, avoid the area on weekends and holidays, when the entire population of El Paso County hauls their extended families into the canyon to picnic by the creek, look at Helen Hunt Falls, or hike one of the many awesome trails. To avoid the dirt road, simply turn around at the top and descend back down through those narrow, gravel-strewn curves—also quite adventurous and potentially very dangerous.

Now, if you feel like taking a nice big bite out of life today, riding this loop is a good start. You can attack this ride from just about anywhere in Colorado Springs. Just get over to the canyon via South Tejon and Cheyenne Boulevard, or head west

The view from Gold Camp Road

out of downtown until you can turn left and south on 26th (or the more direct, less interesting 21st). The west-side routes require some substantial climbing to get over to the canyon. If you're driving to the bottom of the canyon, you can start in a few places. The route described below starts at the Stratton Open Space parking lot off Ridgeway Avenue; there are other good lots farther up the canyon at Starsmore Discovery Center, near the fork in the road where North and South Cheyenne Canyons come together. North Cheyenne Canyon is the right fork; South Cheyenne Canyon is the left fork (see Zoo Loop ride).

It doesn't matter where you start. Just get to the canyon and start riding up. The climb starts moderately but without any shoulder, leaving little room for skittish flatland drivers to pass. That theme will continue as you go. If you've collected too many tourists trailing behind at any point, you might consider just pulling over and letting them go by.

The canyon winds deliciously past crumbling granite walls next to the little gurgling creek, looking so inviting in the hot summer sun. There are several small parking areas at trailheads and picnic areas along the side of the road. Steadily, the slope ramps up. On Mine Hill the incline is a respectable 14 percent or so, wheel-slipping territory on the gravelly edges of the road. You'll know it when you get to it.

Gold Camp Road is really fun or really messed up, depending on your point of view.

The incline flattens again on approach to Helen Hunt Falls, the destination for most of the car traffic. It's strange that they didn't call it Helen Hunt Jackson Falls, because that was the poet and activist author's name when she died in 1885. Hunt was Helen's first husband, who died in a military accident; Jackson was a rich banker she met while visiting the area in the 1870s. In fact they met one canyon over, at nearby Seven Falls, while the resort city of Colorado Springs was being created on a flat, treeless plain a few miles away.

Sadly, death followed Helen Hunt Jackson like her own shadow. Two of her three siblings, both her parents, her first husband (Hunt), and both of her own children met early deaths. Left alone, she became a fierce advocate for Native Americans, writing a history of their mistreatment by the government called *Century of Dishonor*, and a novel, *Ramona*, which is said to have sold over a half-million copies. The falls were named for her after she died of stomach cancer in 1885.

Her views about Native Americans would not have been popular, to say the least, with many who lived in the area in the nineteenth century—her views would not be popular with many Springs residents today. She is an interesting hero for a town like this. One could make an argument that her memorialization was largely a product of the collective guilt of the area's settlers and developers, in the wake of the Sand Creek Massacre and other disasters that occurred not that long before her death.

The parking area up here is surprisingly busy. Beyond the falls, the road climbs through a few switchbacks and then finally tops out at yet another surprisingly large and busy parking area. This one is in the red dirt where Gold Camp Road, High Drive, and the North Cheyenne Canyon Road all come together. This is a popular starting point for hikers and mountain bikers. Stay to the right and continue slightly downhill on Gold Camp Road.

Dirt! If you don't think riding on dirt is a glorious good time, the best bet is to turn around promptly and head back down from whence you came. Gold Camp Road isn't one of those super-mellow dirt roads that is smoother than the nearby paved roads, like many of the dirt roads I point riders to in this guide. It's a bit of a gravel pit, and there will be washboard sections. Even—on occasion—baby-head-size rocks. And, as mentioned, the tunnels with their deep potholes. The dust, the teen-age drivers who think they have rally skills, the body droppers. This one is more for advanced riders and riders who are used to this sort of thing.

Gold Camp, an old railroad grade, curls around the east side of the range, past Point Sublime, and steadily descends northbound along the front of the mountain. It transforms back to pavement as it turns north. Hang a right into suburbia and drop like a rock to Cresta Road (the continuation of 21st Street), which provides the fast final leg of the loop back to Cheyenne Canyon.

I grew up near here, in another life it seems now. My dad was an English teacher at Cheyenne Mountain High School for 41 years. By far the coolest thing about living over here on the west side of the Springs was the proximity to the mountains. The weather is intense and awesome. It comes at you hard every afternoon: lightning, hail. And I distinctly remember some tornados. When I was a kid, a tornado demolished the Husky gas station on 21st Street about a mile away from our house.

If the clouds are rolling in when you start this ride, I recommend carrying a jacket. Even though it's a short loop, there is a decent probability of being caught out in a violent storm.

Miles and Directions

0.0 Start from the Stratton Open Space parking area and ride down Ridgeway Avenue to Cheyenne Boulevard.

0.1 Take a right onto Cheyenne Boulevard.

0.6 Veer right at the fork, onto North Cheyenne Canyon Road.

3.7 Pass Helen Hunt Falls.

3.9 Stay right at the big dirt parking lot and start descending Gold Camp Road. The surface turns to dirt.

7.5 Take a right onto Bonne Vista Drive.

7.8 Turn right onto Vista Grande Drive.

8.0 Turn left onto Constellation Drive.

9.0 Turn right onto Cresta Road.

9.9 Turn right onto Cheyenne Boulevard.

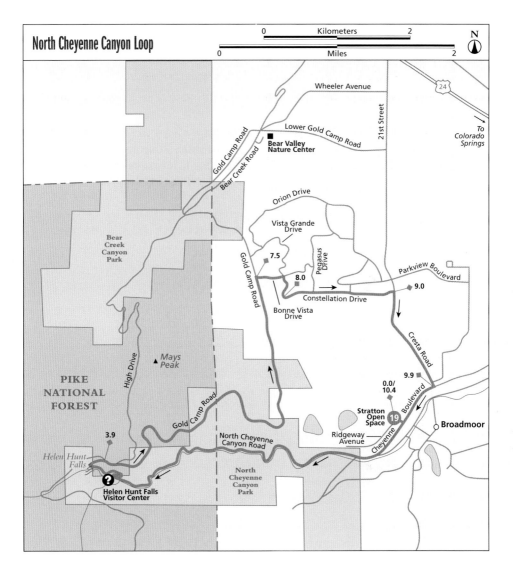

North Cheyenne Canyon Loop

10.3 Turn right onto Ridgeway Avenue.

10.4 Back at the parking area.

Bike Shops

Colorado Springs Bike Shop. 622 W. Colorado Ave., Colorado Springs; (719) 634-4915; coloradospringsbikeshop.com.

Criterium Bicycles. 6150 Corporate Dr., Colorado Springs; (719) 602-4397; criterium bicycles.com.

Old Town Bike Shop. 426 S. Tejon St., Colorado Springs; (719) 475-8589; oldtownbike shop.com.

ProCycling. 415 W. Pikes Peak Ave., Colorado Springs; (719) 266-4047; procyclingware house.com.

REI. 1376 E. Woodmen Rd., Colorado Springs; (719) 260-1455; REI.com.

Ted's Bicycles. 3016 N. Hancock Ave., Colorado Springs; (719) 473-6915; tedsbicycles .com.

Food

Edelweiss. 34 E. Ramona Ave., Colorado Springs; (719) 633-2220; edelweissrest.com. German food, German beer.

La Casita. 306 S. 8th St. at US 24, Colorado Springs; (719) 633-9616; lacasitamexigrill .com. Fast Mexican food, a Springs institution. It's the tortillas.

Shuga's. 702 S. Cascade Ave., Colorado Springs; (719) 328-1412; shugas.com. Interesting.

Adam's Mountain Cafe. 26 Manitou Ave., Manitou Springs; (719) 685-1430; adams mountain.com.

Lodging

The Broadmoor. 1 Lake Ave., Colorado Springs; (719) 623-5112; broadmoor.com.

Avenue Hotel Bed and Breakfast. 711 Manitou Ave., Manitou Springs; (719) 685-1277; avenuehotelbandb.com.

The Cliff House. 306 Cañon Dr., Manitou Springs; (719) 785-1000; thecliffhouse.com.

20 Zoo Loop

A short, interesting, and fun loop from Cheyenne Canyon through the Broadmoor and up to the Cheyenne Mountain Zoo, the route gains most of its elevation on quiet and pleasant Marland Road South, tucked behind the Broadmoor golf course.

Start: Stratton Open Space trailhead parking area on Ridgeway Avenue in Cheyenne Canyon
Length: 8.0 miles
Terrain: Hilly, swanky residential zone that starts in a canyon and climbs up onto a mountain.
Traffic and hazards: Tourist traffic can be heavy in the canyon, but speeds tend to be low. Traffic can be heavy and slow around the Broadmoor hotel and the zoo itself. Moderate traffic on the rest of the loop. Some fast descending around traffic.
Things to see: South Cheyenne Canyon, the Broadmoor, the "Mountain Course," Cheyenne Mountain Zoo

Getting there: From downtown Colorado Springs, go south on Tejon Street to Cheyenne Boulevard. Go west on Cheyenne Boulevard to Ridgeway Avenue. Turn right on Ridgeway and then right into the Stratton Open Space parking lot. From I-25, take exit 140 and go south on South Tejon Street, then west on Cheyenne Boulevard to Ridgeway Avenue and the Stratton Open Space parking lot. **GPS:** N 38 47'43.52" / W 104 51'28.79"

Ride Description

This loop starts, somewhat arbitrarily, from the Stratton Open Space parking area in lower Cheyenne Canyon. The truth is you could start from anywhere over there, from the Broadmoor or, for that matter, from downtown or Manitou Springs. The basic idea is to head up South Cheyenne Canyon (left at the fork), just to enjoy that delightful, too short section of winding road, then crank a sharp left and bob along fast rollers to the Broadmoor hotel. At the lake, go left.

When I was a kid, the lake and the whole hotel were wide open to the public. We used to ride our bikes around the lake. These days, probably because of the violations committed by townie whippersnappers, the hotel is locked down like a military base.

Curl around past the front of the hotel, which aspired to impress nineteenth-century Viennese barons, and cruise steadily uphill next to the

The Will Rogers Shrine of the Sun is not legally accessible by bike, but its chimes are helpful if you're on a tight schedule.

If you want to see the zoo, bring a lock. They won't let you take your bike in.

world-famous golf course. Instead of heading straight up the hill, jog left briefly to find Marland Road. This is the back way to the back way to the Cheyenne Mountain Zoo.

Not only is there little traffic on Marland Road South, but the climb is really nice. Not easy but not steep, the road eases out of the farthest reaches of suburban residences and climbs past the southernmost golf course, the "Mountain Course," lined by scrub oak and big ponderosa pines. It runs into the main zoo road after a mile of steady climbing. Turn left and continue uphill for another 0.5 mile to the zoo entrance.

It's not exactly a family ride! I want to make this clear because some will be tempted to herd their kids up to the zoo on bikes. The climb is probably a bit much and traffic hazards too plentiful for young kids to ride. For parents with kids on board, however, this is probably the least problematic route to the zoo. Traffic near the Broadmoor hotel isn't great, but then it really thins out until you get up to the main zoo road, which can be bumper-to-bumper. Marland Road South tends to be nicely empty, with as many deer as cars.

Miles and Directions

0.0 From the Stratton Open Space parking lot, ride down Ridgeway Avenue toward Cheyenne Boulevard.

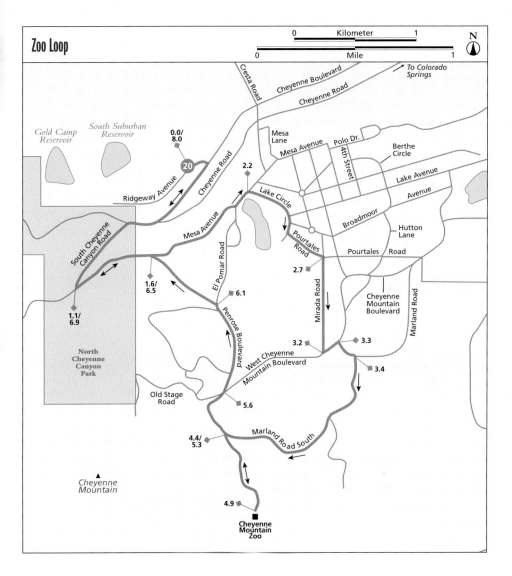

Zoo Loop

0.1 Turn right onto Cheyenne Boulevard.

0.6 Veer left at the fork, onto South Cheyenne Canyon Road. (**Note:** You could also take a sharp left here onto Evans Avenue and cut off the South Cheyenne Canyon portion.)

1.1 Take a sharp left onto Mesa Avenue.

1.6 Turn left, continuing on Mesa Avenue.

2.0 At the intersection, continue on Mesa Avenue.

2.2 At the traffic circle, turn right onto Lake Circle.

2.5 After passing by the Broadmoor and its golf club, continue pedaling as the road becomes Pourtales Road.

2.7 Veer right onto Mirada Road, next to the golf course.

3.2 Turn left onto West Cheyenne Mountain Boulevard.

3.3 Turn right onto Marland Road.

3.4 Turn right onto Marland Road South.

4.4 Turn left onto Cheyenne Mountain Zoo Road.

4.7 Pass the lower entrance to the zoo lot.

4.9 Arrive at the main entrance. Turn around! (Or go see the animals.)

5.3 On the way back down, pass the intersection with Marland Road South and continue descending on Cheyenne Mountain Zoo Road. (**Option:** Turn right here and go back the way you came.)

5.6 Continue straight through the intersection, onto Penrose Boulevard.

6.1 Continue straight through the big intersection.

6.5 Veer left onto Mesa Avenue. (You're now retracing your route back to the start.)

6.9 Take a sharp right onto South Cheyenne Canyon Road.

7.4 Continue straight through the intersection, onto West Cheyenne Road.

7.5 Stay left at the fork, onto Cheyenne Boulevard.

7.9 Turn left onto Ridgeway Avenue.

8.0 Back at the Stratton Open Space parking lot.

Attractions

Cheyenne Mountain Zoo. 4250 Cheyenne Mountain Zoo Rd., Colorado Springs; (719) 633-9925; cmzoo.org.

Bike Shops

Colorado Springs Bike Shop. 622 W. Colorado Ave., Colorado Springs; (719) 634-4915; coloradospringsbikeshop.com.

Criterium Bicycles. 6150 Corporate Dr., Colorado Springs; (719) 602-4397; criterium bicycles.com.

Old Town Bike Shop. 426 S. Tejon St., Colorado Springs; (719) 475-8589; oldtownbike shop.com.

ProCycling. 415 W. Pikes Peak Ave., Colorado Springs; (719) 266-4047; procyclingware house.com.

REI. 1376 E. Woodmen Rd., Colorado Springs; (719) 260-1455; REI.com.

Ted's Bicycles. 3016 N. Hancock Ave., Colorado Springs; (719) 473-6915; tedsbicycles .com.

Food

Edelweiss. 34 E. Ramona Ave., Colorado Springs; (719) 633-2220; edelweissrest.com. German food, German beer.

La Casita. 306 S. 8th St. at US 24, Colorado Springs; (719) 633-9616; lacasitamexigrill .com. Fast Mexican food, a Springs institution. It's the tortillas.

Shuga's. 702 S. Cascade Ave., Colorado Springs; (719) 328-1412; shugas.com.

Adam's Mountain Cafe. 26 Manitou Ave., Manitou Springs; (719) 685-1430; adams mountain.com.

Lodging

The Broadmoor. 1 Lake Ave., Colorado Springs; (719) 623-5112; broadmoor.com.

Avenue Hotel Bed and Breakfast. 711 Manitou Ave., Manitou Springs; (719) 685-1277; avenuehotelbandb.com.

The Cliff House. 306 Cañon Dr., Manitou Springs; (719) 785-1000; thecliffhouse.com.

MORE COLORADO SPRINGS AREA RIDES

Air Force Academy Loop. Check in with the sentry at the gate of the North entrance. Much more locked down than it was in the past, the US Air Force Academy contains quite a bit of wonderful paved mileage for road riders. There are several moderately hilly roads winding through the forests around the striking campus, between the steep mountains and the highway.

These roads once hosted the world championship road race. On a freakishly cold day in 1986, Lemond, Hinault, and other legends looped the academy dozens of times. Moreno Argentin was first to the line. Due to new restrictions, which have closed some roads to the public, it may not be possible to ride the whole '86 course, but a strenuous and satisfying experience is still there for the taking.

Garden of the Gods. With its unique and amazing scenery and smooth, rolling roads, the Garden of the Gods is one of the time-honored favorites of local riders. Start a Garden ride from one of several parking areas within the park itself, or remotely from elsewhere. There are cool routes connecting the Garden of the Gods to just about anywhere in town. It's easily linked to downtown via Pikes Peak Avenue, a nearly direct, as-the-crow-flies route. The Pro Challenge stage race has been using a circuit encompassing downtown and some of the Garden's roads, like Ridge Road, a tough little climb that has hosted "Big Mig" Indurain and served as a launching pad for one of Jens Voigt's doomed attacks. The racecourse uses Colorado Avenue to reach the Garden from downtown, but you'll do better to avoid Colorado Avenue, the main drag through Old Colorado City and into Manitou Springs, when it's not cleared of traffic for race day. One block north, Pikes Peak Avenue gets you there nicely. Pikes Peak doesn't go under I-25, so use West Bijou to cross, then zigzag south to Pikes Peak. Alternatively, use the Midland Trail, which follows Fountain Creek and US 24 west, all the way to Ridge Road. (Check a map or, better still, a recent satellite image. The trail appears to end at 21st Street but continues on the south side of Fountain Creek at 25th Street.) The Midland Trail links to the Pikes Peak Greenway Trail that runs by Monument Creek, allowing you to ride almost entirely on path between Ridge Road and downtown.

For a completely different route to the Garden of the Gods from downtown, find Mesa Road off Uintah Street. (There are several fun ways to get over to Mesa Road. Note the bike-ped overpass crossing the highway south of Uintah. Rolling down West Dale to Glen Avenue, past the pond in Monument Valley Park, is also a nice little jaunt.) Mesa eventually drops in on the Garden from above, after passing the Kissing Camels gated community, summer playground for old-school Texas oil zillionaires.

You'll find there isn't too much actual road mileage within the Garden itself, but the quality is high. The tourists drive slow in the park, and most of the roads have a painted bike lane.

Manitou. West of Garden of the Gods is Manitou Springs, a unique type of American hill town. If you like biker gangs and witches, quaint nineteenth-century architecture, funky galleries, and cotton candy, then Manitou is your jam. To get there, use your preferred route to reach Garden of the Gods (see above) but continue west and find El Paso Boulevard to cross under US 24, then get on Lovers Lane, one of the most awesome little stretches of pavement in the region. Lovers Lane gives you a precious behind-the-scenes view of Manitou. Notice how the buildings here are built right over the creek. Once in town, loiter at the Ruxton Park bandstand, drink from one (or several) of the springs, eat food, and buy trinkets. The steep roads of Manitou are fun to explore by bike, if you don't mind getting lost and don't hate gravity.

Palmer Park. In the northeast quadrant of town sits Palmer Park, a large parcel of rugged open space known primarily for its cache of technical mountain-bike trails. But road riders can also have a lot of fun here on a few tight, twisty ribbons of pavement. It's not a bad ride to pedal to the park from downtown, either. Use the wide residential boulevards or Shooks Run Trail to go north, then find the Rock Island Trail to take you east to Paseo Road, which takes you northeast into the park. Ride up to the Palmer Park overlook and gaze back on where you just were, with the mountains in the background.

21 Pikes Peak

An extremely long and steep high-altitude challenge with spectacular views, this climb could be more difficult than any climb in North America or Europe.

Start: Crystal Reservoir Visitor Center, Pikes Peak Highway
Length: 26.2 miles up-and-back
Terrain: One monster hill
Traffic and hazards: Tourist traffic can be fairly heavy. The road is quite narrow in spots. Tricky descending. High-altitude weather and potential altitude sickness. Vertigo.
Things to see: Half the United States from up here
Fee alert: This ride is on a toll road and requires a fee of $12 per person (subject to change).

Getting there: From Colorado Springs, go west on US 24, up the hill past Manitou Springs. Exit onto the Pikes Peak Highway (Fountain Avenue) in Cascade. Drive up the Pikes Peak Highway (toll road) to the Crystal Reservoir Visitor Center. **GPS:** N 38 55'17.67" / W 105 1'31.59"

Ride Description

This ride could be called "Big Daddy."

Pikes Peak could be the toughest road ride you will ever attempt. It's certainly the most difficult climb in Colorado, having displaced Bob Cook Mountain (aka Mount

Cloud world

Crystal Creek Reservoir is roughly the same elevation as the summit of the Col de l'Iseran, the highest paved pass in Europe.

Evans) at the exact moment that bicycling on the recently paved Pikes Peak Highway was legalized.

The Pikes Peak road is noticeably steeper than the Mount Evans road (see Squaw Pass–Mount Evans ride). That's the biggest difference between the two. In general, Pikes Peak is a bit more intense, with steeper slopes and more exposure. Along some stretches above timberline it feels like you might roll off the edge of the asphalt and fall through space for a while. Clouds float up from below and appear suddenly next to the road, like giant, curious ghosts.

Lack of oxygen will batter cyclists on this road like it will on few roads in the world. The starting point for this ride, at Crystal Creek Reservoir, sits at roughly the same altitude as the summit of the tallest paved pass in Europe, the Col de l'Iseran. After mile 12, with the summit still looming overhead, you'll pass a point that is exactly twice as high as the fabled Col du Tourmalet. So take that, Europe.

We cheated a bit on this one. Instead of starting at the toll booth, the most obvious start point, we drove up about 5 miles and parked at Crystal Creek Reservoir, where you'll find a big parking lot, bathrooms, and a visitor center. Starting from here cut about 2,000 ridiculously difficult feet of elevation gain from the climb. This made us feel like chumps when we were driving up past some fellow cyclists as they struggled valiantly on the steep lower slopes. Some of them, no doubt, had started all the way back in Colorado Springs. We almost turned around and went back to Chipita Park. But later on, after tackling the 13-mile, 5,000-foot "abbreviated" route, we were very relieved that we didn't. We'd probably still be up there.

The route from the reservoir starts off, well, fast and easy. Rolling terrain. After about 2 miles the real climbing begins. Except for a half-mile breather before mile 10, it doesn't let up. You'll get used to seeing 10 to 12 percent

The smile of pain

ramps disappearing into distant clouds every time you come out of a hairpin turn.

If you've never been up to the top of Pikes Peak before, you'll be freaked out to see a large parking lot, a sprawling gift shop, and a horde of tourists up there. The gift shop is built of rock and has a low profile, which prevents it from being blasted into the plains by the harsh wind. The tourists are huddled together in small groups and have on all their available gear, which prevents them from freezing. They have arrived on foot, by bike, in cars, and via the Pikes Peak Cog Railway, which produces a new batch of gawkers several times per day. Buying freshly made high-altitude doughnuts from the greasy spoon in the gift shop is a minor tradition for some. You'll see them inside huddled near the doughnut machine.

Feeling sick? Headache, nausea? That's probably altitude sickness. (Note that altitude sickness is difficult to distinguish from doughnut sickness.) It's not a big deal unless it gets severe, but you'll want to get back down the mountain pretty soon. Drink lots of water in the meantime. Descending a few thousand feet will make a world of difference to your well-being. If you're suffering from acute altitude sickness, a quick descent could save your life. Get thee down the mountain! For those already suffering at the bottom of the mountain, before the ride even begins, this is probably not a good day to try climbing another 7,000 feet.

Obviously a ride like this requires a little more preparation than the typical excursion. Keep a close eye on the weather, first of all. I don't recommend attempting Pikes Peak if there's sketchy weather in the forecast. It will be hard to believe until you experience it firsthand, but even on a hot, clear summer day, the summit will be very windy and cold, so you can imagine what it's like up there if it's cool and blustery at the bottom. Pack all your winter gear, even on a clear day. You'll be glad you did. Hats, gloves. Regular tights may not be enough.

Lightning is the other obvious concern. Never strikes in the same place twice? Nonsense. Lightning strikes the top of Pikes Peak all summer long. The later you

You can't, you won't, and you don't stop.

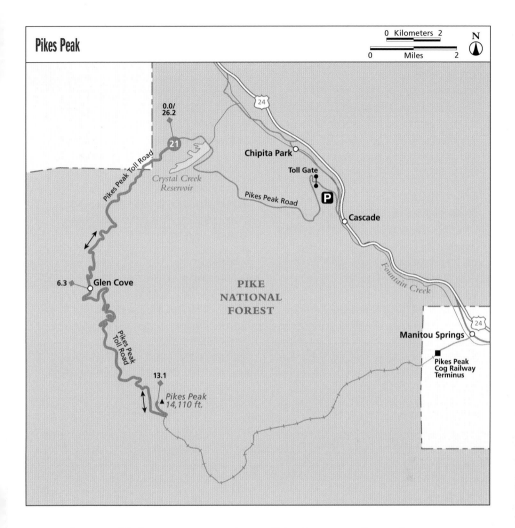

0 Kilometers 2

N

0 Miles 2

0.0/
26.2

21

Pikes Peak Toll Road

Chipita Park

Toll Gate

Crystal Creek
Reservoir

Pikes Peak Road

P

Cascade

6.3 Glen Cove

PIKE
NATIONAL
FOREST

Fountain Creek

Manitou Springs

24

Pikes Peak
Cog Railway
Terminus

Pikes Peak
Toll Road

13.1

Pikes Peak
14,110 ft.

start, the more likely you are to run into a lightning storm. But early starts are no surefire solution either (my dad thinks any problem can be solved simply by getting up at 4:30 a.m., but sadly this is not true).

Thankfully, with a diner at the top and another one halfway up, hauling calories and water isn't as much of an issue as it could be. But don't skimp on water or food; you'll need a lot of it. Sunshine is also a serious concern up on the big mountain. You'll do yourself a favor to use a good sunscreen and some lip balm, too. And don't forget to bring your toll money.

Miles and Directions

0.0   Start riding up the road from the Crystal Creek Reservoir visitor center parking lot.

6.3   Pass the gift shop and diner at Glen Cove, near the halfway point.

13.1 Summit (14,110 feet above sea level).

26.2 Back at Crystal Creek Reservoir.

Attractions

Pikes Peak Highway. (719) 385-7325; pikespeak.us.com. Closed on Christmas and Thanksgiving. Opens at 7:30 a.m. in the summer and 9 a.m. after October 1. Toll is $12 per person. These details are subject to change. Please call for updated information.

Bike Shops

Criterium Bicycles. 6150 Corporate Dr., Colorado Springs; (719) 602-4397; criterium bicycles.com.

Old Town Bike Shop. 426 S. Tejon St., Colorado Springs; (719) 475-8589; oldtownbike shop.com.

Ted's Bicycles. 3016 N. Hancock Ave., Colorado Springs; (719) 473-6915; tedsbicycles .com.

Team Telecycle. 615 S. Baldwin St., Woodland Park; (719) 687-6165; teamtelecycle.com.

Food

Edelweiss. 34 E. Ramona Ave., Colorado Springs; (719) 633-2220; edelweissrest.com. Pricey German food, German beer.

La Casita. 306 S. 8th St. at US 24, Colorado Springs; (719) 633-9616; lacasitamexigrill .com. Fast Mexican food, a Springs institution. It's the tortillas.

Adam's Mountain Cafe. 26 Manitou Ave., Manitou Springs; (719) 685-1430; adams mountain.com.

Lodging

The Broadmoor. 1 Lake Ave., Colorado Springs; (719) 623-5112; broadmoor.com.

Avenue Hotel Bed and Breakfast. 711 Manitou Ave., Manitou Springs; (719) 685-1277; avenuehotelbandb.com.

The Cliff House. 306 Cañon Dr., Manitou Springs; (719) 785-1000; thecliffhouse.com.

RIDES IN SOUTHERN COLORADO

Arkansas River Trail. An off-street path rolling from downtown Pueblo along the river to the Pueblo Reservoir west of town. A 16-mile round-trip with year-round goodness.

Department of Transportation (DOT) Test Track Road. Could be just what you're looking for if you're craving some flat pedaling. The Test Track Road (CR 3) heads off northeast of Pueblo, skirting the surreal Army Depot, and dead-ends at the Federal Railroad Administration's Transportation Technology Center, run by the Association of American Railroads. This secure facility covers more than 50 square miles. The center's employees and bicyclists are generally the only people on the road. There are some nice curves, but it's mostly dead-straight, dust bowl prairie schooner action. Really hot in the summer; probably dry in the winter. Watch for tarantulas. Start from the airport or from town.

Greenhorn Highway. A hilly, moderately trafficked road between Colorado City (the one near Pueblo) and CO 96 near Hardscrabble Pass. If you're really feeling strong, go for an out-and-back along the whole length of this pretty road. After the initial 2,000-foot climb from Colorado City, the road goes up and down and up and down across mini passes, adding up to well over 7,000 feet of vertical gain over the total 65-plus-mile round-trip.

The Hardscrabble Century. A circular ring of roads in south-central Colorado, from Florence to Wetmore, Westcliff (over Hardscrabble Pass), the Arkansas River, Cañon City, and back to Florence, happens to be almost exactly 100 miles long.

This classic route, what we once simply called "Hardscrabble," isn't quite what it used to be. The lonely farm roads around Florence and Cañon City sure have changed their tune as the incarceration industry has blossomed throughout this valley, with various super-max mega-prisons now dominating the landscape. There has been a huge amount of suburban-style development and growth in population and traffic. The first leg of this 100-miler, from Florence to Wetmore, was never a huge amount of fun, but now it's boring with traffic. Once you escape the prison zone, however, the route is still fabulous.

Hardscrabble Pass is a long, gradual climb into the pines, a welcome change of scenery. On the other side of the pass lies one of the nicer roads in the state, through the Wet Mountain Valley: rolling hills with the snowcapped Sangre de Cristo Mountains looming above. The next phase is a long, loud cruise on snaky US 50 next to the Arkansas River.

There's one more sizable climb before Cañon City. Finally, you're subjected to more serious traffic on the "back" road between Cañon City and Florence to finish the loop.

You get to see all kinds of Colorado on this ride, from the dry flats to the wet forests, from the windblown green hills to the dry rock trench of the Arkansas River. While it may not be suitable for all riders, Hardscrabble is worth a mention. If nothing else, consider riding back and forth on the rolling road between Hardscrabble and the Arkansas River.

22 Chimney Rock Loop

This is a long loop on the roads west of Pagosa Springs. CO 151 is a real gem, with rolling terrain and relatively light traffic.

Start: Intersection of US 160 and CO 151 west of Pagosa Springs
Length: 67.5 miles
Terrain: In the hills, but avoiding the mountains. Moderate climbs through forest and semiarid land.

Traffic and hazards: High-speed traffic is a consistent theme on this ride. Heavy traffic on US 160. Slightly less heavy on the Buck Highway. Boat pullers use CO 151 in the summer.
Things to see: Chimney Rock, Bayfield, Arboles, Navajo State Park, a beautiful part of the state

Getting there: From Pagosa Springs, go west on US 160 about 13 miles from the edge of the development and turn left onto CO 151. Park in the informal dirt lot on the side of the road. **GPS:** N 37 12'35.37" / W 107 15'48.67"

Ride Description

The centerpiece of this long, gorgeous, and slightly obscure loop is Chimney Rock, not because the phallic rock formation is particularly wonderful to look at, but because of the amazing prehistoric ruins that are located up there, along the sharp

Pagosa hot springs   Photo by Jerry Hurst

Chimney Rock, viewed from the ruins   PHOTO BY JERRY HURST

ridge just below the rocks—the remains of a mysterious 200-room "palace" made of exquisitely shaped stone. An ancient road runs straight from Chimney Rock to Chaco Canyon, the home base of those who built and lived in the structures on the ridge. Chimney Rock is considered a classic outlier of the Chaco civilization. The archaeological site was upgraded to national monument status in 2012.

Archaeologists seem to have formed a consensus that the Chacoans were the overlords of the people who lived in this valley, and that the structures below Chimney Rock housed something akin to a territorial governor, who kept the subjects under an iron fist and critical commodities, like timber, flowing from here down the road to Chaco. Many feel that the site was more ceremonial than anything, noting that the full moon can be observed from the palace rising between the rock spires during "lunar standstills." In 1125 all the humans left the area, and all the buildings were burned—a mystery for another day.

If you've got a little time (which you might not have before or after a nearly 70-mile loop), go check out the Chimney Rock National Monument up close. You can ride up the dirt road if you want. From the top parking lot, a short but steep hiking trail leads up to the ruins. There are regular tours conducted by charming and knowledgeable guides. As of 2015, cost is $12 for adults. The last tour of the day is at 3 p.m., although there are some nighttime tours through the year. Pick up tickets at

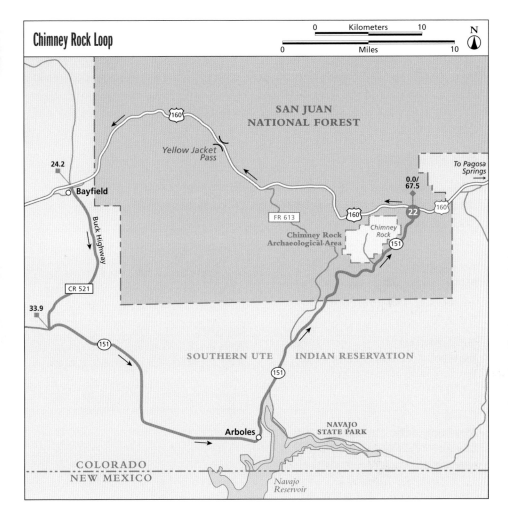

0   Kilometers   10   N

0   Miles   10

SAN JUAN
NATIONAL FOREST

160

Yellow Jacket
Pass

24.2

To Pagosa
Springs

Bayfield

0.0/
67.5

160

160

22

FR 613

Chimney
Rock

Buck Highway

Chimney Rock
Archaeological Area

151

CR 521

33.9

151

SOUTHERN UTE   INDIAN RESERVATION

151

Arboles

NAVAJO
STATE PARK

COLORADO
NEW MEXICO

Navajo
Reservoir

the ranger's cabin at the base of the mountain (or at the museum or visitor center—if it's ever built). It'll blow your mind up there, on a few different levels.

The loop starts with a moderate climb over Yellow Jacket Pass on US 160—not a real pass—then coasts into Bayfield. Traffic along the whole stretch of US 160 can be uncomfortable. Speeds can be really high, with not enough space to accommodate such high speeds. It's not my favorite type of riding, but old hands will get by without too much trouble. Cyclists ride US 160 regularly, but in my opinion it's not a destination ride on its own.

Unless you're facing a wicked headwind, which is entirely possible, you'll speed down the so-called Buck Highway (CR 521) from Bayfield into the farmland, steadily losing altitude. Pick up CO 151 near Ignacio and roll east. The final third of the ride, though steadily uphill the whole way, is what makes the rest of the loop worthwhile. The road curves deliciously as it meanders into the rolling hills toward Chimney Rock.

There are other ways to enjoy this great section of CO 151. You could out-and-back it to Navajo State Park, for instance. If you're ready for some dirt and extra adventure, consider a shortened loop using Fossett Gulch Road (FR 613) to cut between US 160 and CO 151. To the east, CO 151 connects to more dirt routes, like Cat Creek Road and Trujillo Road. Make sure you bring the right stuff if you go rolling deep into the hills, though. Services and cell phone reception are few and far between out there.

Miles and Directions

0.0   Start riding west on US 160 from the intersection of US 160 and CO 151.

24.2   Turn left at Bayfield and begin riding southbound on the Buck Highway (CR 521).

33.9   Turn left onto CO 151.

67.5   Back at the intersection of US 160 and CO 151.

Attractions

Chimney Rock National Monument. 3179 CO 151, Chimney Rock; (970) 883-5359; chimney rockco.org.

Bike Shops

The Hub. 100 Country Center Dr., Suite F, Pagosa Springs; (970) 731-2002; ridepagosa springs.com.

Food

Alley House Grille. 214 Pagosa St., Pagosa Springs; (970) 264-0999. Reservations recommended.

River Pointe Coffee Cafe. 445 San Juan St., Pagosa Springs; (970) 264-3216; riverpointe coffeecafe.com. Breakfast and lunch.

Lodging

Alpine Inn. 8 Solomon Dr., Pagosa Springs; (970) 731-4007; alpineinnofpagosasprings .com.

Fireside Inn Cabins. 1600 E. US 160, Pagosa Springs; (970) 264-9204; firesidecabins.com.

23 Animas Valley Loop

This loop, known to locals as the "Long Valley Loop," is a mellow river ride touring the beautiful Animas River Valley north of Durango—a rare option without big hills.

Start: Riverview Sports Complex, Durango
Length: 27.9 miles
Terrain: Mellow or flat slopes in a river valley flanked by rocky foothills

Traffic and hazards: Moderate traffic on two-lane roads
Things to see: Animas Valley, Baker Bridge, Hermosa, Trimble Hot Springs

Getting there: From Main Street/US 550 in Durango, go east on 15th Street; 15th becomes Florida Road (CR 240). Florida Road curves to the northeast and angles along the edge of town. Take Florida Road about 1 mile and turn due north briefly on Angel Lane. Take the first left off Angel Lane onto Plymouth Drive and park in the lot by the softball fields (Riverview Sports Complex). Obviously, this is a ride that could begin anywhere around Durango. If you ride from some other place, Florida Road will likely be the best way to reach CR 250. **GPS:** N 37 17'36.01" / W 107 51'41.79"

Ride Description

The full name of the river is El Rio de las Animas Perdidas. The River of Lost Souls. It was named by Spanish explorers about 500 years ago, and the "lost souls" in question belonged to people who had vanished from the area a few hundred years prior to the Spaniards' arrival. It seemed like the souls abandoned their homes, or were driven from them, in a hurry. The trappings of their civilization were all around, but the people were missing.

It turns out that many of the people who populated this area may have migrated east to the other side of the Continental Divide. A brutal decades-long drought is the most likely cause of the mass abandonment, although the complications of the drought, things like war and general chaos, may have been more immediate reasons to exit. We can't help noticing that many of the lost souls' leftover structures appear to be defensive battlements.

On any bike ride around Durango, you can feel your smallness relative to human history, which in turn is a mere sliver of a fraction of a speck of dust falling off the corner of the history of the earth. You might also feel the presence of the ancient ones who populated this valley, if you're tuned in to that sort of thing.

One thing you won't feel very strongly on this particular loop is your smallness in relation to the mountains, because this ride sticks to the valley floor almost exclusively. It climbs, but not more than a few feet for every 100 traveled, plus a few scattered lumps here and there. Toward the end of the valley, it enters terrain that could be described as rolling. That qualifies as an easy ride around here.

The route is simple, heading north out of town on well-known CR 250, right next to the mountain. After about 14 miles, it cuts across to the other side, joining the

Columbine PHOTO BY JERRY HURST

wide shoulder of US 550 for a few miles on the way back down. At Hermosa, the route joins CR 203, which is like a mirror image of its cross-valley cousin CR 250.

If you're looking for a big climbing workout, this ain't it, but it can be connected to climbs paved and unpaved. The most obvious is US 550 itself, which begins a serious chug up Coal Bank Pass from the top end of this loop. On the other side of Coal Bank, of course, lies Molas Pass and Silverton. Local pros love to ride the Old Shalona hill, which is the extension of CR 250, at the very end of the valley. It ascends smartly for about 600 feet then reconnects with US 550 higher up.

Traffic is pretty subdued on the two-laners of this loop, but so are the shoulders. Shoulders are almost nonexistent on some segments, so a little talent for the dance of traffic is helpful. The mellow slopes and simple route make this a good ride for gravity-averse folks who don't mind sharing pavement with cars and trucks that much. An option to cut the mileage in half by taking an earlier turn across the river makes the loop even more attractive for all kinds of riders, especially those on a tight schedule.

Miles and Directions

0.0 Start from the park and go west briefly on Plymouth Drive, then turn right (south) onto Aspen Drive.

0.1 Turn left onto Florida Road (CR 240).

0.9 Turn left onto CR 250.

1.1 Cross East 32nd Street (CR 251) and continue straight on CR 250.

7.5 Continue past the intersection with CR 252 (aka Trimble Lane). (**Option:** Turn here and cut across to Hermosa and CR 203, cutting the ride in half.)

14.4 Continue around the curve toward the highway. (**Option:** Turn right here and ride the Old Shalona hill, adding about 5 miles and a lot of exertion to the loop.)

14.6 Turn left onto US 550.

17.8 Turn right off US 550 onto CR 203 at Hermosa, continuing south.

19.9 Pass the intersection with CR 252. (**Option:** Turn left here and recross the valley, then return on CR 250.)

24.7 Carefully join US 550 (Main Avenue) and continue south. (**Option:** Cross the highway and continue south on CR 203, which makes its way about 1.5 miles south before it hits the highway again.)

26.7 Turn left onto East 32nd Street.

26.9 Turn right (south) onto East 3rd Avenue.

27.3 The road curves to the east and becomes East 29th Street.

27.6 Continue straight ahead on a bike-path connector by Riverview Elementary School.

27.7 Continue straight on Mesa Avenue briefly, then turn left onto Plymouth Drive.

27.9 End the ride back at the parking area.

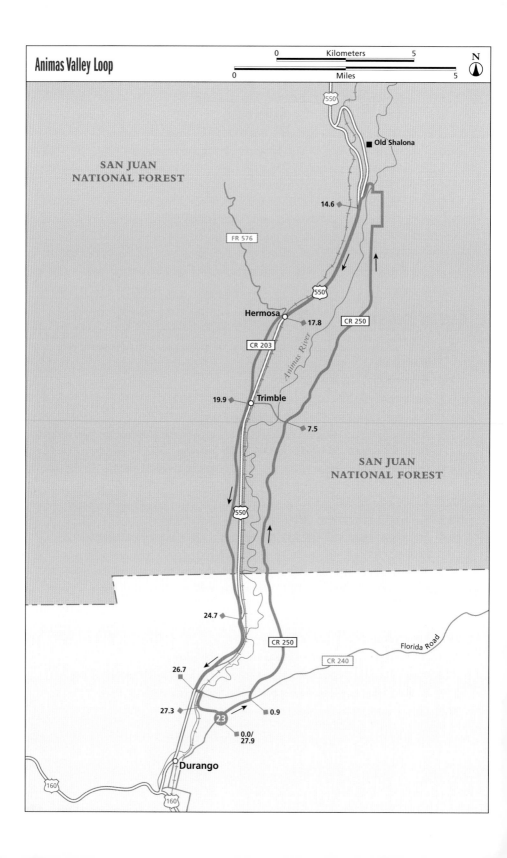

Animas Valley Loop

SAN JUAN
NATIONAL FOREST

Old Shalona

550

14.6

FR 576

550

Hermosa   17.8   CR 250

CR 203

Animas River

19.9   Trimble

7.5

SAN JUAN
NATIONAL FOREST

550

24.7

CR 250

Florida Road

26.7

CR 240

27.3   0.9

23

0.0/
27.9

Durango

160

160

Events and Attractions

Durango & Silverton Narrow Gauge Railroad & Museum. 479 Main St., Durango; (888) 872-4607; durangotrain.com.

Iron Horse Bicycle Classic. ironhorsebicycle classic.com. This weekend of races has been run continuously since 1972, typically on the last weekend in May. The signature race is a road race from Durango to Silverton on US 550, but the mountain-bike race is a pretty big deal, too.

Bike Shops

Durango Cyclery. 143 E. 13th St., Durango; (970) 247-0747; durangocyclery.com.

Hassle Free Sports. 2615 Main Ave., Durango; (970) 259-3874; hasslefreesports.com.

Pedal the Peaks. 598 Main Ave., Durango; (970) 259-6880; pedalthepeaks.biz.

Velorution Cycles. 1077 Main Ave., Durango; (970) 259-1975; velorutioncycles.com.

Food

Durango Diner. 957 Main Ave., Durango; (970) 247-9889; durangodiner.com. Unparalleled carbo loading.

J. Bo Pizza & Rib Co. 1301 Florida Rd., Durango; (970) 259-0010; jbosdurango.com.

Serious Texas Bar-B-Q. 3535 Main Ave., Durango; (970) 247-2240; serioustexasbbq .com.

Tacos Nayarit. 2477 Main Ave., Durango; (970) 385-1595.

Lodging

Adobe Inn. 2178 Main Ave., Durango; (970) 247-2743; durangohotels.com.

Leland House & Rochester Hotel. 726 E. 2nd Ave., Durango; (970) 385-1920; rochester hotel.com.

Strater Hotel. 699 Main Ave., Durango; (970) 247-4431; strater.com.

OTHER RIDES AROUND DURANGO

Durango to Silverton. This 48-mile, double-humped, one-way challenge is the route of the annual Iron Horse Bicycle Classic race and a traditional rite of passage. It's on a highway, but a nice highway. If you're going to ride that far, you may as well keep going. This section of road is often used as part of a big touring loop.

Florida Loop. Not Florida the state, Florida the road. And they pronounce it Flo-REE-da around here. Take Florida Road (CR 240) out of town, up into the hills. There's plenty of development up there and plenty of traffic on the road, but it's fairly civilized. CR 240 rises about 800 feet over Durango before it intersects with CR 234. Hang a right there and cruise down to US 160 and back to Durango. It's a little over 20 miles with an option for a much bigger loop reaching all the way to Bayfield.

Junction Creek Road. This awesome gravel-grinding opportunity right out of town reaches to the high mountains and becomes increasingly rustic as it goes. The climb is gradual. To find it simply head west out of town on West 25th Street.

TOURING SOUTHWEST COLORADO

There are many possible cycle-touring routes around southwestern Colorado, but two classic loops approach must-do status if you're a dedicated tourer. *Tourer.* Not sure if that's a real word, but it should be. Tourers are different than tourists. Anyway, here are the tourers' favorites:

Lizard Head Loop. This shares the Million Dollar Highway portion with the next loop but otherwise breaks to the west. Starting in Durango and rolling clockwise, head west on US 160 to Dolores, then north up the Dolores River on CO 145. The climb from Dolores to the top of Lizard Head Pass, named for the iconic rock formation up there among the towering peaks, is gradual but super long—a 50-mile stretch that will probably consume most of the calories and water you can carry. On the other side, of course, is Telluride, slightly off the loop. Stick around if you can. Then it's a long but beautiful curl around the Mount Sneffels massif. A massive massif. A massive, beautiful massif. Over the moderate Dallas Divide lies Ridgeway. Here you join the legendary highway to Ouray, Silverton, and Durango, over three passes. Conquering that whole stretch of Million Dollar Highway in one day is a tall order.

Lake San Isabel near Lake City   PHOTO BY JERRY HURST

Southbound riders will be pedaling on the exciting side of the road, staring into the abyss, while climbing Red Mountain Pass. Make sure your camera game is strong if you try this route. Starting the loop in Durango or Ridgeway and rolling counterclockwise is also a good time. Try it in all possible configurations and report back to us on which is best.

Million Dollar Loop. Nobody calls it that, but they might start now. You could begin anywhere along the loop, but the starting point and direction will have a big effect on the overall feel of the ride. Assuming a clockwise direction of travel and a Gunnison start, the first showpiece section is between Lake City and Creede, over Slumgullion Pass and accompanying Spring Creek Pass, down the Rio Grande headwaters. Unbelievable country. Wolf Creek Pass is the next challenge, and it's a big one. They wrote a song about it. The views as you roll off the pass into Pagosa Springs are stunning.

The southern section of the loop along US 160 is pretty but could be less stressful from a traffic standpoint. Consider augmenting with some dirt roads and such if you've got the time and equipment. North out of Durango the ride enters its second top-shelf section: US 550, aka the "Million Dollar Highway." This highway does some amazing things between Durango and Ouray. Coal Bank, Molas, Red Mountain Pass. You'll never forget Red Mountain Pass and Ouray. From there you roll out of the mountains into the sagebrush desert of US 50 for a final push into Gunnison.

24 Colorado National Monument

One of the must-do rides in Colorado, this loop takes you from the flatland near Grand Junction into the spectacular Colorado National Monument, a world of red cliffs and pinnacles of sandstone jutting into the sky, on an amazingly well-engineered and fun road.

Start: The parking lot at the trailhead of the Redlands Second Lift Canal Trail, on South Broadway west of Grand Junction
Length: 32.8-mile loop
Terrain: Canyons, cliffs, buttes—Wile E. Coyote and Road Runner-type stuff. Plenty of climbing.
Traffic and hazards: Traffic can be heavy and occasionally oppressive. The road through the Monument is narrow and very curvy. Heat!

Especially in high summer, heat and sun can reach the danger zone.
Things to see: Intense landscape of eroded sandstone
Note: Two things are required to attempt this loop: (1) $7 fee to enter the park by bike, and (2) front and rear lights. The lights are required because of the tunnels along the route.

Getting there: From Grand Junction, take Redlands Parkway (24 Road) southwest, crossing Broadway (CO 340). Redlands Parkway becomes South Broadway as it turns due west at the intersection with South Camp Road. Continue on South Broadway for another 1.5 miles and find a parking lot on the right side of the road. (If you're coming from Fruita, it's probably easiest to head due south on CO 340 [Broadway] and begin the ride from a parking area near the north entrance to the Monument, where Broadway intersects Rim Rock Drive.) **GPS:** N 39 4'40.98" / W 108 39'58.57"

Ride Description

Old-time bike nuts may recall the Coors Classic, a big-stage race that took place in Colorado decades ago. One of the iconic stages of that race was known as the "Tour of the Moon," because it sent the racers through the otherworldly Colorado National Monument. It doesn't really look like the moon, but it is exotic country, totally unlike the mountains and plains that compose the rest of the state.

The race through Colorado National Monument was portrayed in the fictional and really quite bad movie *American Flyers* (1985), starring Kevin Costner and Rae Dawn Chong and some other people. Much of *American Flyers* was filmed on location around Grand Junction.

In the movie, Kevin Costner's character is a veteran bike racer with a brain aneurysm that is starting to act up. He teaches his talented little brother how to race and, with the help of Rae Dawn Chong and a sketchy Polish sports doctor, they go on to win the big one. I think I made some of that up.

When big-time stage racing came back to Colorado, in the form of the US Pro Challenge, everyone wanted to see a revival of the "Moon" stage. But the Park Service has denied the organizers' permit applications. It's hard to muster too much

Colorado National Monument catches the afternoon sun.

bitterness about the decision. Bringing crowds up here to watch a race could cause all kinds of problems. The venue could be especially dangerous for both spectators and racers. You'll see what I mean when you get up here. Pros would be *flying* along this road. There are countless diminishing-radius turns that are tricky at high speed, and if you misjudge and go off the road—as pro road racers do with impressive frequency—there's a good chance of going over a 700-foot cliff. That's like a 15-second coyote drop.

It's cool how close the road comes to the edge in some places around the loop. When it seems like the cliff is right there, it usually is. Check for yourself, carefully. You get the impression that the engineers weren't anticipating that people would be outside of cars along the road anywhere but the established rest areas.

You can stage an assault on the Monument from just about anywhere around Grand Junction or Fruita. There is a somewhat obvious and natural route across the flats in front of the cliffs—the boring part of the loop—and there are three or four good parking areas along it. If you're driving in to do the ride, it makes sense to start there, as described below.

It takes some time to traverse the flats and rolling hills to the entrance to the Monument. Nothing special about this portion of the ride, through quasi-rural suburbs of Grand Junction. There's a bike path of sorts by the road for some of the way,

Huge oxbow turns keep the slopes moderate.

but when I was there, it dead-ended rudely in a vacant lot. Take a good look at the map before you start heading off this way and that.

When you find the entrance, 7 bucks will get you in (as of 2015). Due to the tunnels along the road, lights are also required. There are three tunnels up there, and you'll see they're just long enough that using lights makes sense. Front and rear. Don't forget them! What's that you say? You say you forgot your lights? Well, it's possible (unless a horde of other people did the same thing) that the friendly individual in the guard shack can lend you some lights to use, if you promise to return them when you exit the Monument on the other side. Don't count on that though.

The road is highly enjoyable in either direction. From either side you'll find a significant climb of about 2,000 feet. (Total elevation gain is quite a bit more than that when you add up all the little ups and downs along the way.) The road is so nicely engineered that there are no gut-wrenching extra-steep pitches. It's a steady, meandering ramp, coiled on itself in delicious, smooth oxbow turns. The climbing doesn't stop once the road reaches the top of the cliffs, because the land up there is also sloped. But after a time the uphill sections alternate with slight downhills. Then, about halfway around, you find more downhill than up. Then, of course, that speedy descent swooping out of the park and back to the flats.

Rim Rock Drive

Bring a camera along on this one. There's nothing like it. But the riding is so fun, photography tends to get put on the back burner.

Miles and Directions

0.0 Start from the parking lot along South Broadway, where the Redlands Second Lift Canal crosses the road, and begin riding east on South Broadway. South Broadway will turn south, then east again.

1.3 Turn right onto South Camp Road. After a few blocks a bike-path-like object materializes next to the road. You can use it if you wish, or not.

4.0 Turn right onto Monument Drive.

4.6 Pay your fee at the entrance to the Colorado National Monument.

22.7 Pass the Colorado National Monument Visitor Center.

27.0 Pass the park exit/guard station.

27.1 Turn right onto Broadway (CO 340).

30.0 Turn right and head due south on South Broadway. Stay on this road as it turns southeast, due east, back to the south, and east again.

32.8 Back at the parking lot.

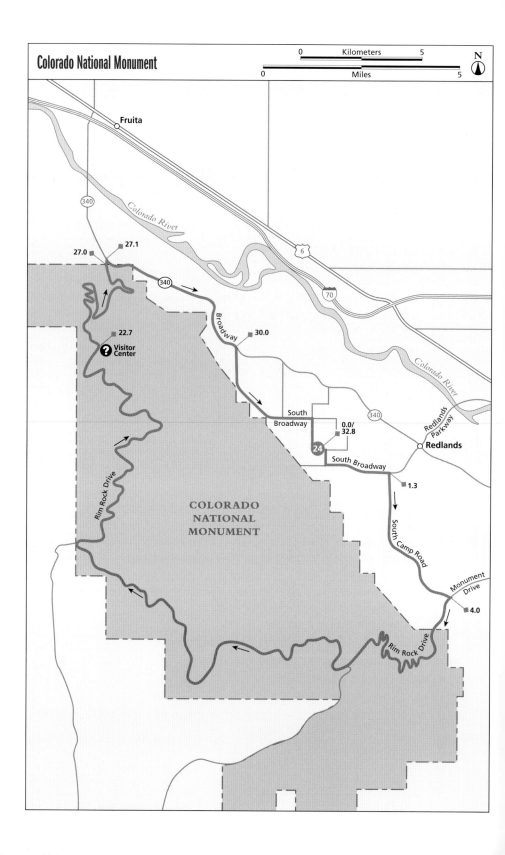

Colorado National Monument

Fruita

Colorado River

340

27.0 ■ ■ 27.1

340

22.7 ■

Broadway

30.0 ■

? Visitor
Center

Colorado River

South
Broadway

340

0.0/
32.8 ■

Redlands
Parkway

24

Redlands

South Broadway

Rim Rock Drive

COLORADO
NATIONAL
MONUMENT

1.3 ■

South Camp Road

Monument
Drive

4.0 ■

Rim Rock Drive

0   Kilometers   5
0   Miles   5

N

Events

Icon Lasik Tour of the Moon Grand Cycling Classic. tourofthemoon.com. This annual supported tour through Colorado National Monument takes place in October.

Bike Shops

Bicycle Outfitters. 537 N. 1st St., Grand Junction; (970) 245-2699; bicycleoutfitters.com.

The Bike Shop. 950 North Ave., Unit #108, Grand Junction; (970) 243-0807; thebikeshopgj.com.

Brown Cycles. 549 Main St., Grand Junction; (970) 245-7939; browncycles.com.

LTR Multisport. 2470 Patterson Rd., Unit #3, Grand Junction; (970) 257-7678; ltrmultisport.com.

Over the Edge Sports. 202 E. Aspen Ave., Fruita; (970) 858-7220; otesports.com. A famous mountain-bike shop in Fruita.

Food

Blue Moon Bar & Grill. 120 N. 7th St., Grand Junction; (970) 242-4506; bluemoongj.com. Closed Sunday.

Famous Dave's. Mesa Mall, 240 US 6, Grand Junction; (970) 245-8227; legendarybbq.com. Barbecue.

Kuniko's Teriyaki Grill. 1133 Patterson Rd., Grand Junction; (970) 241-9245; kunikojap.com.

Nepal Restaurant. 356 Main St., Grand Junction; (970) 242-2233; nepalgj.com.

Lodging

Grand Junction has all the chain hotels but not many interesting options for overnight lodging.

Columbine Motel. 1498 28¼ Rd., Grand Junction; (970) 241-2908; columbinemotel.com. Humble place on the south side of town, right next to a bike shop.

Melrose Hotel. 337 Colorado Ave., Grand Junction; (970) 242-9636; historicmelrosehouse.com. Small, old hotel.

OTHER RIDES AROUND GRAND JUNCTION

Grand Mesa. The Grand Mesa Scenic Byway (aka CO 65) provides one of the longest climbs in the state: over 30 miles and, would you believe, a whopping 6,000 feet of elevation gain. Find CO 65 shooting off I-70 northeast of Palisade. There's a little parking area not far from the interstate. The ride begins with about 10 miles of easy, winding road, then it turns south and up. Bring all the water and whatever you've got in your pantry for this 60-plus-mile out-and-back. Services are minimal other than a general store in Mesa.

Unaweep Divide. A 40-mile, 2,500-foot canyon-climbing up-and-back, with an option to double the mileage and elevation gain by descending to Gateway and the Dolores River before turning around. Plenty of trucks and trailers, not much shoulder. The road (CO 141) begins in Whitewater on US 50, southeast of Grand Junction. Parking is scarce, but there's a little dirt trailhead lot off Coffman Road west of Whitewater.

25 Glenwood Canyon

A bike-path cruise unlike any other, following the Colorado River and I-70 down Glenwood Canyon.

Start: The parking area at the Bair Ranch exit (exit 129) off I-70, on the east end of the canyon
Length: 13.8 miles one way
Terrain: For the most part, slightly downhill cruising, encased in the deep canyon and under the highway viaducts
Traffic and hazards: Entirely concrete off-street path, but not without hazards. There are some blind corners and speedy downhill sections that could be dangerous. In some spots the trail spills into rest area parking lots and briefly shares service roads. Pedestrian traffic can be heavy around the Hanging Lake rest area.
Things to see: 1,000-foot-high walls of Glenwood Canyon, the Colorado River, the engineering masterpiece of I-70, Glenwood Springs

Getting there: From Denver, take I-70 west over the mountains and exit at Bair Ranch (exit 129). If you're already in Glenwood Springs, you may prefer to start the ride from there and do an out-and-back rather than drive to the other end of the canyon. **GPS:** N 39 36'50.31" / W 107 8'21.50"

Ride Description

Do you think they'll go for it?

Here you are, hurtling down I-70 to visit your in-laws in Salt Lake City, or the trails of Moab, when you have a fascinating thought. *Maybe I can get these nice people to drop me and my bike off at the east end of Glenwood Canyon, so I can cruise down that incredible-looking bike path I've always wanted to ride. Maybe I can convince them to hang out and wait for me in Glenwood Springs. . . . Should only be an hour or so . . .*

I don't know, it's worth a try.

A one-way, mostly downhill cruise from the east side is certainly the easiest way to bike the Glenwood Canyon Recreation Trail. The most convenient starting point for such a ride is the Bair Ranch rest stop at exit 129. If you can't get someone to drop you off, there are a few little outfits in Glenwood Springs operating that shuttle on a regular basis, and they'll rent you a bike, too, if needed.

The Glenwood Canyon highway project was a showcase for the alleged human mastery over nature when it opened in the early '90s, after a decade of construction. Expanding the freeway to four lanes meant putting half of it on a serpentine viaduct over the other half, and constructing dozens of bridges and several tunnels. They would have removed the Colorado River if that were feasible. The concrete bike path is integral to the project, tucked away under the highway or just next to it. Where I-70 dives into tunnels, the trail breaks away and follows the river. The path's surface has seen better days but maintains a generally very smooth attitude.

It takes some nifty engineering to fit railroad tracks, a bike path, and an interstate in this canyon with the Colorado River.

There are three more rest areas with parking lots and bathrooms spaced out through the canyon. The trail runs through parking lots and service roads as it passes through these zones. Be on the lookout for pedestrians, especially around the rest area at the Hanging Lake exit, where the concrete path serves as the approach to a very popular hiking trail. You're sure to find someone on the other side of one of the path's blind corners.

The path really disappoints on its final approach to town. After showcasing all that engineering prowess, it devolves into a straight strip of asphalt separated from the highway by concrete barriers. The anticlimax sucks a bit of glamour out of the trip.

At the end of the line is Glenwood Springs, a unique and homey town. A river town, a highway town. An old railroad town, of course, as they almost all are. A tourist town, but not for high rollers. Glenwood is well-known for its big family-friendly hot-springs pool that can be seen from the highway—the largest hot-springs pool in the world, according to the local boosters. But there are other popular attractions here, like dreamy Hanging Lake, and the gondola and the huge apparatus built into the side of a cliff that swings thrill seekers out into the sky at the Glenwood Caverns Adventure Park. You can obtain pretty much whatever provisions and services you need here.

How long before a flood eats the whole thing?

A jaunty one-way journey down the canyon may be unrealistic, depending on your situation and the mood of your traveling companions. An out-and-back from either Bair Ranch or Glenwood Springs may be more appropriate. If you want to ride the path from the Glenwood side, it can be found at the end of East 6th Street. Keep going past the hot-springs pool, past the Yampah Spa and Vapor Caves, the easternmost structure in Glenwood Springs, and just keep going. There is some public parking available near the end of 6th Street by the spa.

Most of us will just be looking for a moderate and fun ride in the canyon, but the Glenwood Canyon Recreation Trail could become part of a much bigger adventure. If you're feelin' your oats, just keep rolling from Glenwood. The River Trail follows the Roaring Fork out of town and joins the Rio Grande Trail, a gently sloped gravel path that goes all the way up the Roaring Fork Valley to Aspen. The Rio Grande's unpaved surface is suitable for road bikes. This opens up some really tempting multiday tour opportunities, for instance, Glenwood Springs–Aspen–Leadville–Eagle, or something similar, just there for the plucking. (If you try that one, consider using the gravel back roads to get from Twin Lakes to Leadville to avoid a boring and dangerous stretch of US 24.) Or Glenwood–Paonia via McClure Pass, then back north via Grand Mesa. For that matter, Glenwood–Carbondale/Redstone–Crested Butte–Buena Vista–Aspen (an extra-difficult route featuring two of the state's toughest

The illusion of permanence in Glenwood Canyon

climbs—Cottonwood and Independence—and a few of the medium-tough ones, too). Any of these tours requires strong fitness and careful preparation.

Miles and Directions

0.0   Start from the Bair Ranch Rest Area parking lot and begin riding west on the Glenwood Canyon Recreation Trail.

3.8   The trail passes a rest area parking lot.

8.6   The trail passes another rest area parking lot, then, after some very sharp turns, another one.

11.5   The trail spills out onto a road (No Name Lane/CR 129). Continue west on the road.

12.1   The road ends, and the trail reappears straight ahead. Continue.

12.8   The trail goes up and over I-70.

13.8   The trail ends near the Yampah Spa and Vapor Caves.

Glenwood Canyon

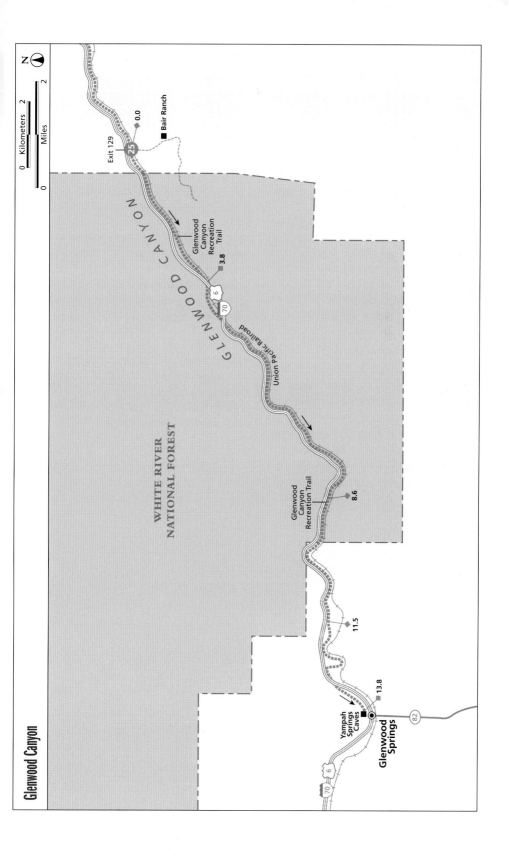

Attractions

Glenwood Caverns Adventure Park. 51000 Two Rivers Plaza Rd., Glenwood Springs; (970) 945-4228; glenwoodcaverns.com. Roller coaster, giant swing, alpine slide, gondola, fairy caves.

Glenwood Hot Springs Pool. 401 N. River St., Glenwood Springs; (970) 945-6571; hotspringspool.com. Ninety-degree water year-round since 1888.

Yampah Spa and Vapor Caves. 709 E. 6th St., Glenwood Springs; (970) 945-0667; yampah spa.com. A unique experience. So I'm told.

Bike Shops

MG Cycle and Sport. 715 Cooper Ave., Glenwood Springs; (970) 945-2453; mgcycleand sport.com.

Bike Rental/Shuttles

Canyon Bikes. 319 6th St., Glenwood Springs (in the Hotel Colorado); (970) 945-8903; canyonbikes.com. Offers rentals and shuttle to Bair Ranch.

Sunlight Ski & Bike Shop. 309 9th St., Glenwood Springs; sunlightmtn.com/rental-shop. Offers rentals and shuttle to Bair Ranch.

Food

Daily Bread. 729 Grand Ave., Glenwood Springs; (970) 945-6253. Breakfast and lunch.

Glenwood Canyon Brewing Company. 402 7th St., Glenwood Springs; (970) 945-1276; glen woodcanyonbrewpub.com.

Jilbertito's. 51241 US 6, Glenwood Springs; (970) 945-2812. One of several intriguing options for budget-friendly Mexican food in town.

19th Street Diner. 1908 Grand Ave., Glenwood Springs; (970) 945-9133; 19thstreet diner.com.

Rosi's Little Bavarian Restaurant. 141 W. 6th St., Glenwood Springs; (970) 928-9186; rosis bavarian.com. Breakfast and lunch.

Lodging

Hotel Colorado. 526 Pine St., Glenwood Springs; (970) 945-6511; hotelcolorado.com. Historic.

Rodeway Inn. 52039 US 6, Glenwood Springs; (970) 945-8817; rodewayinn.com.

26 Aspen-Snowmass Loop

Here's a fun and challenging loop with gravel and paved bike paths and some cool roads in the foothills between Snowmass and Aspen.

Start: The Rio Grande Trail's Slaughterhouse Gulch trailhead near Aspen
Length: 18.1 miles
Terrain: The ride starts nearly flat by the Roaring Fork River and then gets hilly, with some steep climbing. Moderate—by Colorado mountain standards.

Traffic and hazards: Some slippery sections of gravel path. The route briefly follows one deceptively dangerous section of road before heading up toward Snowmass. Some fast descending and moderate traffic on Owl Creek Road.
Things to see: The Roaring Fork, the valley of Brush Creek, Snowmass Village

Getting there: From central Aspen, head northwest on CO 82, toward Glenwood Springs. At the edge of Aspen, turn right onto Cemetery Lane. Follow Cemetery Lane through the neighborhood, down the hill to the Roaring Fork. Start from the trailhead parking area on the left, just beyond the river. **GPS:** N 39 12'41.89" / W 106 50'23.91"

Ride Description

Aspen boomed into existence as a silver town in the 1800s. When the price of silver collapsed, causing the "Panic of 1893," Aspen and other silver towns went into a long

Brush Creek bike path, on the way to Snowmass

decline. The town's population dwindled. But wasting away to ghost-town status, or settling into existence as a sleepy, off-beat mountain town with a few hundred hermit-like inhabitants, would not be Aspen's fate.

Immediately after World War II, Aspen started a new life as a ski resort. The ski mountain was world-class and would have been enough by itself to get a successful venture started, but Aspen became much more than a ski town, thanks in large part to Walter and Elizabeth Paepcke. The Paepckes founded the Aspen Music Festival, the Aspen Institute, the International Design Conference, and other cultural institutions, and they redeveloped a number of properties around town. Their vision of attracting huge money and great thinkers to a near-defunct silver town was wildly successful. Quite too successful, according to some.

Today Aspen is home—make that second or third home—to countless hyper-successful tycoons and entertainers. The real estate here is the most expensive in the United States; the average price of a home or condo is well over $4 million. In 2014 a four-bedroom condo in downtown Aspen sold for almost $16 million. The deal included "air rights"—a guarantee that the owner's view of the mountain from the condo's deck would never be blocked.

Start the ride from this incredible town, where the Rio Grande Trail (or, option-ally, McClain Flats Road) embarks to the northwest, along the Roaring Fork. To reach this part of town, find Cemetery Lane and follow it all the way to the river. Just on the other side, the path crosses the road and there's a little parking area and even a bike fix-it station with tools and a pump. It's easily reachable by bike from anywhere in town, but it's also a nice place to drop your motor vehicle if you have one.

The path is composed of fine gravel, but it's still suitable for road bikes. If you really want to stay on the pavement, or the path's surface is muddy, use McClain Flats Road and rejoin the route at mile 4.5, before it crosses the highway and heads toward Snowmass.

Even path users will have to jump off onto McClain Flats Road for a brief stint in order to continue the loop. This is a deceptively dangerous section of road, invit-ing riders to speed down a hill as oncoming trucks crank left turns. The route joins another path to the left at the bottom of the hill, requiring a road crossing against truck traffic. A little patience could be a lifesaver here. Leaving the road, the path climbs sharply, cruises across the flats, and dives under CO 82.

The climb to Snowmass continues on a bike path. This one is paved, moderately but undeniably sloped, and features sweet views up the valley to Capitol Peak and Snowmass Mountain. It starts out by itself on the edge of a wide-open field but soon crosses back over Brush Creek and unfortunately hugs the road, for the most part, until the turn onto Owl Creek Road. Take note, map readers: This is the valley of Brush Creek, not Snowmass Creek. One would think Snowmass resort would be on Snowmass Creek, but Snowmass Creek is farther north, several valleys away. Tricky!

The Owl Creek turnoff is unsigned and easy to miss, or so I found. If you're still feeling super strong and craving some pain when you get to it, continue straight up

The Brush Creek path heads into open space for a few delicious miles before hugging the road.

through Snowmass Village, using the path as long as you want and then jumping onto the road. The road gets famously steep—15 percent or more—as it ascends about 700 more feet to the top of the last condo building. A system of hot pipes beneath the surface keeps the road ice-free in winter. If you're hungry, there are a few restaurants and cafes at Snowmass Village.

Owl Creek Road is really fun to ride, but lots of folks prefer the path that accompanies it. There is a path following the road much of the way back to Aspen, but it's steeper than the road and the surface is rougher. Either option is good.

Whether you take the road or path, there's quite a little climb in the way of your return to Aspen, gaining about 300 feet in a little under a mile. Once over the top it's almost all coastable downhill back to the start/finish.

Miles and Directions

0.0 Start from the Rio Grande Trail trailhead off Cemetery Lane, and begin riding northwest along the Roaring Fork River.

3.8 Continue straight on the Rio Grande Trail as another trail branches off to the left. (**Option:** If you're feeling a little cyclocrossy, you can take this trail down the hill and rejoin the route at mile 4.5, thus cutting off the section of McClain Flats Road.)

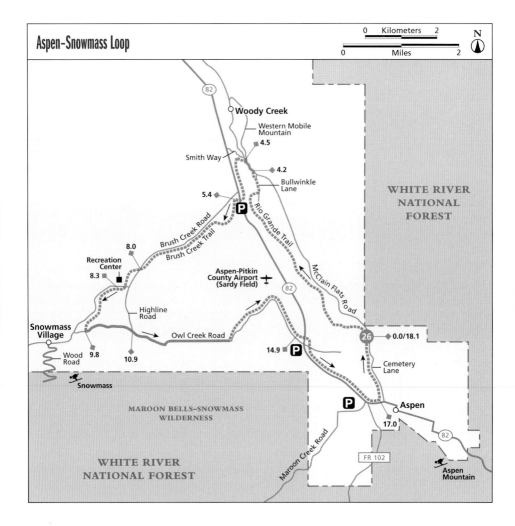

Aspen-Snowmass Loop

3.9 The Rio Grande Trail veers to the left, hugging Lower Bullwinkle Road. Lower Bullwinkle Road! Hey Rocky, watch me pull a rabbit out of this hat! Again?!

4.2 Carefully turn left onto McClain Flats Road and descend. Be extra wary of potential left-turners as you descend.

4.5 Take a left onto the bike path and ascend sharply through the trees.

5.3 The path enters a big parking lot used by bus riders. Continue straight across and find the path continuing on the other side.

5.4 The path goes under CO 82. On the other side, veer left onto the Brush Creek Trail.

8.0 The Brush Creek Trail crosses Brush Creek Road.

8.3 The path crosses back over Brush Creek Road near the rec center (bathrooms and water available here). Continue climbing beside Brush Creek Road.

9.8 Take a left onto Owl Creek Road. (**Option:** Continue climbing to the top of Snowmass Village, just for kicks. Then return to this spot and turn onto Owl Creek Road. There are bathrooms and food at Snowmass Village.)

10.9 Turn right, continuing on Owl Creek Road.

14.9 After the road flattens out behind the airport, jump onto the Owl Creek Trail on the left side of the road, as this will allow you to cross back under CO 82 and avoid the intersection.

15.1 The Owl Creek Trail crosses beneath CO 82. On the other side, take a right.

15.2 Stay right as the trail forks and go under Harmony Road, continuing next to CO 82.

15.6 The trail crosses a road.

16.2 The trail crosses another road at the golf club.

16.6 Continue as another bike path intersects on the right.

17.0 Stay on the path as it curls to the left and begins to follow Cemetery Lane.

18.1 Back at the trailhead.

Bike Shops

Ajax Bike & Sport. 400 E. Cooper, Aspen; (970) 925-7662; ajaxbikeandsport.com. They also have a shop in Carbondale.

Aspen Velo. 465 N. Mill St., Aspen; (970) 925-1495; aspenvelo.com.

Fly Cyclery. 614 E. Durant Ave., Aspen; (970) 925-9539; flycyclery.com. Closed Sunday.

Hub of Aspen. 315 E. Hyman Ave., Aspen; (970) 925-7970; hubofaspen.com.

Ute City Cycles. 231 E. Main St., Aspen; (970) 920-3325; utecitycycles.com.

Food

Cache Cache. 205 Mill St. #106, Aspen; (970) 925-3835; cachecache.com. Upscale French bistro where you might see Lance Armstrong having sharp words with Tyler Hamilton.

Grateful Deli. 223 Main St., Aspen; (970) 925-6647.

Hickory House. 730 W. Main St., Aspen; (970) 925-2313; hickoryhouseribs.com. Barbecue and huge breakfasts.

Johnny McGuire's Deli. 730 E. Cooper Ave., Aspen; (970) 920-9255. Good pastrami sandwiches.

Fuel Coffee Shop. Snowmass Village. (970) 923-0091. Breakfast burritos, bagels with cream cheese, sandwiches, smoothies, and more.

Woody Creek Tavern. 2858 Upper River Rd., Woody Creek; (970) 923-4585; woodycreektavern.com. Down-valley in Woody Creek. Some say that the food here is the reason Hunter Thompson committed suicide. It's not bad though.

Lodging

Tyrolean Lodge. 200 W. Main St., Aspen; (970) 925-4595; tyroleanlodge.com. Centrally located and surprisingly budget-friendly.

27 Maroon Bells

Ride one of the iconic climbs in the state, on a road that is closed to auto traffic much of the year.

Start: The parking lot of the Aspen Recreation Center
Length: 16.8 miles out-and-back
Terrain: A shallow-sloped canyon road that steadily ramps up as it gets higher
Traffic and hazards: Depending on the time of year, traffic could be virtually nonexistent—shuttle buses only. At other times, car traffic is moderate. The descent is fast with associated hazards.
Things to see: Maroon Creek Canyon and the Maroon Bells

Getting there: From Aspen, head west-northwest out of town on CO 82, briefly, toward Snowmass and Glenwood Springs. Just out of town, take a left at the roundabout onto Maroon Creek Road (CR 13). Go up the road past the high school and find the Aspen Recreation Center parking lot on the right. **Note:** This start/finish is easily accessible from town via the off-street bike-path network. **GPS:** N 39 11'16.11" / W 106 51'604"

Ride Description

On paper, this is a straightforward ride. Just a simple climb up and coast down. But this is a very special road.

One of the reasons Maroon Creek Road is special: It's closed to cars for the summer. Between June 15 and September 1, tourists who want to see the Maroon Bells have to take a shuttle bus—or get there under their own power. No cars allowed! (Well, not exactly. There are a number of loopholes and exceptions: The road is always open to parents with little kids in car seats, backpackers, and those pulling horse trailers. The road is also open to cars between 5 p.m. and 9 a.m.) It's too bad they don't give the road to the bikes through September, the best month for mountain rides.

Another reason this is such a special ride, of course, is the destination itself, which is sublime, ethereal. Also a bit overrun with humans at times. It's often said that the Maroon Bells are the most photographed mountains in North America, and that may be true. I think we've all seen that photo.

The striking tableau is formed by three pyramidal, sharply striated peaks folded together into one colossal massif. Trailing off to the north of the 14,000-foot chunk is a rugged, crumbling ridge called the Sleeping Sexton. The intense alpine scene is framed by steep pine- and aspen-covered slopes on both sides, and—pulling it all together—the natural reflecting pool of Maroon Lake, which seems to fill the valley. It's almost too perfect. To really get the whole experience, get off the bike and hike around a bit by the lake. (No bikes in the wilderness area, by the way). Take that picture. From the road itself, the Bells come into view only intermittently.

Sharp peaks, round pedal strokes   PHOTO BY JERRY HURST

Yup, there it is. PHOTO BY JERRY HURST

On the bike, the climb is moderately difficult. The first mile is flat and fast, still in the residential zone, then after a little bit of climbing, it eases back to flat again. The road toys around like this until it hits the toll booth before mile 4, then it starts to get more serious. By mile 6 the occasional flat respites have disappeared and it's a steady 6 to 8 percent slope all the way to the top. The route lacks switchbacks or sharp curves of any kind, but it's far from boring.

The climb gains a little over 1,500 feet, topping out around 9,600 feet above sea level. Personally I would bring a real jacket and some kind of thermal jersey along, as tempting as it is to travel light. Unless the weather pattern is exceedingly stable, you stand a good chance of getting harshed on. The extra gear may slow you down a bit, but it will also allow you to ride on into uncertain weather instead of retreating back to Aspen in fear.

Miles and Directions

0.0 Start from the parking lot of the Aspen Rec Center and start riding up Maroon Creek Road (or the bike path next to it).

3.8 Pay your dues at the ranger's toll booth.

8.4 Arrive at the Maroon Bells parking lot.

16.8 Back at the Aspen Rec Center.

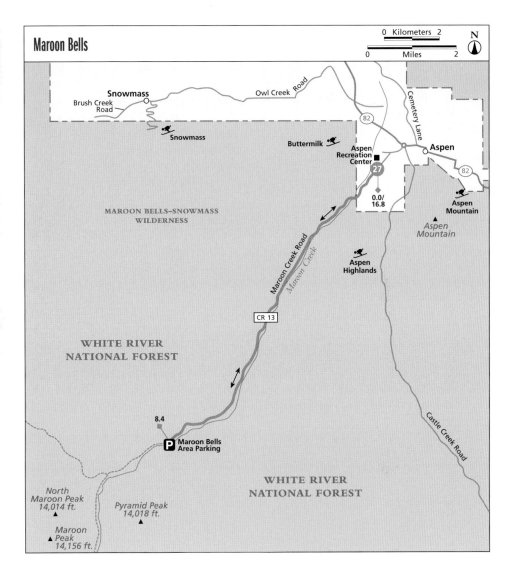

Maroon Bells

0 Kilometers 2

N

0 Miles 2

Snowmass

Brush Creek Road

Owl Creek Road

Snowmass

82

Cemetery Lane

Buttermilk

Aspen Recreation Center

Aspen

82

27

MAROON BELLS-SNOWMASS WILDERNESS

0.0/ 16.8

Aspen Mountain

Aspen Mountain

Maroon Creek Road

Maroon Creek

Aspen Highlands

CR 13

WHITE RIVER NATIONAL FOREST

8.4

P Maroon Bells Area Parking

Castle Creek Road

WHITE RIVER NATIONAL FOREST

North Maroon Peak 14,014 ft.

Pyramid Peak 14,018 ft.

Maroon Peak 14,156 ft.

Bike Shops

Ajax Bike & Sport. 400 E. Cooper, Aspen; (970) 925-7662; ajaxbikeandsport.com. They also have a shop in Carbondale.

Aspen Velo. 465 N. Mill St., Aspen; (970) 925-1495; aspenvelo.com.

Fly Cyclery. 614 E. Durant Ave., Aspen; (970) 925-9539; flycyclery.com. Closed Sunday.

Hub of Aspen. 315 E. Hyman Ave., Aspen; (970) 925-7970; hubofaspen.com.

Ute City Cycles. 231 E. Main St., Aspen; (970) 920-3325; utecitycycles.com.

Food

Cache Cache. 205 Mill St. #106, Aspen; (970) 925-3835; cachecache.com. Upscale French bistro where you might see Lance Armstrong having sharp words with Tyler Hamilton.

Grateful Deli. 223 Main St., Aspen; (970) 925-6647.

Hickory House. 730 W. Main St., Aspen; (970) 925-2313; hickoryhouseribs.com. Barbecue and huge breakfasts.

Johnny McGuire's Deli. 730 E. Cooper Ave., Aspen; (970) 920-9255. Good pastrami sandwiches.

Woody Creek Tavern. 2858 Upper River Rd., Woody Creek; (970) 923-4585; woodycreek tavern.com. Down-valley in Woody Creek. Some say that the food here is the reason Hunter Thompson committed suicide. It's not bad though.

Lodging

Tyrolean Lodge. 200 W. Main St., Aspen; (970) 925-4595; tyroleanlodge.com. Centrally located, this tidy establishment provides nice rooms for a surprisingly low price.

OTHER ASPEN AREA RIDES

Aspen to Crested Butte. With an all-terrain bike you could take a more direct route, over Pearl Pass. On skinny tires, the Aspen–Crested Butte run is a meandering, all-day epic. Head down-valley on the Rio Grande Trail to Carbondale, then hang a left onto CO 133 toward Redstone and McClure Pass. (Consider the Redstone Castle for a lunch stop.) After topping McClure Pass, turn left onto Kebler Pass Road (CR 12) at the Paonia Reservoir. The stunning Kebler Pass Road sheds its pavement as it climbs, adding difficulty and adventure to the journey. The dirt shouldn't be much of a problem if the weather is dry; in wet conditions, however, things can get pretty exciting for road bikers. By this point, wet or not, there's no turning back. Crested Butte sits right at the bottom of the pass on the other side.

Castle Creek. One canyon over from the Maroon Creek Road, and sprouting from the same roundabout on CO 82, is Castle Creek Road (CR 15). Castle Creek Road climbs steadily to tiny Ashcroft, another first-class canyon climb. The difficulty of the climbing is about the same as the Maroon Bells road. I recommend riding both roads if you've got multiple days in Aspen. Completing both on the same day is a tall order, but many local bikies have been known to pull it off and live to tell the tale, loudly, later that evening.

Fryingpan Road. A delightful 20-mile climb to Ruedi Reservoir from Basalt, but expect trailer pullers. Go northeast on Midland Avenue in Basalt to find Fryingpan Road.

Independence Pass from Aspen. This is a distinctly different ride than the east-side Independence Pass climb described elsewhere in the book. The climb from Aspen is even longer and more difficult. Plus, it's a bit sketchy. Famously, the road narrows to a single lane in a few places along the way, a feature that has traumatized Colorado drivers for decades and claimed countless side mirrors. Being on a bike instead of in a car doesn't exactly improve the outlook in the narrows. So this adventure requires not only serious power and endurance but a high tolerance for snaggly, awkward traffic situations in a sublimely beautiful alpine setting.

The Monastery. The inhabitants of Saint Benedict's Monastery on Capitol Creek Road (CR 9) are used to bicyclists rambling up to their abode and coughing up a lung. It's a natural destination that can be accessed from Aspen via the Rio Grande Trail or the road through

Woody Creek. Usually an out-and-back, you can turn it into a big dirt loop using Snowmass Creek Road (CR 11), which branches off from Capitol Creek Road.

Rio Grande Trail. This family-friendly bike path rolls all the way from Glenwood Springs to Aspen. That's right, the entire valley. The surface is crushed gravel most of the way, fine for any type of bike. Slopes are generally very shallow. The trail is a bit elusive to nonlocals as it enters Aspen, tucked away on the far side of the Roaring Fork. The Slaughterhouse Gulch trailhead, accessible via Cemetery Lane on the northwest side of Aspen, is a nice place to get on. On the Glenwood side, there is an off-street path all the way through town to Two Rivers Park. The path is known as the River Trail through Glenwood.

28 Ohio Pass

Ohio Pass is the road biker's backdoor to Crested Butte. This awesome part-gravel road connecting Gunnison to Kebler Pass Road is delightful in its scenery as well as its obscurity. Cruise back to Gunny on the highway to complete a classic loop.

Start: CO 135 and the Gunnison River
Length: 57.0-mile loop
Terrain: From the sage hills to the aspen-covered mountains and back along a wide river valley. The climbing is unmistakable but relatively manageable.

Traffic and hazards: Light-to-moderate traffic on Ohio Pass and Kebler Pass Road. The highway return is less pleasant, but the shoulder is ample.
Things to see: Gunnison River Valley, Ohio Pass, Kebler Pass, Crested Butte

Getting there: From Gunnison, head north on CO 135 toward Crested Butte. About 5 miles from town, turn left off the highway where it crosses the Gunnison River and park in the dirt parking area by the river. **GPS:** N 38 34'54.37" / W 106 55'20.89"

Ride Description

It kind of amazes me that this isn't on everybody's list of go-to rides. The route's ongoing obscurity only adds to its world-class awesomeness.

I guess the reason more people don't pedal Ohio Pass is the surface of the road (CR 730). The pass itself is dirt, and it spills out onto Kebler Pass Road, which is also partially dirt, and that scares away a lot of road bikers. On the other hand, the mileage leading up to the pass is paved, and that scares away the mountain bikers. Meanwhile, the tourists in cars are satisfied with the more direct but still scenic CO 135, or else they stick to Kebler Pass. What we have here is a rare opportunity to ride a top-notch route that isn't infested with motorists or crawling with other riders.

This ride makes a whole lot of sense if you're staying in Gunnison. (**Note:** It's probably not worth it to drive to the start as described here if you're already in Gunnison. Ride from town, either on the CO 135 shoulder or the pleasant public paths by the river and West Elk/Castle Mount Road, to the Ohio Pass Road [CR 730].) Though it is home to a number of incredibly fit bicyclists, this gritty little town doesn't exist just to indulge our sports fantasies. It benefits from the nearby ski resort but doesn't depend on it. Like Durango, Gunnison is a real working town that just happens to be situated near some of the best cycling on the planet. While Durango was a smelting and mining community, Gunnison was an agricultural hub.

You really feel that agricultural heritage during the opening miles of this ride, across the wide Gunnison River floodplain, headed diagonally for the valley of Ohio Creek. Much of the farmland has been divided into nonworking private land, but in large part the old paradigm has been preserved. There are no lawns up here, but the

Kebler Pass Road   Photo by Jerry Hurst

whole area is still lavishly irrigated—"under ditch" as they used to say—and it looks like a bright green patch in a sea of brown when viewed from above.

Subtly the road transitions from farm cruiser to mountain climber as the Ohio Creek valley narrows. Fittingly, the pavement disappears. Let's hope your sky is looking pretty tame and clear at this point. If not, it's not too late to turn back. Don't push off into uncertain weather on this or any mountain ride without some extra gear. You're likely to see a few different weather situations arise on a ride this long.

Ohio is a low, easy pass. But it's still a big hill, about 20 miles long and rising 2,000 feet—gaining most of its vertical in a 5-mile finale. (From the other direction the climb is noticeably steeper and shorter.) It flirts with 10,000 feet in elevation, but doesn't get too close. There is one squiggly section of road with some switchbacks, but the rest of the pass is pretty straightforward.

As you might imagine, being so close to Crested Butte, it's beautiful up there.

Drop into Crested Butte without delay via the Kebler Pass Road, which is also off-and-on dirt. It was proven once and for all that wispy road bikes could handle the Kebler descent in 2014 in a stage of the US Pro Cycling Challenge. Well, sort of. In one of the more bizarre episodes in American pro-racing history, race officials neutralized the Kebler Pass stage due to alleged dangerous conditions on the dirt in the rain. It was puzzling because they stopped the race *after* the riders had already

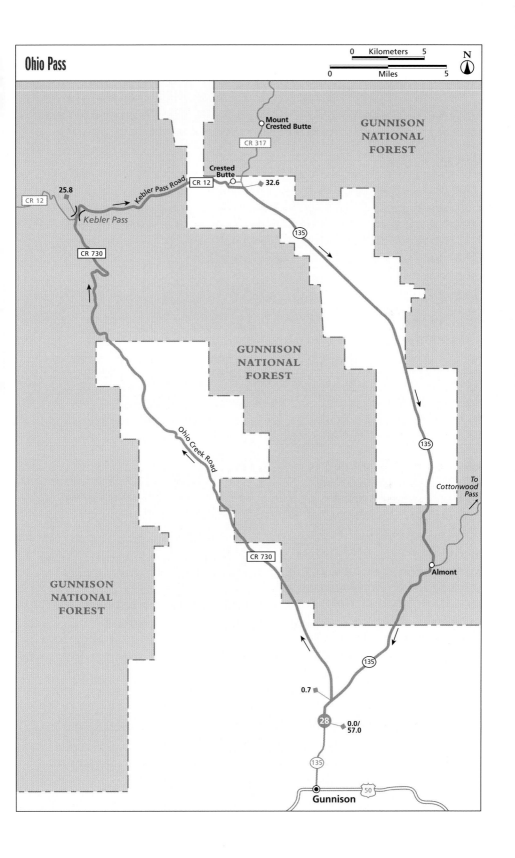

Ohio Pass

0   Kilometers   5

0   Miles   5

N

Mount Crested Butte

GUNNISON NATIONAL FOREST

CR 317

Crested Butte

CR 12

25.8

CR 12

Kebler Pass Road

Kebler Pass

32.6

135

CR 730

GUNNISON NATIONAL FOREST

Ohio Creek Road

135

To Cottonwood Pass

GUNNISON NATIONAL FOREST

CR 730

Almont

135

0.7

135

28

0.0/ 57.0

135

50

Gunnison

completed the descent. The moral of that story is don't panic! But if you're going to panic, panic early and often.

Not only is this a great journey, but the reward at the other end is pretty sweet. You're in Crested Butte, baby! One of these times I'm just going to stick there and never come back. Everything seems so non-crested in comparison.

Miles and Directions

0.0 Start riding north up CO 135.

0.7 Turn left onto CR 730 (Ohio Creek Road). Stay on CR 730 past all intersections until . . .

25.8 Turn right onto Kebler Pass Road (CR 12). You can stay on the same road as it becomes Whiterock Avenue and shoots right through Crested Butte.

32.6 Stop and get some food? Then turn right onto CO 135.

56.2 Pass the turnoff to CR 730; continue.

57.0 Back at the parking area.

Bike Shops

Double Shot Cyclery. 121 W. Virginia Ave., Gunnison; (970) 642-5411; doubleshotcyclery .com. Coffee and food, too.

Race Townie Bicycles. 620 W. New York Ave., Gunnison; racetownie.com.

Rock 'N' Roll Sports. 608 W. Tomichi Ave., Gunnison; (970) 641-9150; rocknrollsports online.com.

Tomichi Cycles. 104 N. Main St., Gunnison; (970) 641-9069; tomichicycles.com.

Big Al's Bicycle Heaven. 207 Elk Ave., Crested Butte; (970) 349-0515; bigalsbicycleheaven .com.

Food

The Bean Coffeehouse and Eatery. 120 N. Main St., Gunnison; (970) 641-2408. Good food and coffee.

Cafe Silvestre. 903 N. Main St., Gunnison; (970) 641-4001. Cheap Mexican food.

Garlic Mike's. 2674 Highway 135, Gunnison; (970) 641-2493; garlicmikes.com.

Las Palmas. 138 W. Tomichi Ave., Gunnison; (970) 642-1108. More cheap Mexican.

Izzy's. 218 Maroon Ave., Crested Butte; (970) 349-5630. Breakfast and lunch.

Pitas in Paradise. 302 Elk Ave., Crested Butte; (970) 349-0897; pitasinparadise.com.

Lodging

Long Holiday Motel. 1198 Highway 50 Frontage Rd., Gunnison; (970) 641-0536; long holidaymotel.com.

The Seasons Inn. 412 E. Tomichi Ave., Gunnison; (970) 641-0700; coseasons.com.

Elk Mountain Lodge. 129 Gothic Ave., Crested Butte; (970) 349-7533; elkmountainlodge .com.

Old Town Inn. 708 6th St., Crested Butte; (970) 349-6184; oldtowninn.net.

MORE RIDES AROUND GUNNISON

CO 92. This ride sprouts north from US 50 at the west end of Blue Mesa Reservoir and crosses the dam. There are various types of public parking lots on both sides of the road as you rise from the water. Views into the Black Canyon of the Gunnison steal your breath, if you have any left to steal. The road's high point is about 22 miles from US 50, and the town of Crawford is another 20 or so. Since Crawford sits about 1,000 feet lower than Blue Mesa Reservoir, an out-and-back reaching all the way to Crawford is a mega challenge.

Ninemile Hill. About 9 miles west of Gunnison on US 50, find CO 149 crossing Blue Mesa Reservoir (dramatically) and chugging southward up into the aggressively sage-brushy hills for 9 somewhat brutal miles, to an elevation of about 9,000 feet. Nine, nine, nine. Makes a fine and painful out-and-back, or stay on this road for a long time and you'll get through "the Gate" to Lake City. Lake City sits at about the same elevation as the top of Ninemile, but there are plenty of ups and downs in between.

Pitkin. From the little hamlet called Parlin on US 50 east of Gunny-sack, a humble and rustic (yet paved) road winds its way up through the sage toward the high mountains. About 15 miles up, the pavement ends at tiny Pitkin.

29 Cottonwood Pass

Cottonwood is a top-notch climb without top-notch hype. An up-and-back on the Buena Vista side of the pass should fill you with enough endorphins for a few weeks.

Start: The bottom of Cottonwood Pass, on CR 306 west of Buena Vista
Length: 12.6 miles one way
Terrain: One long climb
Traffic and hazards: The route follows a two-lane highway. Traffic is moderate. Trucks with trailers are common on this route, with lots of people pulling boats or quads up over the pass to Taylor Park. The road is relatively wide.
Things to see: Unforgettable Cottonwood Pass

Getting there: From Buena Vista, head west on East Main Street/CR 306 for about 7 miles and find a parking spot on the side of the road. There's a good parking area on the left, just below the turnoff to Cottonwood Lake (CR 344). **GPS:** N 38 48'20.13" / W 106 14'32.81"

Ride Description

At some point in your journey through the bike culture, you might have heard some guys bikesplaining about the relative difficulty of climbs in Colorado versus those in Europe. Quite often I hear occasional soapboxing about Colorado climbs being so much easier. I doubt any of these dudes have attempted Cottonwood or Independence, the big-and-tall climbs around here, or their proclamations would be less absolute.

European climbs may rival the big climbs in this book in terms of slope and vertical gain. But there's one thing the climbs in Europe have in abundance that our Colorado climbs do not: air. Lovely, invisible air. Oxygen. Cyclists in the Alps and Pyrenees enjoy noticeably higher air pressure in their lungs when pedaling uphill. This has some significant positive effects on performance, to put it mildly. If we could take Cottonwood Pass and transfer it to the Alps, it would be so much easier to deal with!

Luckily for us, Cottonwood Pass is right here in the middle of Colorado, 2 miles above sea level.

I'm not a big fan of the straight run-up to the mountains on the two-lane highway west of Buena Vista (pronounced Byoona Vista around here). Doesn't do much for me. In fact I've been sort of avoiding this kind of road section for a while now, if the option is available. Drivers don't pay attention to what's in front of them and start drifting around, shoulders tend to be thin or nonexistent, and the riding is pretty boring. Given the services of an internal combustion engine, I like to drive up and park somewhere near the bottom of the hill itself and start pedaling from there. But starting right from town is always satisfying in its own way, certainly more eco-friendly, and it can make up for a lot of boring road. It is very possible to ride the pass from

Nearing the summit on Cottonwood Pass Road

Byoona, but if you try it, allot a good deal more time than you would for the route described below.

There are many suitable parking spots along the road after it starts to point up, but there's a more formal paved parking area about 7 miles outside of town on the left. Starting here leaves about 13 miles to the top—plenty. If you want to drive a little farther up, you can park in the Colorado Trail's huge trailhead lot.

The first 5 miles or so are on the forgiving side, with steeper pitches augmented by flat sections. The last 7 or so make up a big climb to the top, relentless but not too bad if there's no headwind. There are some rudely steep pitches along the way, flirting with double-digit slopes for way too long. Thankfully, the last few miles are moderate and steady. The grade is remarkably consistent on final approach, thanks to huge, awesome oxbow turns in the road. The top of Cottonwood is every bit as tall as Independence, at around 12,100 feet. The view is intense.

On the other side of the pass, the road turns to dirt and drops about 15 potentially bone-jarring miles to the Taylor Park Reservoir before finding pavement again. Below the reservoir, the road twists down the Taylor River Canyon to the collection of fishing cabins called Almont, which sits on the highway between Gunnison and Crested Butte. In either direction, rolling the whole distance between Buena Vista and Almont is a mega-challenge that will consume much of the day and about two days' worth of energy.

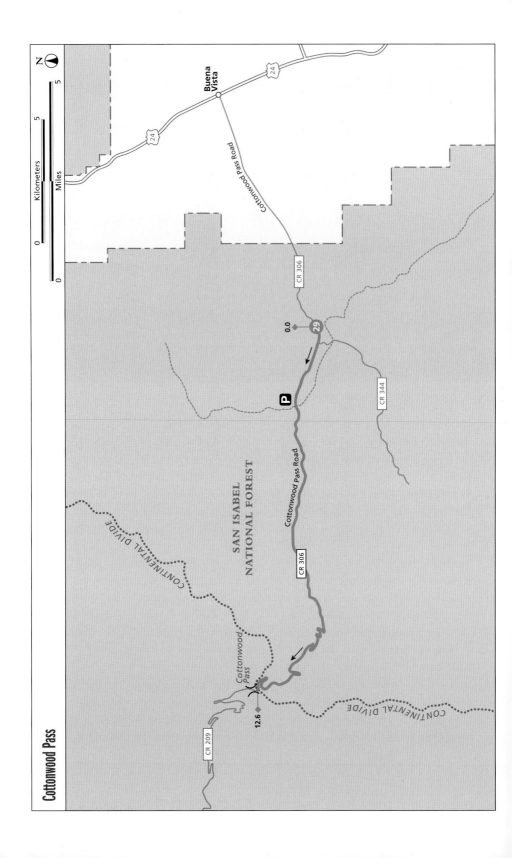

Cottonwood Pass

Miles and Directions

0.0 Start riding up Cottonwood Pass Road (CR 306) from the parking area. (There are many suitable parking spots, but the one I have in mind is on the left side of the road about 7 miles from Buena Vista, just below the junction with CR 344 to Cottonwood Lake.)

12.6 Top of the pass: 12,127 feet.

Bike Shops

The Trailhead. 707 US 24, Buena Vista; (719) 395-8001; thetrailheadco.com.

Food

Evergreen Cafe. 418 US 24, Buena Vista; (719) 395-8984; evergreencafebv.com. Nothing fancy.

Las Girasoles. 708 US 24, Buena Vista; (719) 395-9998.

Lodging

Lakeside Motel. 112 W. Lake St., Buena Vista; (719) 395-2994; lakesidebv.com. Clean motel, nice location, owners very excited about not allowing smoking.

Topaz Lodge. 115 US 24, Buena Vista; (719) 395-2427; topazlodge.biz. A basic motel, centrally located.

Vista Court Cabins & Lodge. 1004 W. Main St., Buena Vista; (719) 395-6557; vistacourtcabins.com.

30 Independence Pass

Climbing Independence Pass is something to write home about. It is one of the most difficult paved passes in North America, and perhaps the most beautiful. This iconic ride is a rite of passage for Colorado road bikers.

Start: Twin Lakes
Length: 17.0 miles one way
Terrain: One very long, tall climb
Traffic and hazards: The route follows a two-lane highway. Motor traffic can be heavy, and speeds are relatively high on the lower portion of the route. The upper portion is narrow in spots. Descent of the pass in either direction demands great care.
Things to see: One of the most beautiful stretches of road anywhere

Getting there: The tiny village of Twin Lakes is on CO 82 about 6 miles west of US 24, west of the actual lakes. From Denver, go west on I-70, then turn south at Copper Mountain onto CO 91. Continue south through Leadville on US 24. About 15 miles south of Leadville, turn right onto CO 82, continue west past the lakes, and park in a trailhead parking area on the left, right across from the Twin Lakes Inn and General Store. **GPS:** N 39 4'53.93" / W 106 22'55.45"

Ride Description

Considered by many to be the ultimate pass climb in Colorado, Independence Pass is frightful in many ways. The climb is scary long, first of all. From Twin Lakes, down

An unnamed lake at the top of the pass

Part of the "Long Valley"

in the valley of the upper Arkansas River, you're looking at 3,000 feet of vertical over 17 miles. The elevation is serious, starting over 9,000 feet and topping out over 12,000. Even the traffic gets scary on this route, with its slightly narrow roads and lack of shoulder.

And it's always raining up on Independence Pass. And that rain is *cold*.

Needless to say, if you embark on this ride, make sure to carry the necessary gear. If there's any question about the weather, it's a good idea to bring a waterproof shell, thermal top, tights—and don't forget the warm gloves and hat. This stuff probably isn't going to fit in your jersey pockets. There aren't any visitor centers or gift shops up at the top, no real shelter from the weather.

Independence Pass is a toughie, but very doable for an enthusiastic rider. There are much more difficult rides—the big fourteeners come to mind, of course—and maybe even more difficult passes in the state. But Independence Pass overflows with majesty, grandeur, and excitement. It has a precarious feel, looking into the abyss below. The road sometimes seems to cling to nothing. The landscape at the summit is intensely beautiful, arguably unmatched for roadside scenery.

The climb has two phases: what I call the Long Valley, and—failing to think of anything good for the top part—the Top Part.

After a few miles of twisting and turning out of Twin Lakes, the route settles into a relatively wide-open and straight attitude as it follows the valley of Lake Creek for 8 miles or so: the Long Valley. The scenery is already divine as the road shoots up the

One of the prettier roads in the book

valley between the monster peaks, Elbert, the tallest in the state, on the right and La Plata, with its jagged ridge, on the left. But the route is otherwise a bit boring down here, and people tend to drive way too fast, as is typical for roads without sharp curves.

To me this long run-up is the least pleasant part of the ride. I get more inspired when the road climbs into the high subalpine valley (about mile 11), where you can look up and see the remainder of the route carved into the mountainside. The Top Part. This is what we think of when we imagine ourselves on Independence Pass.

This exciting second phase begins without ambiguity at mile 12.8, where the road switches and starts chugging up the side of a very steep mountain. Soon you gain a bird's-eye view of the valley. This is what we Colorado kids remember from our youths, when we hid on the floor of the Pontiac as our parents, who were not particularly skilled drivers even on flatland, drove up the narrow road. It was a good bet that the steering or brakes would fail and the Pontiac would end up on the floor of the bright green valley, sending up a column of black smoke from the thick shrubs by the meandering creek. But we lived to tell the tale, most of us.

The incline gets much more serious, popping into 10 to 15 percent territory for a quarter mile here and there, although you'll see the road engineers managed to keep those inclines down pretty well overall, even on this upper portion. The Top Part looks like a twisted paper clip on the map, with three hairpins and three 90-degree curves.

Independence Pass

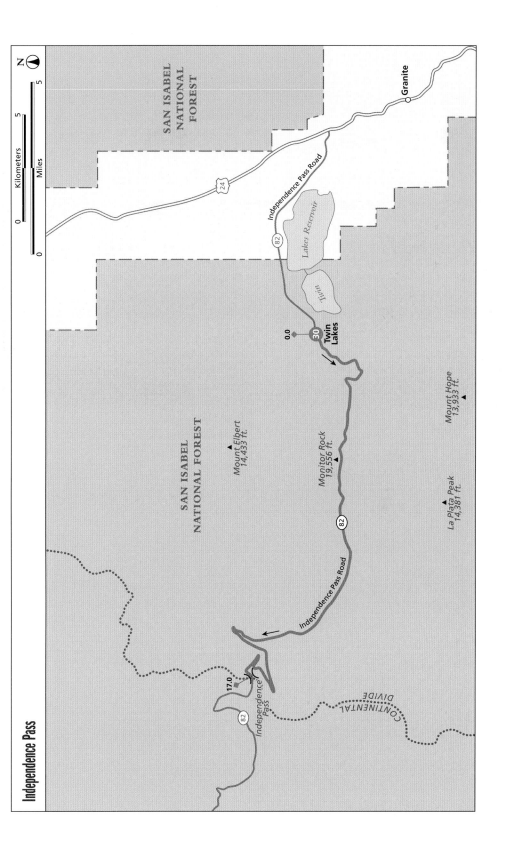

N

Kilometers
0   5
Miles
0   5

SAN ISABEL
NATIONAL
FOREST

Granite

24

Independence Pass Road

82

Lakes Reservoir

Twin

Twin
Lakes

0.0

30

SAN ISABEL
NATIONAL FOREST

Mount Elbert
14,433 ft.

Monitor Rock
19,556 ft.

Mount Hope
13,933 ft.

82

La Plata Peak
14,381 ft.

Independence Pass Road

CONTINENTAL
DIVIDE

17.0

Independence
Pass

82

Independence
Pass

The upper portion narrows enough that some drivers will have difficulty passing a bicyclist even if the bike is tucked over to the side. There could be some bottlenecks and frustrated drivers, and aggravated bicyclists, too. Everything will work out just fine if we can bring a little extra patience and awareness to the Top Part.

On the other side of the pass, of course, is Aspen. Riding all the way down to Aspen and back up the pass is possible, but more for extreme athletes. I won't pretend to have tried it. Note that the other side of the pass is longer and, arguably, a more difficult climb. Start early if you try that. Or, better yet, stay overnight in Aspen and ride back the next day. (For more on the Aspen side of Independence Pass, see Other Aspen Area Rides.)

Miles and Directions

0.0   Begin riding up Independence Pass from the parking lot across the road from the Twin Lakes businesses.

17.0   Top of the pass. Minimal services.

Bike Shops
The Trailhead. 707 US 24, Buena Vista; (719) 395-8001; thetrailheadco.com.
Cycles of Life. 309 Harrison Ave. (US 24), Leadville; (719) 486-5533; cyclesoflifepb.com.

Food
Twin Lakes General Store. 6451 CO 82, Twin Lakes; (719) 486-2196; twinlakesgs.com.
Twin Lakes Inn. 6435 E. CO 82, Twin Lakes; (719) 486-7965; thetwinlakesinn.com. A bit upscale, lunch and dinner.

Lodging
Twin Lakes Inn. 6435 E. CO 82, Twin Lakes; (719) 486-7965; thetwinlakesinn.com.
Twin Lakes Roadhouse Lodge. 6411 E. CO 82, Twin Lakes; (719) 486-9345; twin lakescolorado.com.
Windspirit Cottage & Cabins. 6559 CO 82, Twin Lakes; (719) 427-0621; twinlakescolorado cabins.com.

31 Turquoise Lake

This deceivingly difficult loop around Turquoise Lake near Leadville is a roadie's dream. The road winds above a gorgeous lake with the state's highest peaks looming above.

Start: Turquoise Lake, at the intersection of CR 4 and Turquoise Lake Road

Length: 14.7-mile loop

Terrain: Hilly road around a beautiful mountain reservoir

Traffic and hazards: Moderate traffic and somewhat technical descending; curvy mountain road; high-altitude weather

Things to see: The lake and surrounding forests, Mounts Massive and Elbert

Getting there: From Leadville, take 6th Street west toward Mount Massive until it ends at McWethy Drive (CR 4), then take a right. Stay on CR 4 as it veers west and continue on CR 4 until you reach the intersection with Turquoise Lake Road. There are several places to park next to the road near this intersection. **GPS:** N 39 15'7.82" / W 106 22'2.27"

Ride Description

It took me so long to learn how to spell the word *turquoise* that I almost gave up.

The Turquoise Lake loop is one of my sleeper favorites. The road surface may not be in great shape, but the twists and turns along the mountainy north shore are

A natural lake turned reservoir

Turquoise Lake in the distance beyond Leadville

delightful. If you can persuade yourself to stop while pedaling from curve to curve up there, check out the view from the overlooks. The setting and terrain make this one of the sweetest road rides in the state.

The almost-15-mile loop might look easy on a map. Don't be fooled! Riding Turquoise might be just as hard as spelling it. There is a hefty climb on the north side; it's pretty steep and gains about 1,000 feet. Even on the south side the road climbs over some humps, about 400 feet worth. It's a humpy, lumpy ride.

If you'd like to add some extra mileage and challenge, start the ride from central Leadville. This adds about 5 miles of cruising on the way in, and about 46 miles of false flats on the way back—or so it seems. In reality the road seems to be the same length in both directions! Hmm. Will have to double-check. Use 6th Street to get out of town, take a right at the T, and keep going until you find the lake. Services are pretty minimal when you get there, other than some bathrooms, so stock up with all the necessary water and food while in town.

Turquoise Lake is one reservoir of the Fryingpan-Arkansas ("Fry-Ark") Project, which collects water from the Fryingpan River and Arkansas River basins and redirects it to the insatiably thirsty people and lawns of southern Colorado. The dam was built in 1969 to enlarge the existing lake and turn it into a reservoir.

In 1967, before the dam was built, the feds tried to kill all the fish in Turquoise Lake with a chemical called Fintrol (antimycin A), hoping to "reclaim" the lake for

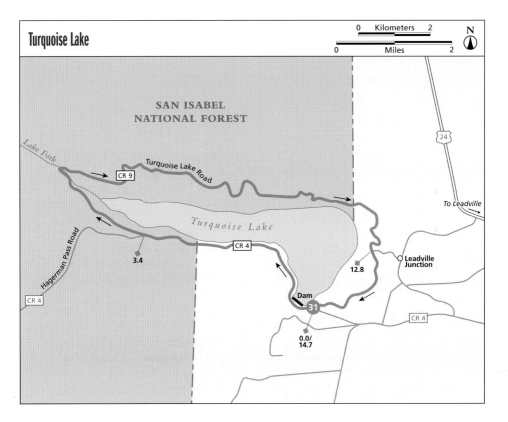

SAN ISABEL
NATIONAL FOREST

native species. The suckers, however, survived. How did all those nonnative fish get into the lake in the first place? Well, don't call them "invasive." They were put there by the government, of course! Mountain lakes all over the United States, many of them "dead lakes" after being inundated by mining waste and other poisons during the nineteenth century, were stocked with sport fish. It didn't take too long before people started to agree what a grand mistake that was, and the re-poisoning began.

Poisoned, stocked, re-poisoned, restocked . . . that's the story of Turquoise Lake and other bodies of water in the western mountains. The lake is currently supplied every year with Snake River cutthroat and rainbow trout raised just down the road at the Leadville National Fish Hatchery. To this day the suckers reign supreme. Almost 400 suckers were reportedly pulled out of Turquoise in 2013—nearly 80 percent of the lake's total catch.

Miles and Directions

0.0 Start from the dam and begin riding clockwise around Turquoise Lake Reservoir.

3.4 Pass the intersection with Hagerman Pass Road. (Turquoise Lake Road becomes CR 9 here, and CR 4 heads up Hagerman Pass.)

5.4 The road curls around the west side of the lake, beginning a long climb.

7.5 False summit!

8.1 Top of the big climb.

12.8 Continue straight past an intersection (CR 9 becomes CR 9C).

14.7 Back at the start.

Attractions
Leadville National Fish Hatchery. 2846 CO 300, Leadville; (719) 486-0189; fws.gov/ Leadville. Open to the public.

Bike Shops
Cycles of Life. 309 Harrison Ave. (US 24), Leadville; (719) 486-5533; cyclesoflifepb.com.

Food
City on a Hill Coffee & Espresso. 508 Harrison Ave. #3 (US 24), Leadville; (719) 486-0797; cityonahillcoffee.com. Bakery and cafe, too.

High Mountain Pies. 115 W. 4th St., Leadville; (719) 486-5555. Pizza, good.

Manuelita's Restaurant. 311 Harrison Ave. (US 24), Leadville; (719) 486-0292. A Mexican place with an emphasis on *mariscos* (seafood), which is pretty strange in one of the most landlocked towns in America.

Quincy's Tavern. 416 Harrison Ave. (US 24), Leadville; (719) 486-9765; quincystavern .com. Meat.

Wild Bill's Hamburgers and Ice Cream. 200 Harrison Ave. (US 24), Leadville; (719) 486-0533. Don't expect too much and you'll be fine.

Lodging
Alert! Don't even try to find a place to sleep in or around Leadville within a week or so of the Leadville Trail 100 mountain bike race, in early to mid-August.

Alps Motel. 207 Elm St., Leadville; (719) 486-1223; alpsmotel.com.

Columbine Inn & Suites. 2019 N. Poplar St., Leadville; (719) 486-5650; columbineinn.com.

Delaware Hotel. 700 Harrison Ave. (US 24), Leadville; (719) 486-1418; delawarehotel .com.

32 Mineral Belt Loop

One of the coolest bike-path rides you'll ever find, this off-street loop cuts through Leadville, then meanders through the woods to a serene landscape marked by old mines and crumbling leftovers of the town's boomtown past.

Start: Ice Palace Park at 11th Street and Harrison Avenue in Leadville
Length: 11.7-mile loop
Terrain: Moderately sloped foothills in the historic mining district outside of Leadville
Traffic and hazards: This ride requires two highway crossings. The trail crosses a few other minor roads as it cuts through Leadville. With lots of curves on the path, other cyclists are a potential hazard.
Things to see: Mount Massive, Mount Elbert, Leadville, and the historic mining district above town

Getting there: Toward the north end of Leadville, find Ice Palace Park at 11th Street and Harrison Avenue. (From the north, enter town on US 24 and take a right on 11th Street. The park and parking area are dead ahead 1 block. From the south, drive through Leadville on US 24, which becomes Harrison Avenue as it turns north. When the main route turns right, at 9th Street, continue straight on Harrison, over the hill. You'll find Ice Palace Park and the small parking area on the other side, at 11th and Harrison.) **GPS:** N 39 15'9.93" / W 106 17'36.47"

Ride Description

What a gem this trail is. It cuts through Leadville, one of Colorado's most genuine mountain towns, and loops up through the woods, perusing the mining district above

The Mineral Belt Trail after an afternoon rainstorm

More enjoyable than the Leadville 100

the town. Despite the hilly terrain, the path twists around severely to find the easier inclines. The path doubles as a groomed cross-country ski trail in the winter, which makes sense. This loop could be a lot shorter, but it wouldn't be nearly as pleasant.

The 11.7-mile loop works nicely in either direction, and it can be ridden from several starting points. The main trailhead is located at the extreme southwest corner of town next to the highway; starting and ending there feels kind of lonely and doesn't really give you that Leadville experience. May as well cruise into town and start from there. (If you've got kids along, consider starting at the main trailhead on US 24 and riding an out-and-back route to the mining district and back. This will keep you from having to cross any highways. There are about 9 miles of nearly traffic-free trail on the backside of the loop—a truly awesome family-ride opportunity.)

Whichever direction you decide to ride the loop, you'll be climbing before too long. As soon as you get out of town and cross the highway, in either direction, the path ramps upward and keeps ramping for several miles. Count on almost 1,000 feet of climbing. So, this isn't exactly an easy loop.

If you're a first-time visitor to the upper Arkansas valley, you'll be surprised to roll into a mountain town, in such a striking location as this, that does not sprout towering hotels built in that faux *alpenhaus* style by golf-shirt-wearing developers named Brandon, and is not ringed with multimillion dollar, four-story homes that are empty almost the entire year, just waiting for their absentee owners to jet off for

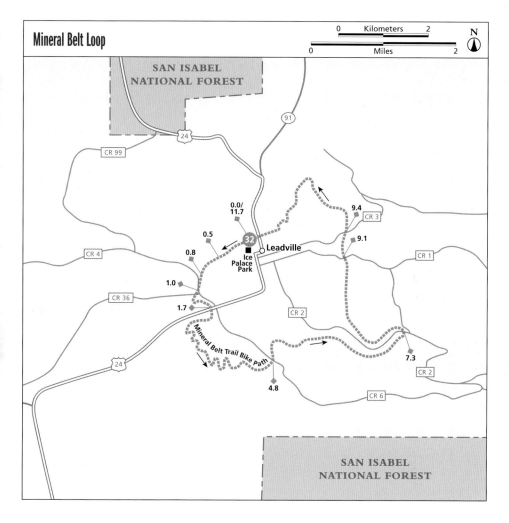

Mineral Belt Loop

a long ski weekend from Houston or Paris or wherever they hang out collecting interest on their inheritances. Not that the people of Leadville wouldn't want to have those things. But such opulence just wasn't in the cards for Leadville. Instead of long driveways and empty mansions among the aspens, Leadville has "suburbs" populated by actual working people. Working people with huge lungs.

Unlike its cousins Crested Butte, Telluride, Aspen, and Breckenridge, Leadville never got its ski resort makeover after World War II. Leadville is still a leftover silver town that supernova'd in the 1890s. It's a sad fact for some of the people in town, but it gives the place a unique sort of awesomeness.

The Leadville Trail 100, a jeep-road mountain-bike race that starts and ends here, has pumped quite a bit of juice into the local economy. A comically huge field tackles the 50-mile out-and-back course each year, usually during the second weekend of August. The likes of Levi Leipheimer, Floyd Landis, and Lance Armstrong have won it. Prior to the era of mega–doped road pros poaching wins here, the race was owned by Dave Wiens, a genuine Colorado dude and nice guy. On the women's side, Rebecca Rusch was the rider to beat, with four straight wins from 2009 to 2012. Now the race carries international prestige and is contested by the top off-road racers in the world.

I'll tell you something. I have competed in the Leadville Trail 100. While that was a memorable experience, this little bike-path loop is a bit more enjoyable in my opinion.

Miles and Directions

0.0 Start from Ice Palace Park and begin riding west (toward Mounts Massive and Elbert) on the Mineral Belt Trail bike path.

0.5 The path crosses James Street.

0.8 The path crosses West 6th Street.

1.0 The path crosses McWethy Drive.

1.5 The path spills out onto Elm Street. Take a right here onto Elm Street.

1.6 Turn left, back onto the Mineral Belt Trail.

1.7 Carefully cross US 24.

4.8 The trail crosses a dirt road (CR 6).

5.0 The trail crosses another dirt road.

7.3 The trail comes to a road (CR 2). Take a left onto this road briefly and find the Mineral Belt Trail continuing on the other side.

9.1 The trail crosses CR 1.

9.4 The trail crosses CR 3.

11.2 Back in Leadville, take a sharp right onto East 12th Street.

11.4 Get back on the Mineral Belt Trail, which has regenerated on the right side of the road.

11.5 Carefully cross US 24.

11.6 Cross East 12th Street.

11.7 Cross Harrison Street and end the loop at Ice Palace Park.

Bike Shops

Cycles of Life. 309 Harrison Ave. (US 24), Leadville; (719) 486-5533; cyclesoflifepb.com.

Food

City on a Hill Coffee & Espresso. 508 Harrison Ave. #3 (US 24), Leadville; (719) 486-0797; cityonahillcoffee.com. Bakery and cafe, too.

High Mountain Pies. 115 W. 4th St., Leadville; (719) 486-5555. Pizza, good.

Manuelita's Restaurant. 311 Harrison Ave. (US 24), Leadville; (719) 486-0292. A Mexican place with an emphasis on *mariscos* (seafood), which is pretty strange in landlocked Leadville.

Quincy's Tavern. 416 Harrison Ave. (US 24), Leadville; (719) 486-9765; quincystavern .com.

Wild Bill's Hamburgers and Ice Cream. 200 Harrison Ave. (US 24), Leadville; (719) 486-0533. Don't expect too much and you'll be fine.

Lodging

Alert! Don't even try to find a place to sleep in or around Leadville within a week or so of the Leadville Trail 100 mountain bike race, in early to mid-August.

Alps Motel. 207 Elm St., Leadville; (719) 486-1223; alpsmotel.com.

Columbine Inn & Suites. 2019 N. Poplar St., Leadville; (719) 486-5650; columbineinn.com.

Delaware Hotel. 700 Harrison Ave. (US 24), Leadville; (719) 486-1418; delawarehotel .com.

33 Battle Mountain

Best known as a leg of the famous Copper Triangle route, US 24 between Leadville and Minturn provides a mostly downhill run through one of the most beautiful places on the planet.

Start: Ice Palace Park at 11th Street and Harrison Avenue in Leadville

Length: 30.0 miles one way

Terrain: Mostly downhill with a few significant climbs

Traffic and hazards: The route follows a two-lane highway between Leadville and Minturn. Traffic is moderate but can be disconcertingly fast. Shoulder varies from wide to nonexistent on this very popular cycling road. Some tricky descending on the back side of Battle Mountain.

Things to see: Leadville, Tennessee Pass, Camp Hale, Battle Mountain, Eagle River Gorge, Minturn

Getting there: Toward the north end of Leadville, find Ice Palace Park at 11th Street and Harrison Avenue. (From the north, enter town on US 24 and take a right on 11th Street. The park and parking area are dead ahead 1 block. From the south, drive through Leadville on US 24, which becomes Harrison Avenue as it turns north. When the main route turns right, at 9th Street, continue straight on Harrison, over the hill. You'll find Ice Palace Park and the small parking area on the other side, at 11th and Harrison.) **GPS:** N 39 15'9.93" / W 106 17'36.47"

Ride Description

This is one of the state's more popular bike routes, and with good reason. The much-loved "Copper Triangle" route—from Copper Mountain to Leadville to Minturn and back to Copper, over two big passes and a few little ones—is possibly just an elaborate excuse to ride this incredible length of mountain highway. So let's just get right to it.

Most people know the road as "Tennessee Pass," but that doesn't make much sense after you ride the thing. Cyclists do climb up and over Tennessee on this route, but it's hardly the most prominent or memorable feature when the ride is headed northbound. Battle Mountain is a steeper, ruder, and more memorable climb, so I'll put its name on the marquee.

You won't believe the subalpine splendor along US 24 as you bomb downhill out of Leadville. The road settles into a dead straightaway for a while as it crosses the flats, but life is good as you cruise in a wide shoulder, gazing off toward Mount of the Holy Cross and other majestic peaks. A strong headwind is about the only thing that could spoil your mood.

Steadily, the road ramps uphill, almost imperceptibly at first. By mile 7 you know you're on a hill, and by mile 10 you've reached the top: Tennessee Pass. It's probably the most forgiving pass in Colorado. Tennessee Pass is especially mellow from the Leadville side, as the summit is only a little higher than Leadville itself. (Coming from

The road climbs above the Eagle River Gorge near Battle Mountain.

the other direction, Tennessee Pass is a lot longer and taller, much more challenging, but the slopes remain notably shallow.)

After coming down from Tennessee Pass, the road flattens for a few miles. At the beginning of World War II the Army decided this flat glacier-carved valley would be a good site for training soldiers to fight in snow-covered mountains. There were around 15,000 soldiers based at Camp Hale during the war, learning skills that would prove indispensable during the invasion of Italy. The remnants of the base, consisting of scars of roads and building foundations, fill the valley on the north side of the road.

Until 1965, when the base was finally dismantled in its entirety, the surrounding valleys were also used for training with all kinds of artillery and ordnance, including land mines and chemical weapons. Now a project is underway to clear the old training grounds of unexploded ordnance (UXO) and other hazardous materials. Users of the Colorado Trail, which crosses the highway close to here, go right through the most heavily affected area.

There is a lot of mystery hanging over this place. From 1959 to 1965, the CIA used Camp Hale to train Tibetan anti-Chinese rebels. The locals were told that the base was being used for atomic testing, and the perimeter was locked down and heavily patrolled. Trainees rode back and forth from the Denver airport in blacked-out buses. The secret training program is now openly acknowledged. Undoubtedly other interesting things that remain in the dark were taking place at Camp Hale.

Leaving Camp Hale behind, the road resumes a more raucous descent down the narrowing valley of Homestake Creek. The second hill begins in earnest by mile 22, when the road climbs up the side of the mountain to bypass the Eagle River gorge (with a connection to the tiny town of Red Cliff). This is Battle Mountain, literally and figuratively. Jens Voigt had a personal battle with this hill in 2013 during the US Pro Cycling Challenge, the crux of a terribly long and ultimately successful solo break.

This isn't a mere hill. On the other hand, it's not like climbing a pass. Sort of a mini pass. Expect serious pushback from the terrain—a very rude awakening after 12 miles of riding with gravity—but the summit arrives before pain reaches soul-crushing levels.

If you are planning on riding back to Leadville the same day, consider turning around when you get to the top of Battle Mountain. Descending to Minturn would be a huge commitment at this point. Climbing back up the other side of Battle Mountain from Minturn will double the difficulty of the ride, and climbing the long side of Tennessee Pass will triple it. In other words, it's twice as hard to ride from Minturn to Leadville as it is to ride from Leadville to Minturn, and a Leadville–Minturn–Leadville out-and-back would be at least three times harder than the one-way journey. Big day in the saddle! Starting from Minturn is also popular, either for a "quick" climb of Battle Mountain (1,250 feet over 5 miles) or a Battle Mountain–Tennessee Pass double scoop (about 3,000 feet of climbing one way).

Minturn, off the beaten path (aka I-70), is a nifty little corner of the world, a great place to start rides or end them. From Minturn, heaping mounds of civilization, with all the services you could possibly desire and then some, can be found just a few miles away along I-70. Access to Vail to the right or Eagle-Vail and Avon to the left is super easy, and it's mostly on bike paths.

Miles and Directions

0.0 Start from Ice Palace Park in Leadville at East 11th Street and Harrison Avenue, and make your way over to US 24 on 12th Street. (**Option:** Use the Mineral Belt Trail for a few blocks or take Harrison Avenue north and then cut over to US 24 by the Safeway.)

0.2 Carefully turn left onto US 24.

0.9 Turn left onto US 24 at the big intersection with CO 91.

9.7 Tennessee Pass summit, 10,440 feet.

22.2 Cross the Eagle River Gorge on a bridge, and pass a road (CR 709) that leads to Red Cliff down below.

23.8 Battle Mountain summit (9,228 feet).

30.0 Arrive in Minturn.

Bike Shops

Cycles of Life. 309 Harrison Ave. (US 24), Leadville; (719) 486-5533; cyclesoflifepb.com.

Mountain Pedaler. 161 Main St., Minturn; (970) 827-5522; mountainpedaler.com.

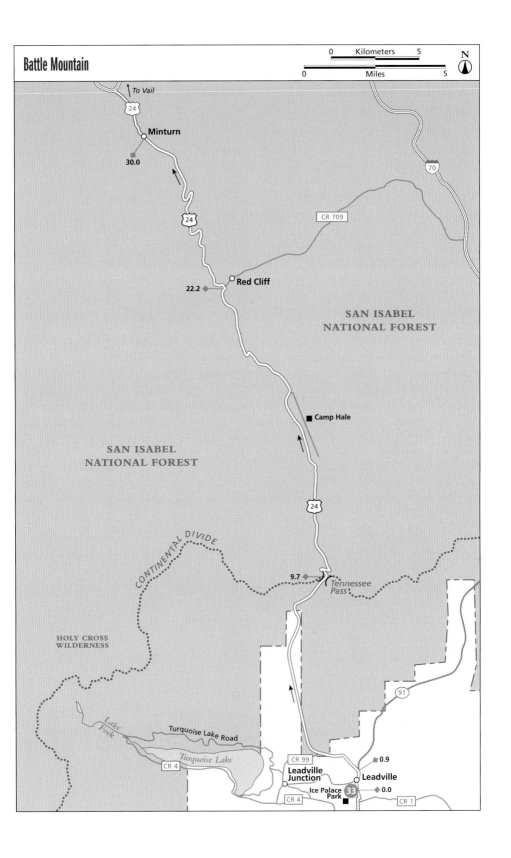

Battle Mountain

0 Kilometers 5
0 Miles 5

N

To Vail

24

Minturn

30.0

24

CR 709

70

22.2

Red Cliff

SAN ISABEL
NATIONAL FOREST

Camp Hale

SAN ISABEL
NATIONAL FOREST

CONTINENTAL DIVIDE

24

9.7

Tennessee
Pass

HOLY CROSS
WILDERNESS

91

Lake
Fork

Turquoise Lake Road

Turquoise Lake

CR 4

CR 99

0.9

Leadville
Junction

Leadville

Ice Palace
Park

33

0.0

CR 4

CR 1

Colorado Bike Service. 41149 US 6 and 24, Dowd Park Business Center, Avon; (970) 949-4641; coloradobikeservice.com.

Pedal Power. 40814 US 6, Avon; (970) 845-0931; pedalpowerbike.com.

Food

City on a Hill Coffee & Espresso. 508 Harrison Ave. (US 24) #3, Leadville; (719) 486-0797; cityonahillcoffee.com. Bakery and cafe, too.

High Mountain Pies. 115 W. 4th St., Leadville; (719) 486-5555. Pizza, good.

Manuelita's Restaurant. 311 Harrison Ave. (US 24), Leadville; (719) 486-0292. A Mexican place with an emphasis on *mariscos* (seafood), which is pretty strange in landlocked Leadville.

Quincy's Tavern. 416 Harrison Ave. (US 24), Leadville; (719) 486-9765; quincystavern .com.

Wild Bill's Hamburgers and Ice Cream. 200 Harrison Ave. (US 24), Leadville; (719) 486-0533. Don't expect too much and you'll be fine.

Minturn Country Club. 131 Main St., Minturn; (970) 827-4114; minturncountryclub.com. Steak house.

Sticky Fingers Cafe & Bakery. 132 Main St., Minturn; (970) 827-5353.

Turntable Restaurant & Motel. 160 Rail Road Ave., Minturn; (970) 827-4164; minturntable .com.

Lodging

Alert! Don't even try to find a place to sleep in or around Leadville within a week or so of the Leadville Trail 100 mountain bike race, in early to mid-August.

Alps Motel. 207 Elm St., Leadville; (719) 486-1223; alpsmotel.com.

Columbine Inn & Suites. 2019 N. Poplar St., Leadville; (719) 486-5650; columbineinn.com.

Delaware Hotel. 700 Harrison Ave. (US 24), Leadville; (719) 486-1418; delawarehotel .com.

Hotel Minturn. 167 Williams St., Minturn; (970) 331-5461; hotelminturn.com.

Minturn Inn. 442 Main St., Minturn; (970) 827-9647; minturninn.com. Bed-and-breakfast.

Turntable Restaurant & Motel. 160 Rail Road Ave., Minturn; (970) 827-4164; minturntable .com.

34 Vail Pass

This is a dreamy route along a fully separated bike path. Slopes are mostly moderate, with a few notable exceptions, but the hill is long and the air is thin.

Start: The start of the Vail Pass bike path southeast of Vail, just east of I-70.
Length: 13.2 miles one way
Terrain: Long climb and descent of Vail Pass. Pine forest, beaver ponds, and I-70.
Traffic and hazards: Other bicyclists! High speeds, sharp curves, and inexperienced riders keep you on your toes. High altitude and associated weather patterns. The route joins roads with motor traffic for a short distance around the top of the pass.
Things to see: Vail Pass, Copper Mountain

Getting there: From Denver, take I-70 west over Vail Pass toward Vail. Take exit 180 and go southeast on Bighorn Road until it crosses under I-70 and ends at a gate. There is parking here near the gate or at the nearby Gore Creek Trail trailhead. From Vail itself, take the I-70 frontage road southeast toward Vail Pass, then turn right onto Bighorn Road and follow Bighorn Road until it ends at the bike path's start. **Note:** If you want to start from Copper Mountain, the path is pretty easy to find from the west end of the resort. There is also some public parking nearby. **GPS:** N 39 37'32.98" / W 106 16'31.93"

Ride Description

As a one-way, out-and-back, or part of a larger ride or tour, the Vail Pass bike path (officially the Tenmile Canyon National Recreation Trail) is one of the must-do rides for recreational bikers in Colorado.

Spot the cyclist in this wooded section.

One of the best rides in the state

The route described here starts on the Vail side and rolls east to Copper Mountain. Most of the folks who start on the Vail side will turn around and ride back after they reach Copper Mountain. The climb is shorter but steeper on the Copper Mountain side. The Vail-to-Copper journey is a popular one-way ride as well as the last leg of a very popular route, the "Copper Triangle," a three-legger, three-passer ride that travels from Copper to Leadville to Vail and back to Copper. (For another leg of this 80-mile route, see the Battle Mountain ride.) The Copper Triangle is not only a traditional route but the name of a popular organized ride that follows the route every year, benefiting the Davis Phinney Foundation.

I encourage you to pedal Vail Pass from both sides, frequently. It's a great ride.

If you want to go into what passes for a town center in Vail, a prefab pop-up place created by developers about 50 years ago to extract money from rich people, know that the prime extraction zone is quite a way down the valley from the start of the path. To be fair, Vail is very nice, especially for those of us who like to ride various types of bicycles. It's easy to roll there, westbound, on good roads. If you start a pass climb from the town center, it takes more time and energy than most realize.

I like to start this eastbounder up-valley at the start of the path, cutting out all the road mileage from Vail. There is good parking where the path begins, and it still leaves all the real climbing. But you could certainly park in one of Vail's massive public parking bunkers and ride from there, adding several miles of gentle terrain. Also, in East Vail, about midway between Vail and the start of the bike path, just off the freeway exit (exit 180), there is a public parking area with a little grocery store nearby. That's a good place to start, too.

Vail Pass

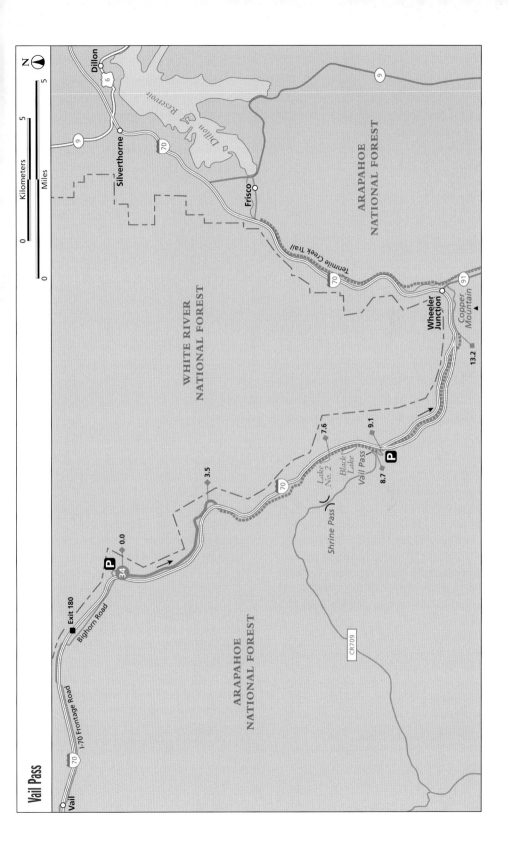

The path is not without hazards. There are some notoriously tight turns, especially on the east side. Couple that with a thriving tourist shuttle business—hordes of rather inexperienced but enthusiastic bicyclists pay to zing down to Vail from the top of the pass on rented bikes—and problems can arise. Head up! Eyes forward! Calm body! Okay, that is all.

Other than a few forays up to the highway, where the path is like a sidewalk next to I-70 for a few minutes at a time, this is a beautiful ride. The path glides along next to beaver ponds and into dark stands of spruce and fir. You could momentarily forget the freeway exists even when it's directly overhead, suspended between massive concrete pylons.

Miles and Directions

0.0 Start riding up the Vail Pass bike path from the Vail side. The mileage cues begin from the gate at the end of Bighorn Road.

3.5 Veer right onto the bike path, descend, and cross under I-70.

3.9 The path runs adjacent to the highway for the next 1.5 miles.

7.6 Continue straight as the path joins a road near Black Lake and Black Lake Number 2.

8.7 Carefully cross the road and continue straight, descending to the lower parking lot at the Shrine Pass rest area. Top of the climb.

9.1 Turn right onto the path and continue the descent.

13.2 The path pops out onto Copper Road at Copper Mountain Resort.

Bike Shops

Bike Valet. 520 E. Lionshead Circle, Vail; (970) 476-5385; bikevalet.net. A bike rental/shuttle operation with no apparent repair service.

Pedal Power. 40814 US 6, Eagle-Vail; (970) 845-0931; pedalpowerbike.com.

Mountain Pedaler. 161 Main St., Minturn; (970) 827-5522; mountainpedaler.com.

Gravitee. 0164 Copper Rd., Tucker Lodge, Copper Mountain; (970) 968-0171; gravitee.com. Another ski/board shop that rents bikes in the summer.

Rebel Sports Rentals. 214 Ten Mile Circle, Copper Mountain; (970) 968-2408; rebel sportsrentals.com/bicycle-rentals. Rents bikes and runs a shuttle to the top of Vail Pass. Call or go online to make reservations.

Food

Joe's Famous Deli & Homemade Ice Cream. 288 Bridge St., Vail; (970) 479-7580; joes famousdeli.com.

Sim's Market. 3971 Big Horn Rd., Vail; (970) 476-6301. Nicely placed grocery store.

Endo's Adrenaline Cafe. 209 Ten Mile Circle, Copper Mountain; (970) 968-3070.

Lodging

If you can afford to stay in Vail, I tip my top hat to you. Consider staying in Frisco, Avon, or even Minturn for far more down-to-earth pricing.

Antlers at Vail. 680 Lionshead Place, Vail; (970) 476-2471; antlersvail.com. I can't believe how expensive this place is. Even on a guidebook writer's salary, it's quite extravagant.

Copper Mountain Lodging. 760 Copper Rd., Copper Mountain. (970) 968-6840; copper vacations.com. Broker of various vacation rentals.

OTHER EAGLE RIVER VALLEY RIDES

Beaver Creek Ups. From the Eagle River path or US 6 in Avon, launch yourself up to the Beaver Creek resort area. Steep stuff, great views. Try to stay off the private roads snaking up through the empty mansions (even though that's the only way to make a paved loop out of it) or you might get chased by a security guard. There are also loop opportunities on the other side of the valley and interstate.

You're a security threat at Beaver Creek.

US 6. It's a highway, but the traffic isn't horrible, since most of it is next door on I-70. You can use US 6 to ride all the way from Vail to the Glenwood Canyon path. Lots of development, Wal-Marts, and such, taking over what used to be bucolic riverside scenery.

Eagle River

35 Tenmile Canyon

A moderately sloped and scenic bike-path ride in Summit County. Though I-70 is never far away, the mountain scenery dominates this up-and-back cruise between Frisco and Copper Mountain.

Start: Frisco, at the Tenmile Creek trailhead on the extreme southwest corner of town
Length: 12.0 miles out-and-back
Terrain: Steady climbing and descending on moderate slopes next to Tenmile Creek

Traffic and hazards: Other riders are the only traffic on this route. The biggest hazard could be weather.
Things to see: Tenmile Canyon, Copper Mountain

Getting there: From Denver, take I-70 west to exit 201, the farther west of two exits near Frisco. Exit the highway and start driving south toward Frisco, but take the first right-hand turn into the Tenmile Creek trailhead parking lot. **GPS:** N 39 34'29.36" / W 106 6'39.35"

Ride Description

Connecting the condo-encrusted enclaves of Frisco and Copper Mountain in the nicest possible way, the Tenmile Canyon National Recreation Trail offers bicyclists a pleasant cruise with moderate climbing.

While the scenery is wondrously subalpine, the path shares the tight canyon with two large and noisy rivers—I-70 and Tenmile Creek. The annoying crackles of your

Surrounded by big ranges on the way to Copper Mountain

A civilized mountain ride

poorly maintained machine will be drowned out by the constant *haaaaaaaaahhhhhh* of cars and semis rolling by just on the other side of the creek.

Make no mistake! (Don't you love it when people say that? I know I do.) This Frisco-to-Copper ride contains about 4 miles of steady climbing. That's enough for most of us. It is not a flat ride. On the other hand, it never gets too steep, maxing out at about 5 or 6 percent. It's just enough of a hill that you won't have to pedal too much after turning around and pointing yourself back toward Frisco.

You'll notice that the path continues up the canyon beyond the Copper Mountain junction. It's been rumored and alleged that the path will be extended all the way over Fremont Pass to Leadville. It hadn't happened yet when I was writing this, but if you're interested and hungry for a bigger challenge, check the current status on that. I've never been a fan of riding on CO 91 out of Copper, so if that dream comes true, I'll be eager to ride it.

Tenmile Canyon is also a natural runway to a Vail Pass excursion. The famous Vail Pass path begins right there on the west side of the Copper Mountain resort, and the top of the pass is only about 5 or 6 miles beyond that. Not that it's easy or anything, but it really doesn't take too long to get up there from Copper. Those wanting a little more saddle time can launch an attack on the pass from Frisco, Dillon, Keystone, or Breckenridge and cruise bike paths almost the entire way.

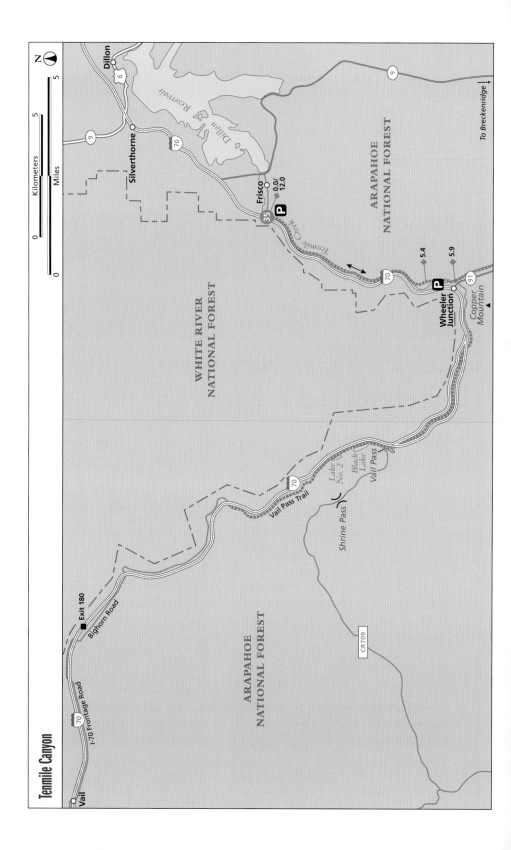

Tenmile Canyon

This path lends itself to various forms of family biking and casual cruising. However, bring plenty of outerwear and thermal goodies if there is any possibility that the weather will turn sour. Getting caught in the rain without gear in the mountains isn't like getting caught in the rain at low elevations. It's potentially dangerous and almost always extremely uncomfortable.

Miles and Directions

0.0 Start from the Tenmile Creek trailhead in Frisco and begin riding up the bike path toward Copper Mountain.

5.4 The path forks. The right fork goes to a trailhead parking area. Go left to continue to the end of the path.

5.9 The path forks again. The left fork continues beside CO 91 (under construction in 2015); the right fork ends shortly at CO 91. Turn around here, visit Copper Mountain, or continue up the path to see how far it goes up Fremont Pass. Then let me know.

12.0 Back at the Tenmile Creek Trailhead.

Bike Shops

Bike Doctor. 32 Lookup Ln., Frisco; (970) 389-7391.
Podium Sports. 720 Main St., Frisco; (970) 668-9996; podiumsportsgroup.com.

Food

Butterhorn Bakery & Cafe. 408 Main St., Frisco; (970) 668-3997; butterhornbakery .com. Breakfast and lunch.
Deli Belly's. 275 Main St., Frisco; (970) 668-9255; delibellys.com. Pastrami.
Himalayan Cuisine. 409 E. Main St., Frisco; (970) 668-3330; himalayancuisinefrisco.com.

Peppino's Pizza and Subs. 610 Main St., Frisco; (970) 668-5128; peppinosfrisco.com.

Lodging

Frisco Lodge. 321 Main St., Frisco; (800) 279-6000; friscolodge.com.
Snowshoe Motel. 521 Main St., Frisco; (970) 668-3444; snowshoemotel.com.

36 Montezuma Road

Rising out of Keystone, Montezuma Road is a moderate climb off the beaten path. Get sweaty, visit a tiny mountain town, then return through the fake bike paths and cul-de-sacs of Keystone.

Start: Parking area on east side of Lake Dillon (aka Dillon Reservoir), near the intersection of US 6 and Swan Mountain Road.
Length: 18.8 miles out-and-back
Terrain: Montezuma Road rises 900 feet in 4.6 miles. The rest of the ride is mostly flat, with short little hills here and there.
Traffic and hazards: Narrow, curvy, cracked bike paths with plenty of foot, paw, and bike traffic. The paths go through a heavily populated tourist resort before the route hits Montezuma Road. Montezuma Road has moderate traffic and seems to have adequate width for safe riding. You'll find some fairly steep descending with sharp curves on Montezuma Road.
Things to see: Lake Dillon, Tenmile Range, Snake River, Keystone Resort, Montezuma

Getting there: From Denver, go west on I-70 and then head south at Silverthorne (exit 205) onto US 6. Go past Dillon and Lake Dillon, then turn right onto Swan Mountain Road. Turn right into the parking area by Lake Dillon. **GPS:** N 39 36'10.21" / W 106 0'40.60"

Ride Description

For those craving a little extra ouch with their Summit County weekend, Montezuma Road is perfectly situated, tucked away on the far side of Keystone in the

Montezuma is a tiny, fiercely quirky community.

Montezuma Road

Snake River Canyon. It works as a nice extension to a Summit County bike-path adventure (see Lake Dillon Loop ride) or stands alone as a relatively quick but satisfying climb. If you're looking for something to do but don't have much time, consider visiting Montezuma.

Starting from the parking area on Swan Mountain Road by Lake Dillon adds mileage and some pizzazz, and maybe a little annoyance, to the route. The Keystone bike-path network is strangely and inconsistently routed and is a bit antiquated, in general. It is not built for fast cycling, or getting from here to there efficiently. There are even some dismount zones through there.

Don't be too alarmed if you get lost navigating through the deliberately serpentine Keystone. Just keep moving up the valley without straying too far up a mountain and you'll find Montezuma Road. The route described below is just one of several possibilities. If finding the route is getting you down, or you don't have time for this garbage, simply ride US 6 to the turnoff, as straightforward as can be. There is also some parking on the side of Montezuma Road itself if you want to eliminate the preliminaries.

Montezuma Road is a fairly popular bike ride and hosts moderate car and truck traffic, but it still has a lonely feel to it. The road is almost flat and straight as it leaves the Keystone development due east, then it grows into a moderate 5-mile climb, angling southeast and getting steeper and twistier toward the top, around the bridge.

Speaking of the bridge, you may notice how fresh and new it looks when you're riding over it, about 8.6 miles up from the bottom. That's because the old one was blasted downstream by a flash flood in 2013. (Seems like most of the bridges in Colorado were destroyed by angry rivers in 2013.) Without the bridge for about a year, Montezuma residents had to hike a half hour just to reach a passable road, leaving their town nicely cut off from the hustle and bustle in the valley below. This, of course, was like a dream come true for many of them.

Imagine Ward without a general store. That's Montezuma. You won't find much in the way of services, food, or water up here. But the people are friendly and helpful if you need assistance.

That's it for the pavement. There are good gravel-grinding opportunities out of town, straight up the valley or up the mountain on your right, but they're the kind of routes that end up on chunky four-wheel-drive roads. Anything above Montezuma belongs to the mountain goats and mountain bikes.

Miles and Directions

0.0 Start from the parking lot on the shore of Lake Dillon (aka Dillon Reservoir) near the intersection of US 6 and Swan Mountain Road, and begin riding up the bike path that leads toward US 6.

0.1 Continue straight past the first path intersection, then turn right and begin riding south up the path next to US 6.

0.3 Cross Swan Mountain Road.

0.5 Continue straight past a path intersection on the right.

0.7 Cross a road.

1.4 Continue on the path past more path intersections.

2.3 Cross East Keystone Road and continue on path. (**Option:** Turn right here onto East Keystone Road, or the path next to it, and rejoin the route at mile 3.1 below.)

2.5 Continue past Keystone Lake.

2.7 Veer right and continue on bike path on the other side of the lake.

2.8 The path joins Decatur Hill Road.

3.0 Decatur Hill curves sharply to the right.

3.1 Turn left onto East Keystone Road.

3.3 Continue straight through the "village" on the other side of the big parking lot. You may have to walk your bike through sections like this.

3.4 Continue around the left side of another bike parking lot and continue on East Keystone Road.

3.9 Turn right onto River Run Road.

4.2 Turn right and head toward the lift, then continue east on the path.

4.5 Turn left onto West Independence Road, or the path next to it.

4.6 Turn right onto Montezuma Road (CR 5).

Montezuma Road

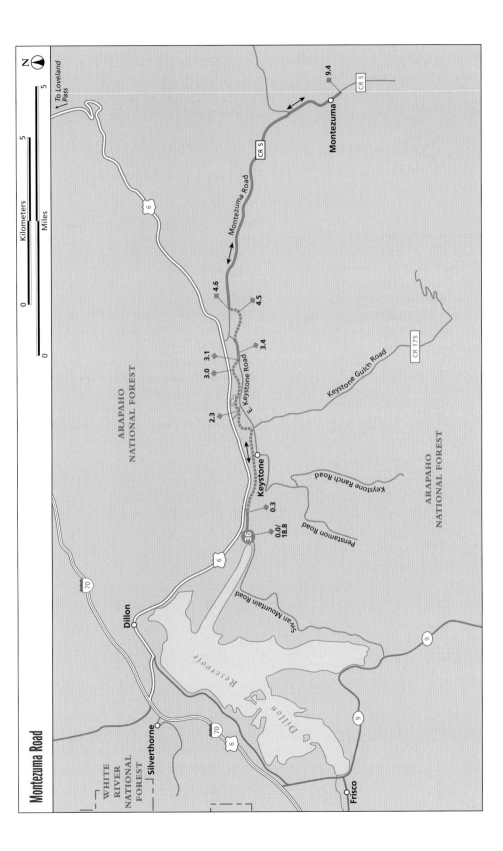

9.4 Arrive in Montezuma. Turn around and retrace your tire tracks.

18.8 Back at Lake Dillon.

Bike Shops

Bike Doctor. 32 Lookup Ln., Frisco; (970) 389-7391.

Podium Sports. 720 Main St., Frisco; (970) 668-9996; podiumsportsgroup.com.

Keystone Sports. 129 River Run Rd., River Run Village, Keystone; (970) 496-4619; keystone sport.com.

Mountain Sports Outlet. 167 Meraly Way, Silverthorne; (970) 262-2836; mountainsports outlet.com. Not exactly a bike shop but may have what you need.

Pioneer Sports. 560 Silverthorne Ln., Silver-thorne; (970) 668-3668; pioneersportscolorado .com. Not really a bike shop but might have what you're looking for.

Food

Butterhorn Bakery & Cafe. 408 Main St., Frisco; (970) 668-3997; butterhornbakery .com. Breakfast and lunch.

Deli Belly's. 275 Main St., Frisco; (970) 668-9255; delibellys.com. Pastrami.

Himalayan Cuisine. 409 E. Main St., Frisco; (970) 668-3330; himalayancuisinefrisco.com.

Peppino's Pizza and Subs. 610 Main St., Frisco; (970) 668-5128; peppinosfrisco.com.

Dos Locos Mexican Restaurant & Cantina. 22869 US 6, Keystone; (970) 262-9185; doslocoskeystone.com. I have not eaten here, but the thought of it doesn't scare me too much.

Pizza 101. 23024 US 6, Keystone; (970) 262-0200; pizza101.biz.

Lodging

Snowshoe Motel. 521 Main St., Frisco; (970) 668-3444; snowshoemotel.com.

Frisco Lodge. 321 Main St., Frisco; (800) 279-6000; friscolodge.com.

Alpine Slopes Lodge. 22859 US 6, Keystone; (970) 513-9009; alpineslopeslodge.com.

Ski Tip Lodge. 764 Montezuma Rd., Keystone; (800) 354-4386; keystoneresort.com/dining detail/Key+-+The+Ski+Tip+Lodge.axd. B&B with fancy dining.

37 Lake Dillon Loop

A memorable and gorgeous path and road loop around Lake Dillon (aka Dillon Reservoir), with one tough climb on Swan Mountain Road.

Start: Parking area on east side of Lake Dillon, near the intersection of US 6 and Swan Mountain Road. (**Note:** There are several potential starting points to this loop, for instance the Frisco marina, or the south end of Swan Mountain Road, where there is a small parking area.)
Length: 18.8 miles
Terrain: Flat on the west side of Lake Dillon, fairly big climb on the east

Traffic and hazards: Popular bike path with associated hazards. Path spills out onto or crosses roads periodically. The route then follows the shoulder/bike lane of Swan Mountain Road, with moderate to heavy motor traffic.
Things to see: Lake Dillon, Dillon marina, Frisco, Tenmile Range, Gore Range

Getting there: From Denver, go west on I-70 and then head south at Silverthorne (exit 205) onto US 6. Go past Dillon and Lake Dillon, then turn right onto Swan Mountain Road. Turn right into the parking area by Lake Dillon. **GPS:** N 39 36'10.21" / W 106 0'40.60"

Ride Description

My wife Christie insists this is an easy ride, but she's like that. I can't agree with her here. This loop contains a 500-foot climb, so in my opinion that takes it out of the

The flat side of the loop

Dillon Reservoir (aka Lake Dillon) is fed by several rivers.

easy category. The climb itself, on Swan Mountain Road, is actually tougher than "moderate." It's like a mini mountain pass over there.

Easygoing types who seek to avoid painful exertion will want to stay away from the eastern portion of the loop, up on the mountain. But almost all of the mileage between Dillon and Frisco is completely flat.

The loop around the lake is not as tidy as we'd like. There are some silly and potentially dangerous features, like contraflow bike lanes next to high-speed traffic on Dillon Dam Road, and big concrete-and-steel bollards that would not be fun to encounter, suddenly, in the dark. There are many tourists, absolute novices, and kids on the path—which is fantastic!—but it makes things a little . . . interesting.

There is also a fair amount of misdirection along the way. Lack of adequate signage. Confusing inlets and peninsulas on the lake, confusing layouts of the paths themselves. Forays onto streets and across a few. It is the kind of route, however, that you'll be able to follow without much trouble the second time.

Now for the good stuff. What a beautiful ride! There are some truly spectacular sections along the way. The hulking Gore and Tenmile Ranges dominate the skyline, above pine- and aspen-covered slopes. Throw in the glistening lake, man-made though it may be, and you've got top-shelf vistas.

I've got you rolling counterclockwise around the lake, but clockwise also works. Swan Mountain Road, which comprises most of the on-road portion of the route, has a little bike lane if you're climbing it, but the downhill lane doesn't have any extra space. It's an interesting trade-off. The clockwise climb on the path up the other side of Swan Mountain Road is an interesting and quite tough start to the loop.

Git some!

Counterclockwise, the smooth, relentlessly winding descent makes a fun finale to this unique and beautiful ride. Try it both directions.

Miles and Directions

0.0 Start from the trailhead parking area and begin riding east out of the parking area on the bike path.

0.1 Continue straight past the path intersection (you'll be coming back that way later), and then hang a left onto the path next to US 6.

0.4 Cross a road and continue.

0.8 Cross another road and continue.

1.4 Cross the Roberts Tunnel Access Road.

2.6 The path spills out onto Tenderfoot Street and follows it.

2.9 Turn left onto Gold Run Circle. (The path runs along the road.)

3.0 Turn left onto the bike path.

3.4 The path spills out onto another street (West Lodgepole Street). Take an immediate left onto Marina Drive, then find the path continuing westbound on the other side of the parking lot.

3.9 Continue westbound past a few more path intersections, and you should be just about on the dam.

5.2 The path becomes part of Dillon Dam Road.

5.8 The path heads off into the woods by the lake. Ignore all the intersections with little paths leading off to picnic areas and benches.

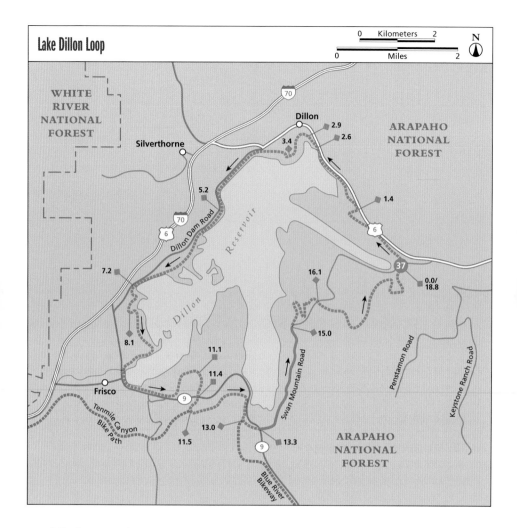

0   Kilometers   2

0   Miles   2

N

WHITE RIVER NATIONAL FOREST

Dillon

ARAPAHO NATIONAL FOREST

Silverthorne

2.9

2.6

3.4

5.2

1.4

70

6

Dillon Dam Road

Reservoir

7.2

6

16.1

37

0.0/ 18.8

8.1

Dillon

15.0

11.1

11.4

Frisco

Swan Mountain Road

Penstamon Road

Keystone Ranch Road

Tenmile Canyon Bike Path

9

13.0

11.5

13.3

9

Blue River Bikeway

ARAPAHO NATIONAL FOREST

6.6 Cross a road.

6.9 Continue straight past a path intersection, then cross a small road.

7.2 The path joins Dillon Dam Road again, briefly.

7.9 Take a sharp left onto the boardwalk.

8.1 Take a left at the T intersection. If your sense-of-direction alarm is going off, you're right. Fear not: The path will make a big right-hand curve and resume cruising south.

9.4 The path comes up to the side path by CO 9 in Frisco. Take a left (south).

9.6 The path turns left away from CO 9.

9.7 Cross Marina Road amid a jumble of parking lots. The path goes through a few right-angle turns, then goes back up next to CO 9 for a while.

10.3 Cross Water Dance Drive.

10.8 Cross a parking lot entrance/exit.

11.1 Cross Peninsula Road.

11.3 Cross another road.

11.4 The path arrives at the intersection of Recreation Way and CO 9. Cross CO 9. The path continues by the road on the other side of CO 9.

11.5 Turn left onto the Blue River Bikeway (the Frisco–Breckenridge path).

11.6 Take a left at the fork.

13.0 Take a left onto another path, headed toward the highway.

13.3 The path arrives at the intersection of Swan Mountain Road and CO 9. Cross CO 9, eastbound this time, and head east on Swan Mountain Road.

15.0 Carefully cross the road and join the bike path on the other side. That's the high point there.

15.2 Be very alert here as the path goes through a busy tourist parking area.

16.1 Cross Swan Mountain Road.

17.8 Continue on the path as you enter suburbia.

18.5 The path joins Cove Boulevard briefly.

18.7 Cross Swan Mountain Road.

18.8 Turn left and end the loop at the parking area.

Bike Shops

Bike Doctor. 32 Lookup Ln., Frisco; (970) 389-7391.

Podium Sports. 720 Main St., Frisco; (970) 668-9996; www.podiumsportsgroup.com.

Keystone Sports. 129 River Run Rd., River Run Village, Keystone; (970) 496-4619; keystonesport.com.

Mountain Sports Outlet. 167 Meraly Way, Silverthorne; (970) 262-2836; mountainsportsoutlet.com. Not exactly a bike shop but may have what you need.

Pioneer Sports. 560 Silverthorne Ln., Silverthorne; (970) 668-3668; pioneersportscolorado.com. One of those Summit County sporting goods stores that offers limited bike service and sales.

Food

Butterhorn Bakery & Cafe. 408 Main St., Frisco; (970) 668-3997; butterhornbakery.com. Breakfast and lunch.

Deli Belly's. 275 Main St., Frisco; (970) 668-9255; delibellys.com. Pastrami.

Himalayan Cuisine. 409 E. Main St., Frisco; (970) 668-3330. himalayancuisinefrisco.com.

Peppino's Pizza and Subs. 610 Main St., Frisco; (970) 668-5128; peppinosfrisco.com.

Dos Locos Mexican Restaurant & Cantina. 22869 US 6, Keystone; (970) 262-9185; doslocoskeystone.com. I have not eaten here, but the thought of it doesn't scare me too much.

Pizza 101. 23024 US 6, Keystone; (970) 262-0200; pizza101.biz.

Lodging

Frisco Lodge. 321 Main St., Frisco; (800) 279-6000; friscolodge.com.

Snowshoe Motel. 521 Main St., Frisco; (970) 668-3444; snowshoemotel.com.

MORE SUMMIT COUNTY RIDES

Blue River Bike Path. The path between Breckenridge and Frisco gets pretty crowded sometimes, but with good reason. It's a great path, providing far more happy riding than the adjacent highway. It's also relatively flat compared to just about any other bike route in the vicinity. Flatlanders take note, however: There are some real climbs toward the end of the 11-mile Breck–Frisco trip, and the Frisco–Breck up-valley ride is a notoriously painful false flat. But this is the best route in the area for families and beginners who want to ride on pavement. The path leads directly to the Tenmile Canyon path and, by extension, Vail Pass and the Fremont Pass trail that was under construction in 2015; with a road crossing or two, the Blue River Bikeway also connects to the Frisco path system and the path around Lake Dillon.

Boreas Pass. One of the sweetest rides in the state, this wide dirt road following an old rail route would be included in the book as a full chapter if there weren't already plenty of gravel rides featured. If you're staying in or near Breckenridge, this is an incredibly well-placed route, rising directly from the south side of town: the last stoplight, Boreas Pass Road (CR 10). The climb starts on pavement, rising on huge round turns as it makes its way up through the residences on the mountain across the valley from the ski area. The pass summit is pretty subdued at around 11,500 feet, strewn with wreckage of the old railroad and support buildings. There are some opportunities for adventurous gravel grinders to loop back to the Blue River from the other side of Boreas Pass, but don't bite off more than you can chew. You can make various smaller loops on the Breckenridge side using Boreas Pass Road and the steep residential roads that cover most of the hillside—roads that could provide a day's workout all by themselves.

Hoosier Pass. The continuation of CO 9 up the Blue River Valley leads to Hoosier Pass. It's a tough climb and a pretty road, popping up all the time in races and tours, but Hoosier could not be called a perennial favorite of Colorado roadies. It's probably the traffic that keeps riders away from this one. Not that there are that many vehicles on the road, but the shoulder is not big, and speeds are high as the road makes a long run up the valley. Still, if you're into collecting passes, you'll want to give Hoosier a try.

Loveland Pass. Use the same lakeside parking area described in the Lake Dillon Loop ride to launch an attack on Loveland Pass. US 6 rises steadily past Arapahoe Basin ski area, then tops a 12,000-foot saddle, about 3,000 feet above Dillon Reservoir. After dropping down the other side past the Loveland ski area, you can find a bike path rolling down the valley. Using a combo of bike path in the woods and frontage road, you can get down to Bakerville, Silver Plume, Georgetown, and beyond. Since the opening of the Eisenhower Tunnel in the 1970s, the only motorists crossing Loveland Pass are truck drivers, occasional sightseers, and goofballs, so it has a unique feel.

38 Guanella Pass

Guanella Pass is among the toughest climbs in the state. Starting from a quaint Victorian town and reaching to alpine meadows, this route is a true test for those who think they can go uphill on a bike.

Start: Georgetown
Length: 21.2 miles up-and-back
Terrain: A high, steep mountain pass
Traffic and hazards: Moderate traffic on Guanella Pass Road (CR 381). The summit may be very crowded with car traffic, but usually it's lighter on weekdays. Negotiating the long descent comes with the usual hazards, almost all of which can be thwarted by keeping your head up and eyes open. This is a high-altitude ride with potentially hazardous weather complications. Bring thermal and waterproof layers, including hat and gloves, if there is any chance of precipitation. Altitude sickness could be a problem for some riders.
Things to see: Georgetown, Guanella Pass, Mount Bierstadt, Mount Evans

Getting there: From Denver, head west on I-70 to Georgetown (exit 228). Go east on 15th Street for a few blocks and turn right onto Rose Street. Take Rose Street into the town center and park somewhere on the street. The mileage cues begin at the corner of 2nd Street and Rose Street; 2nd Street becomes Guanella Pass Road (CR 381). **GPS:** N 39 42'13.62" / W 105 41'52.58"

Ride Description

First of all, let's just acknowledge that the name of this pass sounds like a venereal disease of some sort. With that out of the way, we can discuss the origin of the name.

Georgetown has its roots in the early days of the gold rush, when prospectors swarmed into the mountains, claiming tracts and digging them up. In the April 4, 1861, issue of the *Rocky Mountain News*, there was a progress report on the budding settlement: "Georgetown at present has only the small number of 40 permanent residents—35 of whom, however, have come in since the 24th of January—who are very much in need of more convenient facilities for doing their trading, and an enterprising man could do well here now with a small stock of assorted goods."

Thomas Guanella was just such a man, although he didn't arrive in Georgetown until 1871. Guanella ran a bakery and general store in town with members of his extended family through the 1870s. Monti & Guanella's store sold maple sugar, fresh butter by the pound, pickled pork, canned and salt fish of every variety, Harkness patent wax candles, glassware, gunpowder, bar lead, buckshot, blasting caps . . . "Anything you want—cheap for cash," was the motto.

Thomas Guanella was enterprising beyond merely selling goods in town. Like many other entrepreneurs-slash-civic leaders of that era, Guanella involved himself in multiple road-building efforts. These ventures were viewed as universally beneficial for the public as well as private business, and the road builders were expected

Guanella Pass hurt Christie, which makes it an HC-rated climb.

to enrich themselves in the process. Today, with Georgetown situated right on the mainline artery (I-70), it can be difficult to imagine how isolated the town used to be. When the residents of Georgetown, tucked away in their valley, craved more roads linking them to other communities, Thomas Guanella helped make it happen. Wagon routes over Berthoud Pass, Loveland Pass, and Guanella Pass were carved in the nineteenth century.

But strangely enough, Guanella Pass is not named for him. It is named, supposedly, for his grandson Byron, who was a Clear Creek County commissioner. In his office Byron Guanella pushed to build a more formal road over the pass, and when those efforts were realized in 1951, the pass was named in his honor. But the pass may have been called Guanella since before he was born. We're not quite sure.

The climb begins in earnest right out of Georgetown. You can see it zigzagging up the mountain from just about anywhere in town. After the initial switchbacking climb, there is a respite for a few miles, some flat stuff and rolling terrain as the road chugs past a series of lakes and reservoirs and a small hydroelectric power plant. Then it's a serious grunt all the way to the top at 11,654 feet above sea level, with plenty of pitches at 10 percent or more.

The summit of the pass is a saddle between the 14,000-foot peaks of Mounts Bierstadt and Evans on the east and thirteeners Squaretop Mountain, Argentine Peak, and Mount Wilcox to the west. The Mount Bierstadt trailhead is here, too; the trail

Guanella Pass summit is also the Mount Bierstadt trailhead.

saunters off across the boggy hinterlands on a series of wooden boardwalks. Bierstadt is one of the easiest and most popular of the fourteener climbs, and the trailhead accounts for much of the car traffic up here.

Not long ago the summit was a much lonelier place, with a potholed dirt parking area. Guanella Pass Road (CR 381) itself has been paved for only a few years; it used to be dirt above the power plant. The current chip-seal surface could hardly be described as smooth, but it also won't turn to mud in wet weather. Paving the road made things a little easier, but somewhat less adventurous, for everybody, cyclists included.

Drop back into Georgetown for a world-class leg-crunching up-and-back, or use Guanella Pass as part of a larger tour. On the other side, the road drops into Grant, with minimal services, on the South Platte at the base of Kenosha Pass. The imminently rideable Kenosha Pass (US 285) is the gateway to South Park. I don't like the idea of riding US 285 between Kenosha Pass and Fairplay—lots of riders do it and live to tell the tale, I just won't be one of them—but if you can get as far as Como, you can take a right and climb over Boreas Pass (dirt) into Breckenridge, and from there return to Georgetown via Loveland Pass.

Altitude alert: Anytime you pedal up this high, be aware of the possibility of becoming sick due to the lack of air pressure. Symptoms of mild altitude sickness can be a lot like the normal discomfort that comes from riding bikes up big hills. Serious

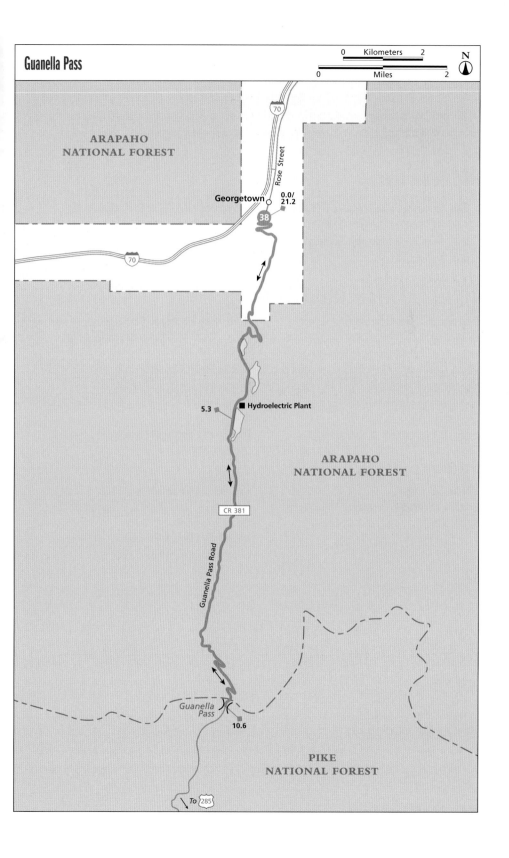

Guanella Pass

0   Kilometers   2

0   Miles   2

N

ARAPAHO
NATIONAL FOREST

Rose Street

70

Georgetown   0.0/
21.2

38

5.3 ■ Hydroelectric Plant

ARAPAHO
NATIONAL FOREST

CR 381

Guanella Pass Road

Guanella
Pass

10.6

PIKE
NATIONAL FOREST

To 285

altitude sickness causes nausea, headaches, disorientation, and, in extreme cases, death. You're very unlikely to die, but if you start to feel sick, the best course of action is to drink plenty of water and roll back down the hill. Getting to lower altitudes cures it. If you're a flatlander who feels the effects of altitude sickness at the bottom of the mountain, or even in Denver, you probably shouldn't attempt a ride like this. Give it a few days and see if you start to adapt.

Miles and Directions

0.0 Starting your odometer or GPS at the corner of 2nd Street and Rose Street, begin riding up Guanella Pass Road (CR 381).

5.3 Pass the hydroelectric power plant.

10.6 Top of the pass.

21.2 Back in Georgetown.

Attractions

Georgetown Loop Railroad. 507 Taos St., Georgetown; (303) 569-2030; georgetown looprr.com. This railroad runs between Silver Plume and Georgetown, looping over itself on high trestles. A must-do for railroad nuts.

Hamill House Museum. 305 Argentine St., Georgetown; (303) 569-2840.

Hotel de Paris Museum. 409 6th Ave., Georgetown; (303) 569-2311; hoteldeparis museum.org.

Bike Shops

Black Diamond Ski & Cycles. 1540 Argentine St., Georgetown; (303) 569-2283.

Food

Dusty Rose Tea Room. 614 Rose St., Georgetown; (303) 569-3100; dustyrosetearoom .com.

Ed's Eighteen Fifty Nine Cafe. 410 6th St., Georgetown; (303) 569-5042.

Happy Cooker. 412 6th St., Georgetown; (303) 569-3166.

Troia's Cafe and Marketplace. 511 Rose St., Georgetown; (303) 569-5014.

Lodging

Georgetown Mountain Inn. 1100 Rose St., Georgetown; (303) 569-3201; georgetown mountaininn.com.

Rose Street Bed & Breakfast. 200 Rose St., Georgetown; (303) 569-2222.

39 Ute Pass

An obscure gem not too far from I-70, Ute Pass is moderately sloped and the perfect observation post from which to gaze upon the intense Gore Range. This quick pass climb works for fitness freaks, cycle-tourists, and afternoon ramblers.

Start: Near the intersection of CO 9 and Ute Pass Road, about 13 miles north of Silverthorne
Length: 10.6 miles out-and-back
Terrain: Moderate but relentless slopes, climbing from the dry, sage-spotted ranchlands to the aspen- and fir-covered mountains.

Wide-open views of the Gore Range across the Blue River Valley.
Traffic and hazards: Traffic is relatively light, but this is a high-speed road with a small shoulder and lots of curves.
Things to see: Ute Pass and the panoramic Gore Range

Getting there: From Denver, take I-70 west to Silverthorne, then turn north on CO 9 (exit 205). Go about 13 miles—if you get to Green Mountain Reservoir, you've gone too far—and find Ute Pass Road on the right. There is a small dirt parking area at the intersection. **GPS:** N 39 47'7.38" / W 106 9'22.23"

Ride Description

Don't confuse this Ute Pass with the better-known Ute Pass that climbs west out of Colorado Springs. There is a third Ute Pass near Durango, and probably several

Storms cross the valley in about 45 seconds.

Ute Pass Road and the Gore Range

others. Like the Ute Pass near Pikes Peak, this one connecting Middle Park and the Blue River was a real Ute trail for a long time prior to the appearance of ranches and fences in the area. Well into the twentieth century, it was known as Big Ute Pass and consisted only of undefined trail and a 6-foot rock cairn near the summit.

In 1866 the world-traveling author Bayard Taylor visited Colorado and toured a large swath of land, including Ute Pass. Here is Taylor's description of topping the pass on horseback from the other side, written just a day or two after the fact and eventually published in a book called *Colorado: A Summer Trip*:

> *Here and there on the trail we could detect the marks of lodge-poles, which, we sup-posed, were made by the Utes in passing from Blue to Grand River [Colorado River]. As this was our only guidance through the unknown portion of the Park, we followed it, although its general direction seemed too much east of south. The mountain range in front was apparently a spur thrust out from the south into the very heart of the Park, and we must cross it in order to reach the Valley of Blue River. The government maps were of no assistance—they omitted the mountains, and inserted streams which have no existence. . . .*
>
> *This part of the Pass was so beautiful, that we reached the summit—much sooner than we expected—almost with regret. We had not risen more than a thousand feet above the general level of the Park. From the top we looked down a narrow, winding*

glen, between lofty parapets of rock, and beheld mountains in the distance, dark with shadow, and vanishing in clouds. The descent was steep, but not very toilsome. After reaching the bed of the glen, we followed it downward through beds of grass and flowers, under the shade of castellated rocks, and round the feet of natural ramparts, until it opened upon wide plains of sage-bush, which formed the shelving side of an immense valley. The usual line of cotton-wood betrayed a stream, and when we caught a glimpse of the water, its muddy tint—the sure sign of gold-washing—showed that we had found the Blue River. We had crossed the Ute Pass, as it is called by the trappers, and are among the first white men who have ever traversed it.

A grand description, but Taylor and his companions were not "among the first white men" to cross Ute Pass. He may have been one of the first fancy authors, though.

The initial mile of this climb doesn't exactly inspire. It's a little drab down there among the windblown sea of sagebrush, and the road seems like it's going to be straight and boring. Don't be discouraged. As the road makes its way around the first big curve, another world opens up. Soon you'll be pedaling past aspen groves, looking down on the valley. At that point your mood is likely to depend mainly on the weather: Clear skies and stable weather make you feel carefree and light, while looming, booming thunderheads fill the ride with nervous energy. It takes about 45 seconds for storms to cross the valley after they appear over the Gore Range.

The pass tops out at about 9,600 feet, but the last mile or so is almost flat. Total gain is about 1,400 feet. Over 5 miles, that's a little over 5 percent average slope. Moderate.

It's a quickie climb by Colorado standards, great if you're short on time but want to try something new. Instead of hurrying to join the Sunday afternoon cattle call down on I-70, head up here for a quick climb instead. Get your ya-yas out, burn off that triple cheeseburger, then join the stop-and-go parade awash in post-ride serenity.

If a 5-mile climb isn't enough to get your juices flowing, check out the other side of the pass. CR 3 continues for another 20 miles or so into the rolling sage hills, passing tailings ponds of the Henderson Mill and the Williams Fork Reservoir, and ends up in Parshall on US 40 and the Colorado River, which Bayard Taylor and his contemporaries knew as the Grand River. Ute Pass would be a great component of a long tour.

Miles and Directions

0.0 Start from the intersection of CO 9 and Ute Pass Road and begin riding up Ute Pass Road.

5.3 Top of the pass. Continue for a longer ride or turn around.

10.6 Back at CO 9.

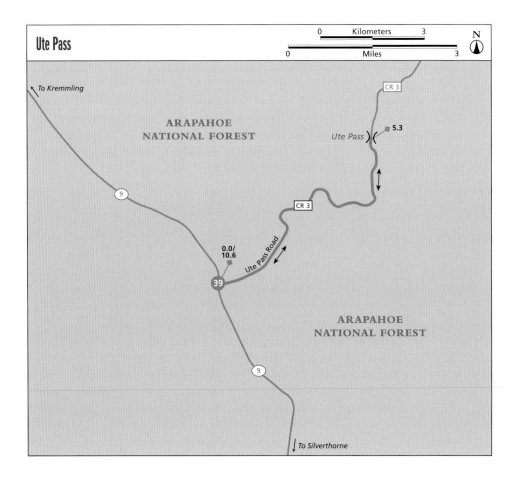

Bike Shops

Mountain Sports Outlet. 167 Meraly Way, Silverthorne; (970) 262-2836; mountainsports outlet.com. Not exactly a bike shop but may have what you need.

Pioneer Sports. 560 Silverthorne Ln., Silverthorne; (970) 668-3668; pioneersports colorado.com. Call ahead to see if they have what you're looking for.

Food and Lodging

Silverthorne is the land of chain restaurants and chain hotels. There are lots of both in the valley here.

40　Steamboat Gravel Grinder

This great loop starts from Steamboat Springs, embarks on rolling Twentymile Road, peruses some gentle dirt roads, and returns along the river.

Start: A parking area on 13th Street where it crosses the Yampa River
Length: 27.5-mile loop
Terrain: Rolling foothills with clusters of aspen. Ranchland. Beautiful.

Traffic and hazards: Traffic is mild to moderate.
Things to see: Wide-open spaces encrusted with aspen and scrub oak

Getting there: From Denver, take I-70 west to Silverthorne, then turn north on CO 9 to Kremmling. Turn north onto US 40, go over Rabbit Ears Pass, and drop into Steamboat Springs. From central Steamboat Springs, head northwest on the main drag, US 40/Lincoln Avenue, then turn left on 13th Street. There is public parking on both sides of 13th Street before it crosses the Yampa River. **GPS:** N 40 29'21.80" / W 106 50'28.93"

Ride Description

Steamboat Springs is in its own beautiful world up here. This is the north country, where Colorado starts to turn into Wyoming. Low hills and big skies. Proud patches

Crunch gravel on CO 41

Along Twentymile Road

of aspen glittering orange and yellow in the September sun, looking down on gently flowing sage-covered slopes.

Steamboat, sitting at 6,800 feet above sea level, is the coolest town in Colorado's northern mountains. Now known primarily for the sparkling powder on its ski slopes, the town began as a cluster of cabins in the 1870s, when the Utes still ruled the valley. This part of the state had been trampled by roving herds of cattle for decades, but, as it was cut off from the big towns by mountain ranges, it was one of the last areas to be afflicted with permanent homesteaders.

For Ute and settler alike, the main attraction here was the hot water bubbling from the ground, the source of mysterious healing minerals and reliable heat in the snowy mountains. (Not all the springs stink of sulfur as bad as the little bubbler near the start/finish of this loop.) The name of the town refers to the sound made by one of the springs.

The Yampa Utes were marched out of the area, which they considered to be their ancestral homeland, by 1879. In that year a proselytizing blowhard named Nathan Meeker became the straw that broke the camel's back, sparking the "Meeker Massacre" on the new White River Reservation, and a brief war between Utes and whites in northwestern Colorado. The Utes were then removed to Utah at gunpoint. After the paroxysm of violence, settlers streamed in to fill up Steamboat Springs.

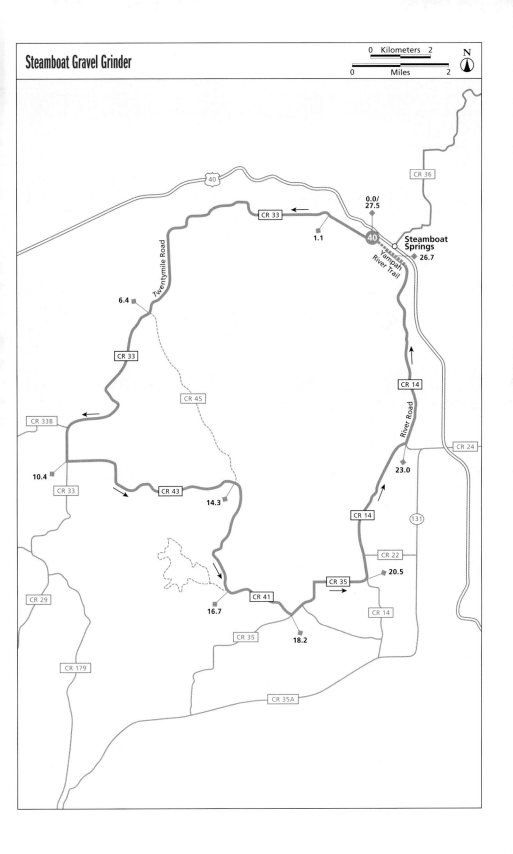

Steamboat Gravel Grinder

0 Kilometers 2

0 Miles 2

N

CR 36

40

0.0/
27.5

CR 33

1.1

40

Steamboat
Springs

26.7

Yampah
River Trail

Twentymile Road

6.4

CR 33

CR 14

River Road

CR 45

CR 33B

CR 24

10.4

CR 33

CR 43

14.3

23.0

CR 14

131

CR 29

CR 22

20.5

CR 35

CR 41

CR 14

16.7

CR 35

18.2

CR 179

CR 35A

The whites called the river Bear River, because grizzlies were so plentiful in the valley. After killing all the bears within a few decades, the settlers found the name unsuitable and reverted to the old one, Yampa, which the Utes had been using seemingly forever. In fact many landmarks were renamed for the Utes after they were forced to leave.

There are a few wonderful bike roads emanating from the Boat. Twentymile Road—officially CR 33—sprouting from the northwest corner of town, is a favorite of the local roadies. Get on there and you'll see why. The road dips and dives through the wavy ranchland, a dark ribbon of chip seal laid across the hills. Is it called Twentymile Road because it goes to Twentymile Park, or because it's 20 miles long?

Lots of folks like to ride Twentymile for a while, then just turn around and retrace their route for a sweet out-and-back. That's great, but there are some cool ways to use this incredible road in a loop, if you don't mind a little dirt.

For this gravel grinder, roll about 10 miles of Twentymile Road before turning off onto CR 43, a wide gravel route that cures into a concrete-like hardness during periods of dry weather. The same super-fine soil particles that make the surface so hard when dry turn it into heinous slop when wet. So this ride—and just about any other dirt-road-involved ride in the book—comes with an extra warning. Mellow, smooth dirt roads may become virtually impassable after heavy rain or wet snow.

If you're still game, you can easily find Twentymile Road (CR 33) shooting off from the northwest corner of town. Just get on 13th Street and go.

Bigger loops are possible here as well. For a 50-miler with lots more climbing, continue on Twentymile Road/CR 33 for another 10 miles to the coal mine, then turn onto CR 27 and make your way toward the little town of Oak Creek. Loop back to Steamboat via Stagecoach Reservoir. It's pretty easy to get lost in these hills, so carry a good map.

Miles and Directions

0.0 From the parking area on 13th Street near the Yampa River, start riding up 13th (CR 33), across the river and away from town.

1.1 Pass the intersection with Shield Drive, veering left on CR 33 (open road).

6.4 Continue straight past the intersection with CR 45.

10.4 Take a left onto CR 43 (gravel road).

14.3 Veer right (south) as CR 45 rejoins from the left. The road is now CR 41, and still gravel at the time of this writing.

16.7 Turn left onto pavement, descending.

18.2 Take a left onto CR 35.

20.5 Continue straight. The road becomes CR 14.

23.0 Take a sharp left at the intersection, continuing north on CR 14, aka River Road.

26.7 Jump onto the Yampa River Core Trail, which has sauntered over next to the road.

27.5 Arrive back at the start, amid wafts of sulfur gas.

OTHER RIDES AROUND STEAMBOAT SPRINGS

Rabbit Ears Pass. This is as uncomfortable traffic-wise as you might expect for a highway ride, but the conditions aren't terrible. Rabbit Ears Pass gets plenty of action from the local riders. There's no substitute for a sustained 2,500-foot climb. This one gains its first 2,000 feet in a big hurry as it overlooks the Yampa River valley and Lake Catamount, then it sucks all your energy and toys with you mercilessly as it drifts over false summits on its way to the top. On the other side, the highway north out of Kremmling is sketchy. Personally I avoid it. Your mileage may vary. After the road climbs out of the sage and into the forest, the ride-ability improves greatly. Some riders who are more tolerant of the worst sections of US 40 use Rabbit Ears as the opening battle in a 100-plus-mile loop. To tackle this monster, turn west onto CR 134 at Wolford Mountain Reservoir and loop back to Steamboat via Phipps-burg and Stagecoach Reservoir.

Yampa River Core Trail. The Core Trail is a concrete multi-use path (known informally as a "bike path") running along the Yampa River, through Steamboat and beyond. The southern end of the trail can be found east of US 40, off Stone Street in the southern "suburbs." It follows the river through town to the north, passing through several parks bubbling with hot springs, and comes to an end up where US 40 curves to the west. This is a relatively good trail for family biking, and it also makes a nice alternate route for riders coming into town from Rabbit Ears Pass or the rolling hills of the loop described above.

Elk River Road. Heading north off US 40 and rolling directly past the airport, Elk River Road (CR 129) is a popular route. Turn around at Clark for a challenging 40-mile out-and-back. Turn around earlier, or keep going to Wyoming. This road, lacking a consistently wide shoulder but also lacking heavy traffic, continues past Steamboat Lake and snakes all the way up to the Little Snake River and the Wyoming border. It loses its pavement along the way, and hooks up with WY 70 (not I-70) in Wyoming, with many epic touring possibilities. There are a number of potential gravel loops to be had using CR 129. If you're looking to go "into the wild" on a big self-supported tour, this would be an interesting place to start.

Appendix: Punctures and Flat Tires

The following material is adapted from the second edition of *The Art of Cycling* (FalconGuides) and includes information about the most likely causes of flat tires in Colorado (especially the Goathead thorn), as well as detailed step-by-step instructions on flat repair.

Flat Repair Equipment

Flats are common enough that cyclists, to achieve any semblance of self-sufficiency, must be able to repair them anywhere they occur in a reasonable amount of time. This means that all the necessary tools—a pump, patch kit, and two tire

The air inside the tube and tire is perhaps the most important component of the machine.

Tire levers, mini-pump, patch kit, and a spare tube

levers—must be carried on every significant ride. Consider this equipment part of the bicycle, and take it wherever the bike goes. Some experienced riders would consider an extra inner tube and cab fare to be included on the essentials list.

Having experienced a host of problems with self-adhesive, or "stick-on," patches, I recommend using the traditional-style patch kits with "glue." (In reality, "glueless" patches are the kind of patches that use glue [the adhesive on the back of the patch], while traditional patch kits really are "glueless." The little tubes of "glue" in traditional patch kits actually contain vulcanizing fluid, which works in a completely different way. Fun facts!) These kits work wonders when the directions are followed. Some folks claim that the so-called "glueless" instant patches have been greatly improved over the decades, but even if they do the job as well (highly unlikely), the time saved by using them would be, at best, about five minutes. And not five minutes of work, mind you, but five minutes of relaxing and sitting around (see below).

Make sure your pump matches the style of valve stem on your bicycle. (Presta valve stems are the thin type with the locking pin, and Schrader valves are the old-school type, like those on car tires.) Many pump heads can be set up to fit either type of valve stem. CO_2 cartridges are easy, fun, and useful—they're nice to have on board, but unfortunately they can't take the place of an actual pump.

Fixing Flats: A Primer

Like sands through the hourglass, so are the flats of the cyclist. It may be glass, a thorn, or some random piece of metal that does the deed. It may be a pinch flat or the dreaded blowout. Chances are you will collect several of each type of flat as time marches on. These occurrences should not send you into fits of frustration, nor should they send you into the bike shop for assistance. Flats should not even raise your eyebrow with the slightest hint of surprise. The inconvenience of dealing with them is easily overcome by a little knowledge and experience.

Fixing flats is no big deal. Here is an opinionated how-to in fourteen steps. Yes, fourteen is a lot of steps for something that is supposedly "no big deal," but don't be alarmed; it's really five general steps broken down into more specific components:

1. Remove the wheel from the frame. (If you aren't completely proficient in this operation, become so by removing and reinstalling the wheels until you get it down cold. The rear wheel can be quite tricky to remove and install, but with practice it becomes a piece of cake. Taking note of which cog the chain is wrapped around and placing it back onto that same cog when reinstalling the wheel will make things much easier. Many of the fork dropouts on late-model bikes have "safety tabs," a product of our lawsuit culture, which undermines the concept of quick-release wheels.)

2. Quickly check the outer surface of the tire to see if you can locate the puncture. There may be a visible thorn or shard of glass sticking out, or an audible hiss of escaping air. If you can locate the point of puncture before actually removing the tube, this will make your job a little easier (because it will give you advance knowledge of where the hole is and what may have created it). If not, no worries.

3. If the tube is still holding some air, release the air by using the valve.

4. Use the tire levers to pry the tire off the rim. This step takes a little bit of practice, but it's not rocket science. The best way to learn is to try it. With the first lever, gingerly crowbar one side of the tire out of the rim in one spot and hook the back end of the lever around a spoke to hold it in place. Then use the second lever, a few inches away from the first, to continue prying one side of the tire off the rim, section by section, all the way around. Be careful not to "pinch" the tube, which would create an additional hole.

5. Pull the tube out of the tire, but leave the valve poking through the rim to make things a little easier. There is no reason to completely remove the tube unless the puncture happens to be right above the valve stem, or you can't locate the hole and need to submerge the tube (see Step 7 below).

6. Very carefully run your fingers (or a wad of easily snagged material, such as pantyhose) all the way around the inside of the tire to find any objects poking through it. What you are looking for is probably very small and very sharp. It's quite possible that there will be nothing at all to find, or there may be several offenders, so be thorough. Remove the objects from the tire and note their location, which will help you find the hole(s) in the tube. At this point, become an active learner. Observe the perpetrator. What is it? Where did it come from? How did you pick it up and how can you avoid it in the future? Refrain from tossing the little beast, whatever it is, back into the street.

7. Use the pump to put about fifteen or twenty pumps of air in the tube. This should give the tube enough air pressure to cause the puncture to reveal its exact location with a hiss. If pumping up the tube fails to give the tube any shape, the hole must be quite large—probably caused by a blowout or a pinch flat–type event. The more air you add to the tube, the louder the hiss will be. Still, it may be difficult to locate the hiss of a tiny puncture, especially if you're attempting to patch the tube next to noisy traffic or on a windy day. If you can't find any puncture, remove the tube entirely, submerge it in water while inflated one section at a time, and look for telltale bubbles. Obviously, this baptism method might be problematic while out on a ride. The problem of mystery punctures is a great reason to carry an extra tube.

8. Once you locate the puncture, use the sandpaper in the patch kit to rough up an area of about 1½ inches in diameter around the hole. This removes the shiny substance that coats the tube. This is residue of a chemical that keeps the tube from sticking to the mold during the production process, and, if left unmolested, this substance will also prevent any patch from sticking well. Also take care to sand off any ridges around the puncture, or these could create tiny air passages under the patch.

9. Using the "glue" in the patch kit, spread a thin layer of the stuff (vulcanizing fluid) around the puncture point, enough so the area covered by it will be easily bigger than the area of the patch.

10. Let the vulcanizing fluid dry, long enough that it no longer feels tacky to the touch. This usually takes a few minutes at least, depending on the humidity. The instructions in the kit usually say to wait for five minutes.

11. Peel the patch away from the foil backing and press it over the hole. Press hard all over the patch. Using a tire lever or similar object might help. There should be no bubbles under the patch or loose edges. It is not necessary to remove the clear plastic, strange as that may seem. Repeat Steps 8 through 11 for any additional holes in the tube.

12. Stuff the patched tube back into the tire—some folks like to add a few pumps of air to the tube to give it some shape prior to this—and work the tire onto the rim with your thumbs. More so than tire removal, reinstallation can be a pain. Some rim/tire combos are extremely problematic. Avoid using tire levers to install a tire. If the last bit of tire refuses to go on the rim, pump up the tube a bit, then let the air out completely and try again.

13. Pump the tire back up to the desired pressure. Make sure it's properly seated, with no sections of tube caught between the tire bead and the rim. Be careful with your pumping action if you are using Presta valve stems because vigorous, uncivilized pumping will break the valve or tear it away from the tube at the base of the stem. (Any tearing of the stem from the tube is very difficult to repair and effectively ruins the tube. However, if the Presta valve stem's pin is broken off, the tire can still be ridden as long as there is good air pressure already in the tube. The air pressure in the tire will hold the valve closed, but you won't be able to add air once the valve pin is broken.) Don't seriously tighten the bolt that holds the Presta valve where it comes out of the rim until you're done pumping.

14. Does the tire feel like it's holding air? Put the wheel back on the bike.

Whatever you do, don't skip Steps 6, 8, or 10. These steps are absolutely crucial to a successful flat repair, but few cyclists give them the respect they deserve.

It's a good strategy to carry a spare tube (or two) while cycling, especially in thorn-prone areas like the Colorado Front Range. That way you can just slap the new tube in and save a lot of time. Fix the bad tube later, and make that your spare tube. If you employ this strategy, don't forget Step 6!

A note on RIM STRIP: "Rim strip" is the piece of rubber, plastic, or cloth that covers the inside of the rim. Its purpose is to protect the inflated tube from the sharp edges of eyelets and spoke nipples on the inside of the rim. The cloth strips are best because they stay in place and last. The rubber strips can move and expose the edges they're meant to cover, and plastic strips fall apart. Here's a hint: Use cloth tape. Usually, rim strip is a no-brainer and demands very little, if any, attention. But if you find yourself suffering multiple flats on the underside of tubes, suspect a disintegrating or improperly seated rim strip.

Broken Glass

Nationwide, broken glass is the most time-honored and feared perpetrator of punctures for cyclists. Its evil powers, however, are much overrated. In Colorado, your flat is much more likely to be caused by a thorn.

There are two general types of broken glass to be found in American cities: tempered glass and "bottle glass." Tempered glass is hardened by forced cooling during the manufacturing process. The faster-than-normal cooling compresses the surface of the glass, leaving it much more resistant to breaking than nontempered glass. This kind of glass is used in the rear and side windows of motor vehicles. (Windshields are made differently, with a thin sheet of plastic sandwiched between two panes of tempered glass. This "laminated glass" is not supposed to shatter at all.) When fractured, a car window made of tempered glass collapses into a pile of soft-edged pebbles. The pieces usually aren't sharp and rarely puncture bicycle tires. Feel free to ignore it. Bottle glass (and the glass from automobile side mirrors) is another matter entirely. It shatters into jagged pieces, any one of which has the potential to cause a flat.

On the street, it's possible to distinguish broken bottle glass from broken tempered glass, even while riding. Along with the obvious difference in appearance, location can provide additional clues. Tempered glass is generally confined to streets and parking lots and, due to car break-ins, is often found in piles in the gutter or just outside the parking lane on narrow streets. Bottle glass, on the other hand, is found everywhere. If there's glass on a bike path or anywhere else that is off-limits to motor traffic, it's almost always bottle glass. Bottle glass is occasionally green or dark brown, a dead giveaway, or has beer-related writing on it, also a dead giveaway.

Avoid the bottle glass if you can. Steer around it if no other vehicles are present, but please keep your priorities straight—flats are the least of your worries as a cyclist. Pick a new route rather than ride over batches of bottle glass each day.

Glassphalt

Don't be afraid. It's only "glassphalt."

"Glassphalt" paving material can cause hopeless glassophobes to suffer flashbacks and convulsions. This special asphalt sparkles in a way that mimics very closely the appearance of a biblical number of glass shards scattered on the road. If it looks like crushed glass, well, that's because it *is* crushed glass. "Glassphalt" incorporates a small percentage of recycled glass, called cullet, into the aggregate mix.

Decades ago, the use of "glassphalt" was driven by economics. There were so many sources of cullet around that it was considered a useless waste product. It was being given away, and those responsible for paving and resurfacing streets had the bright idea that it could be used in the road mix as a way to cut expenses. Today, however, with the widespread use of plastic bottles and the general decrease in sources of glass, asphalt containing crushed glass costs more than regular asphalt. Even with the added expense, it is still used occasionally, because it significantly increases the durability of the road surface.[*]

Like some sort of cruel prank, the sparkly bits of embedded glass disappear as you ride toward them, while still more come into view beyond, flashing like mad. Even

---

[*] Charles Cohen, "All That Glitters Is Not Road," *City Paper* (Baltimore), March 1–March 7, 2000.

knowing that "glassphalt" won't cause flat tires, it's hard not to experience a tiny panic attack while gazing upon what appears to be a vast sea of broken glass.

Tribulus Terrestris

Puncture Vine, Goathead, Sandbur, African Devil Weed . . . call it what you want, it doesn't matter. The thorny seeds produced by *tribulus terrestris*, as it is known in the science books, are the number one cause of punctures for cyclists in Colorado. Thorns in the west, rust in the east.

Tribulus terrestris forms a mat along the ground, with tough vines that sprout very small, dark green leaves and nice-looking little yellow flowers, in addition to the spiked seeds that start out green and soft but mature into thorns as solid as hardwood. The mat formed by one tribulus plant, from a single taproot, can easily grow 6 feet across, and it can produce several thousand seeds. Tribulus seeds fall away from the plant, and some of the lucky ones go off to see the world. (**Note:** Technical information on Puncture Vine is derived from multiple sources, such as the University of California Statewide Integrated Pest Management Program.)

Strangely enough, hopeful weightlifting-type guys have been buying supplements said to contain extracts of the *tribulus terrestris* weed, which is supposed to give them bigger muscles and more serious erections—you know, the usual. To just about anyone else, tribulus is considered to be a noxious weed, an invasive species, and a major source of frustration. Accidentally introduced with a load of Mediterranean livestock sometime in the 1800s, low-maintenance tribulus is now fully living the American Dream. It thrives in so-called areas of disturbance, the sandy, infertile, chemical-soaked soils where other plants fail. That's why it loves cities so much—a city can be described as a vast area of disturbance, and cities are full of rolling rubber, which is tribulus's best friend.

In the early years of the automobile, tires were essentially the same on cars and bicycles, so goathead thorns frequently stranded motorists along with cyclists. In California, where the Mediterranean-like climate is particularly friendly to tribulus, the highway department used to douse the roadsides with diesel fuel hoping to vanquish the evil weed, to no avail. Making very thick tires was the only answer. (See Ashleigh Brilliant, *The Great Car Craze*, pp. 126–27. The irony is not lost on Brilliant: "The remarkable thing was that the Puncture Vine had not been at all common in California until the advent of the Mass Automobile.") Ironically, tribulus was the mortal enemy of the rubber car tire, yet the rubber tire was the best thing ever to happen to tribulus. Having adapted over millions of years to stick in the fur and paws of passing beasts, the patient tribulus plant was gifted one of the greatest windfalls in all of evolutionary history with the near-simultaneous inventions of the rubber pneumatic tire, the safety bicycle, and the automobile. Together, these technologies provided the perfect mechanism to transport tribulus's seeds across the continents.

Once confined only to the dry southwestern states, tribulus has now been found in all states except Massachusetts, New Hampshire, Vermont, and Maine.

Sharp!

We can only assume that New England is next on its list. The various agencies responsible for controlling tribulus have failed primarily because of the remarkable properties of the thorns. Not only do goathead seeds hitch rides cross-country and around the world, they can also lie dormant in the ground for many years, perhaps decades, before sprouting—spiky little time bombs. Back in the 1960s, the government recognized, for a moment, the futility of dumping chemicals on Puncture Vine and imported tribulus-eating weevils into the States. The success of this plan has obviously been limited, although the weevils seem to be enjoying their new home.

Tribulus terrestris is the most well-known member of the Caltrop family (Zygophyllaceae). In medieval warfare, a caltrop was a small iron device composed of four spikes. It was designed in such a way that it could be tossed on the ground in front of advancing cavalry and, no matter how it landed, one of the spikes would always be sticking up.

Tribulus thorns work much the same way. With one impaler always pointed skyward, those little caltrops cut right into your rubber, effortlessly. Tubes advertised as "thorn-resistant" should be looked upon with a healthy degree of skepticism, as should tubes that are supposed to patch themselves with green goo. The thick knobs of mountain-bike tires, by simple virtue of their being thicker than the thorns themselves, can keep the thorns from making contact with the inner tube. But since the knobs cover only part of the mountain-bike tire, protection is incomplete. Some brands of touring tires are said to be thick enough to foil thorns, and some cyclists report good results from protective plastic strips, but these exact a significant toll in increased weight and rolling resistance.

It's time we started giving this plant the respect it deserves after a century of royally kicking our ass. Hail tribulus! We surrender! Those living and cycling in the thorn zone should get to know the plant that produces the thorns. Learn not only what *tribulus terrestris* looks like, but also where and when it likes to grow. Where it now lives, it's there to stay. Where it doesn't live, it's probably on its way.

How to Avoid Goathead Punctures

Technology probably won't save you from thorns, but a little bit of common sense might. The most effective strategy for avoiding thorn flats involves using the thorn's own frightening power against it—thorn jujitsu. The thorns are collected by any tire or soft-soled shoe that presses down on them, so simply ride where other bicycles, cars, or pedestrians have gone before. When possible, ride near the center of bike paths and away from debris fields that collect in the least-used areas of streets. If you find yourself cruising through a vacant lot or across some random dirt patch, find the most established path and don't stray from it. Riding this way will drastically reduce your chances of being stung.

A Thorny Dilemma

Let's say you look down at a stoplight and notice a nice-looking goathead thorn stuck in your front tire. Despite your consistent practice of thorn jujitsu, you've been stung. This presents a dilemma—to pluck or not to pluck. Eyeing the disposition of the goathead, you ask yourself a tough question: Has that damn thorn pierced the tube? Probably, but maybe not. There is the small chance that the thorn is askew and has somehow failed to penetrate the inner tube. There is also the nagging possibility that the thorn has yet to puncture but will do so if it is not removed. You reach down and press on the tire with your thumb. Seems full enough, but that still doesn't answer your question. If the thorn has already pierced the tube, the leak of air caused by the perforation could be quite slow or nonexistent—thorns, you see, have a way of nicely plugging their own holes. In such a case, pulling the thorn out would only open the hole and allow the tube to deflate rapidly.

Do you feel lucky? It takes a confident and experienced cyclist to roll the dice and pluck away, happily and fearlessly, knowing that deft tube-patching skills will handle whatever consequences await. Those more fearful of having to fix a flat on-site will want to leave the thorn in the tire for as long as possible, where it serves as the perfect custom-sized plug for any hole it makes.

These painful dilemmas become more urgent when the cyclist's tire is stuck with multiple thorns, a demoralizing but fairly common occurrence in thorn country. Two extra tubes, one for each wheel, provide some peace of mind when nothing else will.

Random Sharpies

Goatheads and bottle glass can be blamed for the vast majority of Colorado cyclists' punctures, but certainly not all of them. A small percentage of flat tires will be caused by a rogue's gallery of random debris. Among this group, nails, screws, and tacks of various kinds form the most common family of objects: the construction-grade fasteners. There are also staples, pop tops, pins, campaign buttons, busted CD covers and other shards of plastic, dress shoe taps, pieces of wire, broken pencils, lawless twigs, valve cores, and an endless variety of unidentifiable machine parts lurking on the streets, waiting for unlucky cyclists to roll over them at just the right angle. It is quite useless to prepare for random encounters with random objects, aside from learning well how to patch a tube.

The punctures caused by this wreckage are generally violent and obvious, and they result in a rapid loss of air from the tube. In the case of nails and other tough, elongated pieces, the foreign object tends to penetrate all the way to the rim, leaving two big holes in the tube. Punctures of this sort can usually be patched in the normal way, provided there are enough patches left in the kit. If the object punches a hole in the tire casing that is large enough that the tube balloons out of the hole when inflated, the tire itself will have to be patched.

An interesting aspect of random object punctures is that these punctures almost always occur in the rear tire rather than the front. We can imagine why. Most of these objects are lying flat on the road and are harmless in their sleeping position. But when a tire rolls over an object such as a nail or shard of plastic, the object snaps to attention, popping up off the ground. With two tires rolling over the object in quick succession, the front tire causes the object to stand up straight and the rear tire receives the brunt of the attack.

The slice in this tire was caused by a shard of plastic in the street. Such a decisive cut is not reparable.

Pinch Flats

In general, pinch flats occur when a tire is underinflated for the conditions at hand. This type of flat is often associated with mountain biking on rocky trails, but it can occur on the road. The mountain bikers developed tubeless tire systems that eliminated pinch flats even at low tire pressures, but tubeless tires also entail a number of fiddly logistical issues and aren't yet in widespread use among road cyclists. Skinny tires are especially vulnerable to pinch flats when striking curbs, railroad tracks, potholes, or rocks in the road. Because they are associated with underinflation, pinch flats are symptomatic of a prior undetected slow leak, or simple negligence on the part of the cyclist. The occurrence of pinch flats on well-inflated tires calls into question the handling skills of the cyclist—fast, furious, and clumsy.

An experienced rider can feel a pinch flat at the exact moment it occurs. The tire "bottoms out" as it strikes an obstacle, and the wheel's rim impacts solidly with a clunk. This impact causes the inner tube to be pinched harshly in the tire casing as it comes together. Pinches like this cause a small but significant slit to open in the tube, or two matching slits arrayed in the familiar double-fanged snakebite pattern—which is why pinch flats are often referred to as "snakebites." When patching a pinch flat, always search for a second hole, usually about 1 centimeter apart from and parallel to the first. But don't stop there. If the cause of the underinflation leading to the pinch flat is a mystery, then search for a third hole and carefully grope the inside of the tire for the cause of a possible slow leak.

Pinch flats can be prevented easily by maintaining proper tire pressure (very firm to the thumb test) and by riding in a less than reckless manner.

Blowouts

The frightening term "blowout" can be used to describe a few different types of events. Most commonly, when a cyclist claims to have had a blowout, it means that the tube has exploded due to improper installation of the tire. Sometimes, when a tire is worked onto a rim, a section of the tube is stuck between the rim and the tire bead. The faulty installation may go undetected even after the tire is pumped up hard. The unsuspecting cyclist goes out to ride, the tube steadily works its way to freedom, then blam! With nothing holding it back, a section of the tube explodes. (Contrary to popular belief, a tube can't explode spontaneously inside the tire.) If the blowout occurs while the cyclist is cornering fast, there could be painful consequences. Blowouts like this can also occur when the bike is just sitting there in your house, which can cause heart attacks. Blam!

To prevent this most-common form of blowout, simply exercise some care when installing a tire. Make sure the tire is seated properly, with no sections of tube visible. As a way of insuring good tire positioning, some like to inflate, deflate, then re-inflate the tube after they install a tire, but this is usually not necessary.

Another form of blowout occurs at the local gas station, when the recreational cyclist attaches the air compressor built for automobile tires to the Schrader valve on his or her bicycle. Damn, that thing fills up fast, don't it? Blam! Remember, if you are tempted to do this, that the gas station compressor is designed to fill tires with vastly more volume than bicycle tires hold. The same source that requires a minute or two to fill a car tire could blow out your bike tire in about fifteen seconds.

A third type of blowout event is associated with excessive tire wear—and I'm talkin' *excessive*. When a tire—a rear tire, more than likely—is so absolutely finished that its rubber is completely gone, and even the inner casing is totally worn away in spots, there is nothing left between the inner tube and the road. The tube pokes out of the opening, grinds onto the road surface, and blam! (Actually, this sort of blowout sounds more like a pifft! than a blam!) Obviously, flats of this sort can be forestalled by replacing the bad tire. If gross tire wear looks likely to cause a flat in the immediate future—say, while you're out on a ride—switch the front tire to the back and you will probably make it home, or to the nearest bike shop.

If a tube pops due to excessive tire wear—pifft!—you must boot the tire in addition to patching the tube, or the tube will flat repeatedly. Ideally, use a small piece of rubber or denim and fit it on the inside of the tire to cover the worn-out spot. Some cyclists claim success using folded-up dollar bills for this application, but paper products will not last long. A strip of electrical tape or the like on the inside of a bedraggled tire can prolong its life another few hundred miles.

Ride Index

About the Author

Robert Hurst is a native Coloradan, ex-messenger, amateur historian, and stay-at-home dad. He celebrates his continued survival by spending time in the mountains and by riding the world's most excellent roads and trails. Robert is also the author of *The Art of Cycling: Staying Safe on City Streets*, *Best Bike Rides Denver and Boulder*, *Mountain Biking Colorado's San Juan Mountains*, *Road Biking Colorado's Front Range*, *The Art of Mountain Biking: Singletrack Skills for All Riders*, and *The Cyclist's Manifesto* (all FalconGuides).

Your next adventure begins here.

falcon.com